A Short History of the Near East

Courtesy of The Macmillan Co., Ltd.

A CURTAIN AT THE DOOR OF THE KAABA AT MECCA Bearing koranic inscriptions which include surahs 1, 106, and 112. The prominent inscription above the center is the first part of surah 48, verse 27.

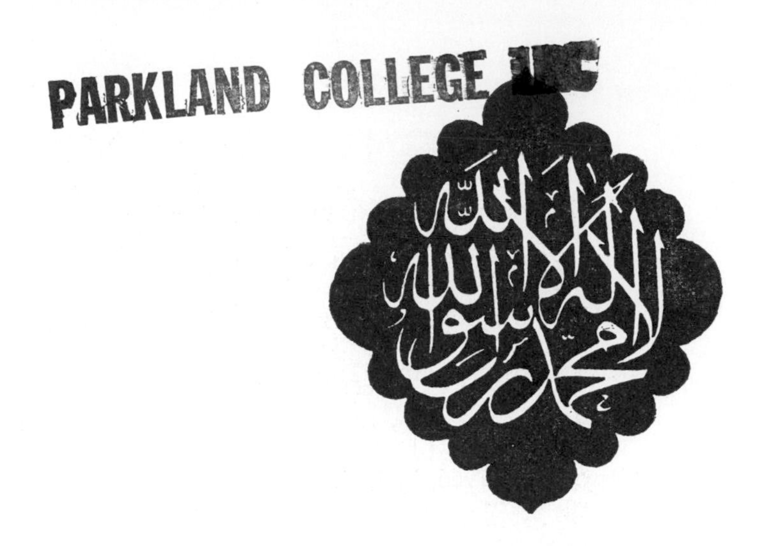

A Short History of the Near East

Philip K. Hitti
Princeton University

D. VAN NOSTRAND COMPANY, INC.
Princeton, New Jersey
Toronto London Melbourne

VAN NOSTRAND REGIONAL OFFICES: *New York, Chicago, San Francisco*

D. VAN NOSTRAND COMPANY, LTD., *London*

D. VAN NOSTRAND COMPANY (Canada), LTD., *Toronto*

D. VAN NOSTRAND AUSTRALIA PTY. LTD., *Melbourne*

Published simultaneously in Canada by
D. VAN NOSTRAND COMPANY (Canada), LTD.

First Published December 1965
Reprinted March 1967, January 1968
September 1968

PRINTED IN THE UNITED STATES OF AMERICA

Preface

What facts to choose from the inexhaustible storehouse of the Near East historical past, how to set these facts in the proper narrative flow—the context of what precedes and what follows—and how to make the whole intelligible and meaningful to the general reader of the present day was the uneasy task confronting the author. The task was made more difficult by the fact that in terms of time the period covered includes all three—ancient, medieval and modern: and in terms of area it is so vast as to contain Egyptians, Babylonians and Assyrians; Phoenicians and Hebrews; Turks, Persians and Arabs. The problem was, to an extent, facilitated by the author's more comprehensive study (*The Near East in History*, first published in 1961) on which this book was based, but in the meantime it was rendered more difficult by having to add condensation to generalization. This resulted in omitting details that illuminate certain facts, and in making sweeping statements hard to defend without the benefit of reservations. But, as in all such cases, the branches and leaves in the historical forest had to be sacrificed in the interest of the trees and the ensemble.

If the attempt serves to open a window through which the reader gains a glimpse of the unique experience of the Near Eastern man and if it further stimulates his appetite for more detailed study, it will not have been made in vain.

P. K. H.

Princeton, N.J.
November 1965

Contents

List of Illustrations

List of Maps

I

Historical Setting

In the length of its recorded history, in the variety and richness of its experience, and in its contribution to human progress the Near East stands unique among the areas of the world. This is the area comprising what is today Turkey in Asia (Anatolia), Iraq and Iran (Persia), Syria, Lebanon, Israel and Jordan, Arabia and Egypt. It is also called currently the Middle East, a term traditionally applied to India and adjacent territory. The unparalleled historic experience of the Near East is, of course, based upon its temperate climate, strategic situation at the intercontinental meeting place of Europe, Asia and Africa and its interoceanic position between the Mediterranean Sea and the Indian Ocean.

History began with writing, and writing began in the Near East. For five thousand years the area has been a going concern. But centuries before the curtain rose on written records, Near Easterners had developed urban life with political, economic and social institutions. Still earlier they had discovered metal, particularly copper, and worked it into tools and weapons that gave them advantage over their stone-using neighbors. Even earlier, some Near Easterner had learned through long and sustained experience, initiated by chance, that certain wild plants growing in his land could be domesticated and that certain wild animals could be tamed. He thereby lifted himself from the status of a food gatherer, roaming from place to place in quest of food, to that of a food producer. This made settled life, with its agricultural pursuit, accumulation of property and increase of population possible. Luckily the area provided the kind of climate, vegetation and animal life without which transition from a nomadic life of grazing and hunting to a settled one could not have been achieved.

What enhances the importance of such history-making prehistoric events is their transmission to regions other than their original. As they passed on to the European mainland they served as a prelude to the classical Greco-Roman civilization, the parent of our European-American. The extent of the material debt Europe owes the Near East was hardly realized until a century ago. The ancestor of the early European wheat and barley, archeologists and botanists assert, should be sought in the wild cereals that still grow in Syria, Lebanon and Palestine. The ancestor of the domesticated European sheep is the one that once roamed the plateau extending from Anatolia to Iran. Early Cretan metallurgy follows Egyptian and Syrian traditions. Primitive eastern European ceramics display similarity to western Asian products. Migration, invasion and trade provided the means of passage. Anatolia, Phoenicia (Lebanon) and Egypt served as bridges. Crete in the Mediterranean and Mycenae in southern Greece were the stepping stones.

Domestication of plants and animals, metallurgy, pottery and other material objects were not the only gifts from the Near East. Embedded in our daily cultural lives are relics of a different kind of legacy. Our seven-day week stems from the Genesis story of creation, itself based on a Semitic system of numeration in which the number seven figures. The early Semites of Mesopotamia (Babylonians) believed in seven planets, to the first of which, the sun, they dedicated the first day of the week. Hence our Sunday. To the second planet, the moon, they dedicated the second day—our Monday. The seventh planet, Saturn, gave us our Saturday. Our division of the hour into 60 minutes, the minute into 60 seconds and the circle into 360 (a multiple of 60) degrees is likewise an inheritance from early Mesopotamia. Our solar calendar was inherited from ancient Egypt through Rome.

Still greater than these cultural strands interwoven into the fabric of our culture are the varied intellectual and spiritual elements from Phoenicia and Palestine. The Phoenicians, ancient Lebanese, perfected the alphabetic system of writing which they bequeathed to the rest of the civilized world. The Mesopotamians (strictly, Sumerians) and Egyptians after them had originated a pictorial system of writing, but it was the Phoenicians who evolved out of pictures the few, simple signs prized everywhere among the most precious and effective tools of intellectual life.

On the spiritual side the Palestinean heritage is unexcelled. Both Judaism and Christianity were born and nurtured therein. Their daughter, Islam, the third great monotheistic religion, was cradled in an adjoining territory. All three religions are the products of the spiritual experience and genius of the same people, the Semites. The recording and dissemination of their sublime message and ethical doctrines were facilitated by the Phoenician alphabet.

In medieval times Moslem Arabs, heirs of the Semitic tradition and to a less extent of the Hellenic, held aloft the torch of enlightenment throughout a large portion of the civilized world. From their Syrian capital Damascus, they ruled an empire extending from the Atlantic to central Asia. From their subsequent capital Baghdad, they spread their translations and renditions of Greek, Persian and Indian philosophy, science and literature throughout that vast domain. From Moslem Spain, Sicily and Crusading Syria, some of these intellectual treasures passed on to Europe to become a vital force in its modern renaissance. Among other words the following testify to the extent of Arab impact: algebra and zero in mathematics; zenith, nadir, Acrab and other star names in astronomy; alcohol, alkali and alchemy in medicine; sugar, coffee, orange, lemon, atlas, satin and damask in agriculture and industry; divan, mattress, sofa and jar in everyday vocabulary.

Such rich and varied historic experience, with its widely disseminated results, was necessarily conditioned by a favorable geographic position in both its local and global aspects. Lying at the crossroads of the ancient world, the area served as a bridge between the three historic continents. Not only is its posture intercontinental but interoceanic, between the Black and Mediterranean Seas on one hand and the Indian Ocean and Arabian Sea on the other. When the world was much smaller, the Mediterranean acquired its appropriate name, "the middle of the earth." This body of water served as a Phoenician lake before it became Greek or Roman. Subsequently its eastern part fell within the embrace of the Ottoman crescent. The advent of the age of air navigation made Beirut and Cairo centers of communication for all-weather round-the-world travel.

Somewhere in this intercontinental, interoceanic region world-empire dreamers from Alexander to Napoleon found themselves battling for the realization of their dreams. The semi-legendary Trojan wars of the twelfth century before Christ were fought not so much for the recovery of the beautiful Spartan queen, Helen, as for the control of the Dardanelles. The Anglo-Egyptian clashes of the mid-twentieth century were occasioned by the desire for control of the Suez Canal. A century earlier rivalry between Great Britain, France and Russia for spheres of influence in the decadent Ottoman Empire precipitated the Crimean War. This makes the story of the Near East not only that of Moses, Christ, Zoroaster and Muhammad but also of Darius and Alexander, Cleopatra and Caesar, Saladin and Richard Coeur de Lion, Chingiz Khan and Hulagu, Napoleon and Allenby.

A new dimension has been added to the importance of the area by the recent discovery of petroleum in fabulous quantities. Estimates make 62 per cent of the total oil reserves of the world embedded in the soil of Arabia, Iraq and Iran. Vital for industry in peacetime, this product is more vital in wartime. Its existence in such quantity has added to the geopolitical importance of the area, especially at this time of tension between East and West.

At this critical period in world history the states of the Near East find themselves still in transition from medievalism to modernism. Under the impact of the West, most of them have started overhauling their traditional political, economic and social institutions, but have not yet achieved stability. The political ferment is aggravated by the adoption of European nationalist and other ideologies. The intellectual awakening through which they are passing, also largely due to European impulses, resulted in their rediscovery of the roles their ancestors played. Contemporary Arabs never tire of reciting the glory of the Moslem caliphate centered successively in Medina, Damascus, Baghdad and Cairo. Modern Iranians awoke to the full realization of the significance of their heritage from Darius and Xerxes, with which went a claim of superiority based on descent. Even Kemalist Turks began to evoke the ghost of the Hittites. Thus is the past of the Near East being relived in the European and American heritage and more fully in the lives and hearts of Near Easterners.

2

The Setting of the Stage

A hundred thousand years or so before Christ, while north Europe was still blanketed with snow and the mountains of south Europe were capped with glaciers, the Near East must have enjoyed more hospitable weather. It evidently received more rain than in historic times. Trees and bushes flourished where nothing but desert grass now struggles for growth. In the centuries preceding the dawn of history desiccation began as a result of the final retreat of the ice cap in Eurasia. River beds became the dry wadies we see today in the Egyptian desert, the Arabian peninsula and the Iranian plateau. Desiccation continued in historic times, but that was due partly to the destruction of irrigation works by wars or negligence and partly to the cutting down of trees by man and to promiscuous grazing by animals. Thus was the soil gradually deprived of plant roots to hold it together. Their loss facilitated erosion and the denudation of hillsides by winds and running rain water. Dried-up springs and deserted settlements on the fringes of the Syrian Desert, ruined villages bordering on neglected caravan routes in the Iranian plateau are produced by man rather than nature.

Mountain ranges along the western border of the area, from Turkey through Lebanon to Arabia, intercept the courses of the westerlies originating in the Atlantic or Mediterranean and bearing the prerequisite moisture for rain. As the mountains tap these resources, they leave the hinterland in a rain-shadow zone. The entire interior is therefore marked by dryness if not aridity. Other than the coastland only the river valleys receive sufficient precipitation in winter and relief from intensive heat in summer to warrant extensive agricultural activity. Whatever rain falls is normally crowded into December to February.

This twofold nature of the land is reflected in the two main categories into which the bulk of the population can be divided: settled farmers and wandering nomads. Accordingly Bedouins populate the desert interiors of Anatolia, Syria, Iran and Arabia as well as the fringes of Iraq and Egypt. The pattern in these two countries is changed because of their three rivers. Lebanon is so mountainous and narrow that it leaves no room for a barren interior or fringe. The Anatolian plateau rises 3000 to 3500 feet above the sea, that of Iran 1000 to 3000 feet and occupies about half of the land. Iran is shielded on the north by the Elburz Mountains and on the south by the Zagoras massif. Both plateaus experience relatively excessive cold in winter and intensive heat in summer (particularly July and August). The average January temperature in central Anatolia is 30° Fahrenheit, the July temperature 86°. Rainfall varies from 10 to 17 inches annually.

The Taurus and Anti-Taurus ranges in southern Anatolia retarded but did not stop communication with the Semitic, later Arab, world to its south. The mountains, together with the climate, however, did keep Anatolia un-Semitic, un-Arabic. Likewise the Elburz-Zagoras barriers kept Iranians from becoming Semitized or Arabicized, despite the fact that the bulk of the population has almost always gravitated westward and maintained closer cultural and commercial relations with the Fertile Crescent than with central Asia.

The Arabian plateau is less elevated and more arid than the Iranian. Starting at a height of some 3000 feet, it dips as it extends eastward to the Persian Gulf. The entire Arabian peninsula is geologically an extension of the African Sahara; its sandy core is continued in the Syrian Desert and eastward through Iraq and Iran to central Asia.

The peninsula's western range stretches all along the Red Sea coast, attaining a height of 9000 feet in Hejaz, birthplace of Islam, and 14,000 feet in Yemen. So complete is the drainage of the mois

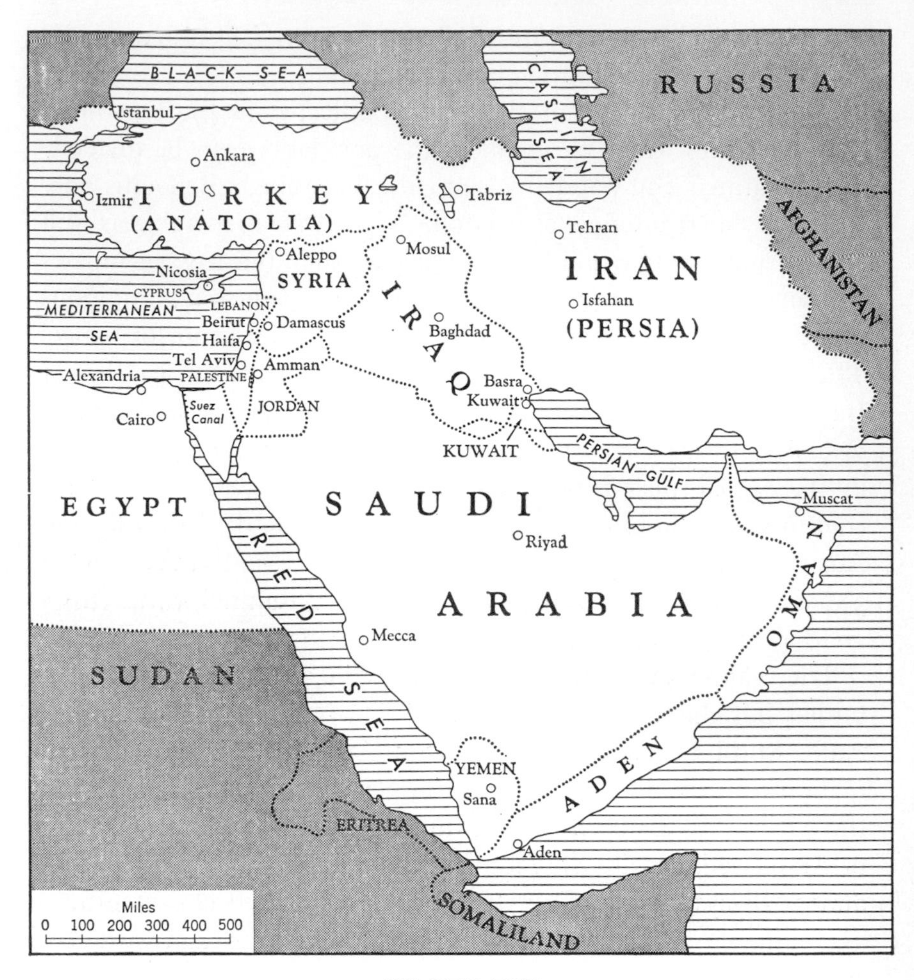

THE NEAR EAST

ture-bearing westerlies during their passage over the mountain that the entire hinterland is left almost rainless. The mean June temperature in Jeddah is 108° Fahrenheit. In all the peninsula only Yemen, the Arabia Felix of the Romans, receives enough precipitation to warrant extensive cultivation. Nejd, nursery of the Wahhabis headed by the Saud (Su'ud) royal family, constitutes the nucleus of the northern interior. The mean June to July temperature in Riyad is 108°F. The peninsula, largest of all Near Eastern countries, cannot boast a single perennial river that reaches the sea, nor does it have a body of water that could be called a lake. Its southern desert covers an area of 400,000 square miles and is appropriately called al-Rub' al-Khali (empty quarter). Treeless and waterless, it was not traversed by a European until the early 1930's.

At the eastern horn of the Fertile Crescent lies the valley of the twin rivers, the Tigris and Euphrates. At the extremity of the western horn lies the valley of the one river, the Nile. Both Egypt and lower Mesopotamia (present-day Iraq) are literally the gifts of the rivers that flow through them. Dry and rainless, they depend on river water for irrigation as well as drinking. Their richly fertile soil is the alluvium deposited through the centuries on a substratum of sand and rock, except at the river mouths, where the build-up has been on the sea. The site of a Sumerian seaport, Eridu, lies today about 150 miles from the head of the Persian Gulf.

In both Egypt and Mesopotamia spring and autumn are short, summers intensely hot and winters relatively mild. Any rain that falls in Egypt is limited to the coast and does not exceed eight inches. The mean July temperature in Cairo is 84°F.; the mean in January is 53°F. Baghdad receives an average rainfall of 5.5 inches and has a mean July temperature of 107°F. Both countries are almost stoneless and treeless (except for the date palm of Mesopotamia) necessitating incursions to Syria or Lebanon for the necessary supply of structural material. Egypt's dryness accounts for the remarkable preservation of its mummies and other buried treas ures. It was these relics of antiquity that furnished Near Eastern archeologists with their earliest opportunity and enabled them to achieve some of the most sensational triumphs in the annals of archeology.

The valley of the Nile enjoys more regularity in climate and topography than that of Tigro-Euphrates. For thousands of miles its life-giving stream moves undisturbed on a generally level surface. Its counterparts in Mesopotamia rise in the Armenian mountains, wind their paths tortuously southward and part company. The Euphrates then suddenly turns southeast, belying its promise to continue toward the Mediterranean, while the Tigris flows close to the Zagoras. The Tigris gives no opportunity for considerable settlement between Mosul and Baghdad, and hardly any worth mentioning between Baghdad and the Gulf. The two rivers unite before emptying into the gulf. Both have shifted their courses considerably within recorded time, a disturbing factor for settlers and archeologists. Their inundations at times have been so violent as to cause considerable damage. Moreover, Egypt is sheltered on all sides by deserts and waters. Mesopotamia is more exposed to invasions from Elam and Iran on the east, to migrations from Arabia on the south and to attacks from neighbors on the west.

These physical differences between the two valleys are reflected in the two civilizations cradled on their river banks. The Sumero-Babylonian society felt helpless vis-à-vis capricious forces personified in gods; it developed a pessimistic philosophy of life. Politically its country was not unified until the eighteenth pre-Christian century under the Semitic Hammurabi. The early Egyptian society felt more secure in its isolated land, enjoyed a long period of peace and became imbued with the sense of homogeneity. It developed a more optimistic outlook. Its gods, like its Nile, were generally beneficent. Egypt achieved political unity a thousand years before Mesopotamia. It experienced no serious invasion until the late eighteenth century B.C., when the Hyksos descended on it from Syria. It waited another thousand years to see another enemy on its soil—the Assyrians.

The mountain range along the eastern shore of the Mediterranean rises to about 5000 feet in Syria and 11,000 feet in Western

Lebanon. Anti-Lebanon parallels Western Lebanon and culminates in Mount Hermon (Jabal al-Shaykh), overlooking Palestine. The two north-to-south Lebanons trap most of the precipitation of the maritime winds, leaving the Syrian hinterland but little. Whereas Beirut receives an annual average of 35 to 38 inches of rain, Damascus gets only 10 inches. In Beirut the mean annual temperature is 68°F., but its summers are more humid and less comfortable than Damascus with its higher temperature. The Lebanese coastal plain with the adjoining mountain slopes makes of the country a garden of the East.

Palestine is geologically a continuation of Lebanon, Transjordan a continuation of Anti-Lebanon and Syria. The Lebanese maritime plain becomes the plain of Sharon, which extends from Mount Carmel to connect with the littoral of Philistia. The highlands of Palestine attain a maximum elevation of only 3935 feet north of Safad. In Jerusalem, 2550 feet high, the average temperature in July is only 75°F., in January 47°F.

Such was the geographic setting of the stage on which our Near Eastern man played his role from primitivism to a dizzy height of civilization.

3

Early Stages of Cultural Evolution

In his lengthy, arduous but steady advance towards a state that could be called civilized, the primitive man, judged by his economy, passed through three principal stages: food gathering, food producing and craftsmanship. These stages marked his evolution from savagery through barbarism to civilization. All three were achieved in his preliterary existence and in the area under study.

The first stage was by far the longest and darkest, lasting perhaps half a million years. Throughout this period man lived on plants and animals in their wild condition. This mode of living kept him on the go from place to place, with no leisure, no settled life, no organized society. Sometime before the end of the period he hit upon one of his first momentous discoveries, that plants and animals could be domesticated. For the first time in his existence he was thereby able to exercise a measure of control over the sources of his livelihood. He was no more in total bondage to his physical environment. His existence became more secure. He thus stepped to the second stage in his economic development. For centuries the two stages must have overlapped. Even today they are not entirely mutually exclusive.

The second stage was considerably shorter, lasting only a few thousand years. In both stages, stone was the only known tool. The predominant early tool was a roughly chipped stone hand-ax, which slowly, gradually gave way to the polished stone instrument that could be used as knife, saw, chisel, ax and weapon. The Old Stone Age developed therewith into the new one. Man was lifted one rung higher on the ladder of progress.

Before the end of his career the new Stone Age man hit—again by chance—on history-making discoveries involving the fashioning of clay into vessels and vases, weaving plant twigs into baskets and animal hair into cloth. More importantly he learned that he could mold a more malleable substance, metal, into more effective tools and weapons. The dawn of the third stage, craftsmanship, began. Pottery, weaving and metallurgy enabled our man to establish urban life, organize society and follow more intellectual, spiritual and artistic pursuits. Savage in the first stage, barbarian in the second, he could now be termed civilized. But he had not yet developed an adequate system of writing. The only records he left came to us in the form of tools, weapons, pottery sherds, and skeletal and other remains.

Climatically, zoologically and botanically the Near East—particularly the Anatolian-Iranian plateau and the Syria-Lebanon-Palestine area—were equipped with the necessary prerequisites for the modes of life described above. The Egyptian and Mesopotamian lands were then too marshy to be habitable. For perhaps ninety-eight per cent of his long age on earth, man subsisted on uncultivated grains, berries, seeds, fruits and vegetables and on such wild animals as deer, gazelle, boar, goat and sheep—all of which abounded in this region. His life was mobile and precarious, exposed to untold perils from nature, wild animals and his fellow man. The area happened to be also rich in flint, whose modules our savage ancestor learned at some time in his struggle for existence to chip on both sides and use as hand- or fist-ax. This gave him not only a useful tool but an effective weapon. Two other dynamic achievements may be attributed to this Old Stone Age man: fire and language. The discovery that he could generate some phenomenon with which he could give his food better taste and protect his body against cold must have been of revolutionary import. Traces of the earliest charcoal left by man have been unearthed in a Carmel cave and dated at about 150,000 years ago. Even more revolutionary and significant was man's development of a vocal means by which he could communicate clearly with his fellow man. Language lifted him above and distinguished him sharply from animals. It contributed immeasurably to welding individuals into groups.

Numberless centuries must have rolled by before man realized that he could further chip his stone implement, improve it and give it a sharper edge. As such polished implements and weapons came to prevail, they inaugurated the New Stone Age, a relatively short one. A complete sequence of stone industries has been found in Syria, Lebanon and Palestine.

Before the conclusion of this era initial steps were taken toward the purposeful cultivation of soil and the taming of animals. Not only cereals but olives, dates, grapes and figs were native to the land. It presumably all began when some wild grain happened to spill from a supply of food near a camping ground and was noticed later by some bright camper as a dense growth. Thus was the way opened for the cultivation of cereals, fruits and vegetables. The first farmer was born. He soon became livestock breeder as well. The domesticability of animals was likewise discovered by chance rather than design. Its long story may be telescoped into a few hypotheses. A wild beast, member of the wolf family, strays to a camping ground, feeds on scattered bones and receives more from a sentimental camper. The animal becomes attached to the place. Mutual confidence is generated. A dog is in the making. This was man's first and has ever since remained his best animal friend. Again a Carmel cave has yielded the first evidence of a domesticated dog. In ancient Egyptian tombs mummified dogs indicate the measure of esteem in which this animal was held. Other animals were tamed in this agricultural age. The earliest representation of a domestic sheep has come to us on a fourth millennium Sumerian vase. The ass was the first beast of burden. The horse came later and was followed by the camel. Both of these animals were domesticated in the area under study. In historic times not a single animal is known to have been added to the list.

With the full adoption of crop and stock raising, man tended to give up nomadism. Settlements grew into villages, villages into towns. Land ownership and personal property became possible. Population increased. Social order evolved. Remains of fifth millennium settlements in Jubayl (Byblus) and Jericho antedate any found elsewhere. Those of Tell al-Judaydah in north Syria and of Nuzi (near Kirkuk) in Iraq follow.

Early in his agricultural career man must have felt the need for a receptacle to store and transport that part of his foodstuff he could not consume at a given time. This need was roughly met by folding animal skins to form bags, and by plaiting twigs of reed or grass and daubing them with mud to form baskets. In due course it was realized that clay could be shaped, hardened and kept in form by heating. The technique gradually improved. The art of ceramics was born.

Courtesy of Oregon State System of Higher Education

PAINTED POTTERY VESSELS FROM THE PREHISTORIC AGE IN MESOPOTAMIA

The earliest specimens of pottery, dating from about 5000 B.C., have come down to us from Tell al-Halaf (on a Euphrates tributary), Tell al-Judaydah and Jericho. A thousand years later the potter's wheel makes its appearance. Its invention, another epoch-making achievement, not only improved and beautified its clay product but led to wheeled cars, carriages, war chariots. It opened the era of land and sea communication. In fact our entire modern economy still runs on wheels.

After pottery came metallurgy. Though copper-ore deposits lay scattered in Anatolia, Armenia, Arabia and Sinai, the metal did not gain widespread employment till about 3000 B.C. Employment involved several complicated processes: mining, extracting, smelting and shaping. Slowly copper displaced stone. A new age was therewith introduced. The metal age, initiated by copper, was designated bronze age after it was realized that copper, if mixed with tin, could be hardened and rendered more effective. The discovery was made in Sumer. The bronze era lasted in our area until about 1200 B.C. In the meantime iron tools were developed evidently in the fourteenth century by Hittites (in Anatolia). Another long forward step was taken when it was realized that steel could be produced from iron.

The employment of metal made man's work easier and his progress in industry and economy quicker. Without metal the opening of adequate roads, the digging of extensive canals, the building of seaworthy boats, the erection of monumental buildings would hardly have been possible. Indeed we have been in the metal age ever since. Metal continues to play a leading role in the material progress of modern man.

Important as these Near Eastern accomplishments were in themselves, they acquired further importance from their dissemination abroad. They all antedated and served as models for their counterparts in Europe. While our New Stone Age man was making advances in farming, cattle breeding, polishing or grinding flint implements, the Western European was still chasing reindeer with his old-fashioned stone tools. Even later, when the Near Easterner was beginning to manufacture pottery, woven cloth and more serviceable metal instruments, the European had not achieved the New Stone Age. In eastern Europe this age began around 3000 B.C. Whether the spread of agriculture and domestication of animals was due to migration of tribes from Anatolia, to cultural diffusion or to both cannot be ascertained. But it has been determined that the ancestry of the European domesticated plants and animals lies in their wild Near Eastern counterparts.

Copper reached eastern Europe about 2000 B.C., a millennium after its widespread use in western Asia. It may be assumed that western Asian traders in search of the metal were responsible for its introduction into Crete, the Aegean Islands and mainland Greece. Iron did not reach Europe until about the tenth pre-Christian century, centuries after its use in western Asia.

All the above-discussed discoveries and inventions belong to prehistory. Prehistory was preliterary. Man lacked ability to record his experience, preserve his knowledge and pass his ideas to later generations. He could not write. It was writing that marked the passage from prehistory to history. Writing is still a criterion for distinguishing between civilization and barbarism.

The earliest extant written remains come from Mesopotamia, dating shortly before 3000 B.C. This date marks the dawn of history. It makes the entire historic period 5000 years, a small fraction of the prehistoric which, in turn, is a minute fraction of the age of the earth. If we could compress man's existence on earth into one single day of 12 hours (from midnight to noon), his literary period would then have begun as late as 11:53 a.m. The Crusades would have been fought about 1 minute and 44 seconds ago, and America's discovery would have taken place 55 seconds ago.

It was the pre-Semitic Mesopotamian (Sumerian) who evolved the earliest adequate system of writing. Its script has been designated cuneiform (wedge-shaped) because of its arrow-shaped characters produced by a stylus pressed on a soft clay tablet. The shredded-wheat-like tablet was hardened in the sun or fire. In another country of our area, Egypt, the second oldest system developed. This was the hieroglyphic (sacred carving), used by priests primary for religious purposes. Both cuneiform and hieroglyphic were syllabic, not alphabetic. Both grew from picture writing. Hieroglyphic displays its pictorial origin. Cuneiform was adopted by Babylonians, Assyrians and others; its script survived in use into the first Christian century. Until its decipherment by an Englishman in 1837, no one could read the language. Shortly before that, hieroglyphic was deciphered by a Frenchman. Since then the undreamed-of treasures—religious, literary, historic, scientific—of the early Babylonians and Egyptians have been revealed.

Scholars could then reconstruct from original literary sources and archeological finds the evolution of man's earliest society. Small settlements on the banks of the Euphrates and the Nile coalesced or grew into towns. Towns developed into city-states. By conquest or pact city-states united to form a larger political unit, a kingdom. The head god of the conquering city was automatically acknowledged as the head of the entire pantheon. By 2900 B.C. the two kingdoms of Lower and Upper Egypt were ready for union under one ruler, Menes. Menes thus became founder of the First Dynasty. He and his Pharaoh ("great house") successors claimed to be the personification of Horus, chief deity of Lower Egypt. In Sumer, not until 2255 B.C. did a monarch, that of Uruk, claim to have "conquered the land from the rising of the sun to the setting of the sun" and "made straight his path from the Lower Sea to the Upper Sea" (Persian Gulf to the Mediterranean).

Ethnically the Sumerians belonged to the still unidentified belt. On the monuments they appear mixed of long-headed Mediterranean and broad-headed Armenoid groups. Their language has no cognate in any one, living or dead. The Egyptians are ethnically designated as Hamites, a traditional name from Noah's second son. The Babylonians, Assyrians, Phoenicians (Canaanites) and Arabs are known as Semites, from Noah's eldest son. In fact both "Hamitic" and "Semitic" are linguistic terms, not biological. The two languages are related. Both the Semitic- and Hamitic-speaking peoples are members of the Mediterranean branch of the Caucasian race.

4

The Imperial Age

The first great Semitic name in history is that of Sargon, who ruled in Akkad (Accad of Gen. 10:10) about 2350 B.C. Sargon destroyed Sumerian power, represented by Lugal-zaggisi, unified and consolidated the Mesopotamian realm and extended its boundaries eastward to Elam (biblical Shushan) and westward to north Syria. This makes him the first empire builder in history. Copper, stone and coniferous wood formed the chief attraction of his westward expansion. A grandson of Sargon extended his authority northward through Assyria, validating his title "king of the four quarters of the world."

Egypt developed its dynastic and political institutions long before Babylonia, but its imperial period was delayed. Menes' successors had no immediate neighbors to threaten, or to be threatened by them. Very early commercial or industrial—but not military—expeditions were undertaken to Lebanon for cedar wood and to Sinai for copper or turquoise. In the step pyramid of Saqqara (ancient Memphis), built by Zoser (*ca.* 2650), have been found the earliest relics of Lebanese cedar. Zoser's court was rendered illustrious by Imhotep, his architect, physician, counselor and magician, deified by Egyptian and Greek traditions for his skill in medicine. The tomb of this first intellectual to impress his name on history was found in January 1965. Cheops (Khufu, *ca.* 2550), founder of the Fourth Dynasty and builder of the greatest pyramid at Gizeh (near Cairo), had his recently discovered barge made of the same wood. The Gizeh pyramids were hoary with age when they were exposed to the eyes of the Holy Family on its flight to Egypt. So impressed were the Greeks with these structures that they counted them first among the "seven wonders" of the world.

Of the seven only this wonder has survived almost intact. Moreover, the pyramids antedate any other monumental structure.

The old kingdom in Egypt was followed in 2200 by the middle kingdom, ushered by the brilliant Twelfth Dynasty. Under this dynasty the country enjoyed a period of peace, progress and prosperity unprecedented. A remarkable hydraulic feat reclaimed the marshy Fayum (Lake Moeris) district to become the fruit and vegetable garden of the country. Another feat, attributed to Sesostris III (Senwosrets, d. 1840) connected the Nile with the Red Sea, establishing maritime navigation with the Mediterranean. Commercial expeditions were undertaken to Punt (roughly Somaliland and perhaps Yemen) for obtaining ivory, ebony, leopard skins, frankincense and spices. National prosperity was reflected in the flourishing of architecture and plastic arts. The period marks the classical age of Egyptian literature and the birth of new genres. An example is Sinuhe's travel story, to be discussed later.

The Eighteenth Dynasty, inaugurated by Ahmose (1570-1545), ushered in the imperial age in Egypt's history. Thebes (Luxor and Karnak) was the sole capital. The complacent, isolationist policy gave way to a dynamic one, involving aggression and expansion. The change was prompted by chasing out of the land the foreign invaders, the Hyksos ("kings of foreign lands," commonly Shepherd Kings), after a hated rule of a century and a half. This was the first national humiliation Egyptian pride suffered. The Hyksos were predominantly Semites from Syria and Lebanon and are credited with having introduced the horse and the war chariot into the Nile valley. It was in their court that Joseph rose to power, leading to the settlement of the Hebrews in the land.

Not content with driving out the Hyksos, Ahmose launched his country upon a career of conquest. A successor, Thutmose III (*ca.* 1502-1448), conducted sixteen military campaigns that took him east of the Euphrates. He was the Napoleon of ancient Egypt. The walls of his Theban temple list the cities he conquered along the coast and cite the spoils. Nubia was added to the rising empire. Thutmose's sister-wife Hatshepsut shared the rule with him for a time. She was the first great woman in history. Her obelisk and his adorn public squares and parks in Istanbul, Rome, London and New York.

Thutmose's successors were not able to maintain the newly acquired possessions for long. Amenhotep (Amenophis IV, *ca.* 1377-1361) was more interested in religion than diplomacy. In face of opposition from the powerful Theban priests of the chief deity

Courtesy of the Metropolitan Museum of Art, Rogers Fund, 1925

PORTRAIT BUST OF QUEEN NEFERTITI, WIFE OF IKHNATON

Amon-Re, Amenhotep raised his favorite god, Aton (the sun disk with its life-giving rays), to the headship of the pantheon. He even changed his name to Ikhnaton (splendor of Aton) and moved his capital to Akhetaton (the horizon of Aton, now Tell al-Amarna). He has been deservedly called the first personality in history, but he could not be considered a monotheist. His beautiful wife, Nefertiti, shared his religious views. The discovery of this Pharaoh's archives in cuneiform script at Tell al-Amarna in the late nineteenth century was a sensational event, and their reading illuminated the history of the period in Egypt and western Asia. More sensational in archeological annals was the finding of the tomb of Ikhnaton's son-in-law Tutankhamon (*ca.* 1361-1352), whose name indicates that he restored the worship of Amon. He moved the seat of government back to Thebes, where the priests buried him with a lavish display of furnishings and art treasures that has not ceased to attract a constant stream of spectators to the Cairo museum.

Nineteenth Dynasty Pharaohs attempted to reclaim the Asiatic provinces, but all they got was Palestine. The long reign of Ramses II (*ca.* 1301-1234) was marked by wars against the Hittites, ending in a pact which maintained a balance of power and temporary stability. But the downward curve in Egyptian prestige continued. Under Ramses' son Merneptah (*ca.* 1234-1215) the Hebrew exodus took place.

In Mesopotamia another Semitic group, known as Amorites, established in Babylon a dynasty whose most distinguished member was Hammurabi (d. *ca.* 1686). The capital city gave its name to the country. Babylon's and Hammurabi's patron deity, Marduk, was automatically elevated to the headship of the pantheon; his cult became a sort of state cult. Hammurabi reunified the country, after a period of disturbances, and extended his domain to the Mediterranean. He boastfully entitled himself king of Babylon, Sumer, Akkad and the four quarters of the world. More than a conqueror, he erected palaces and temples, dug new canals and renovated old ones. Under him Babylon attained a position of eminence and prosperity not again experienced until Nebuchadnezzar's days, a thousand years hence.

Hammurabi's crowning achievement, however, was the compilation of a code of laws that ranks among the oldest, most comprehensive and enlightened of its kind. What makes it especially interesting to us is its parallelism with the Mosaic code. Hammurabi, like Moses, received his code from a god, Shamash (the sun deity of justice), seated on a mountain. Striking as similarities may be between certain articles in the two codes, they can be explained on

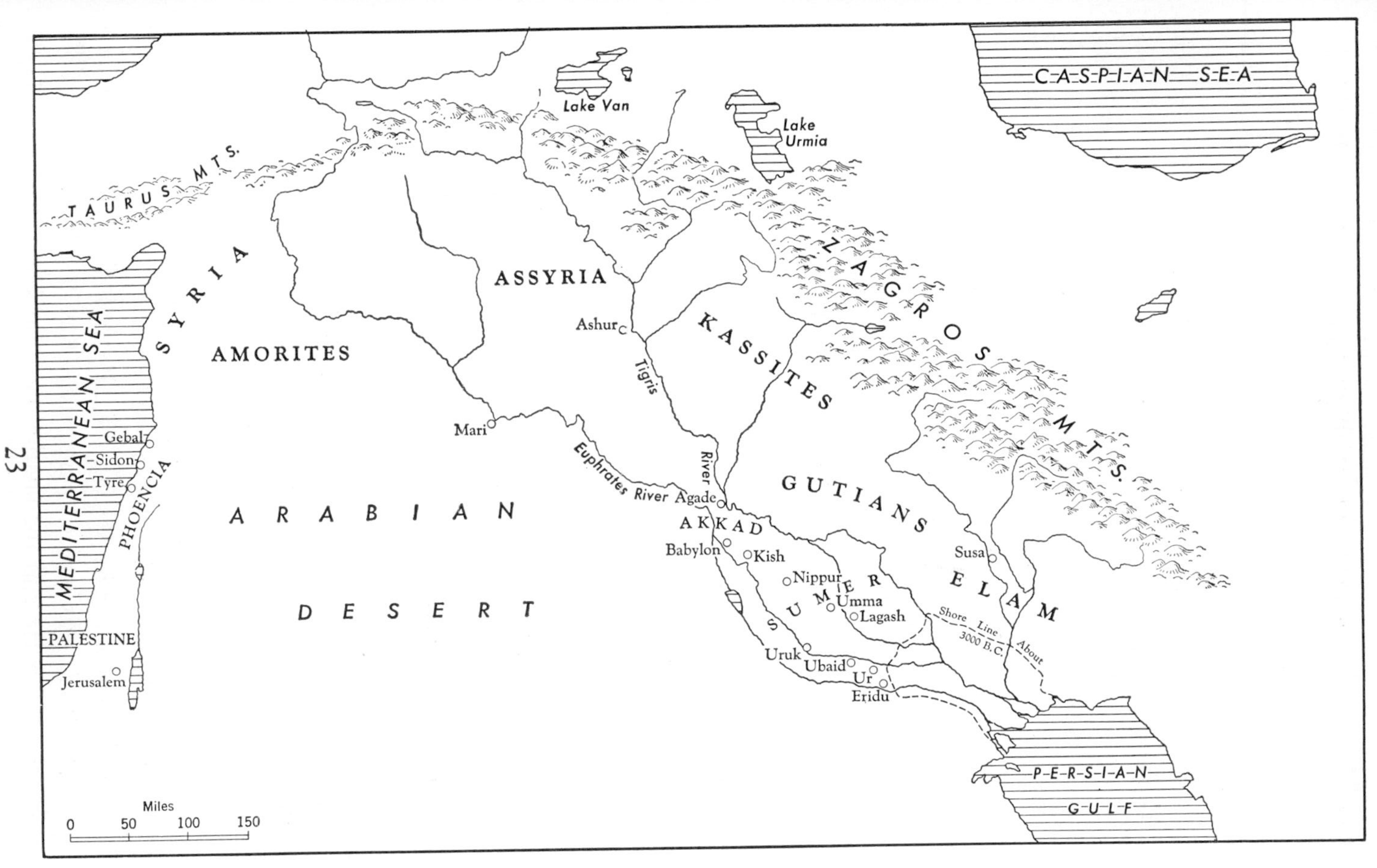

WESTERN ASIA WHEN BABYLON WAS SUPREME: EARLY SECOND MILENNIUM B.C.

the basis of descent from a common Semitic background, rather than borrowing. In criminal cases, for instance, the time-honored principle of retaliation is maintained in both codes.

The main value of the Babylonian code, however, lies in the light it throws on the political, social and economic aspects of life. The family is revealed as the basis of society. The society comprised three classes. The upper class filled the high political and religious offices and enjoyed special rights and privileges. Punishment for injuring an aristocrat could be more severe than for injuring a commoner, but a guilty aristocrat could be punished more severely than a commoner committing the same crime. The slave class constituted a substantial part of the population, and as in all antiquity, its members were considered the property of their owners. In between came the commonality of merchants, shopkeepers and artisans. The code provided for marriage contracts, breach of promise, divorce and concubinage. Adultery was punishable by death. In general the rights of women were safeguarded as in no other code until Roman legislation. Physicians, artisans and other skilled laborers were often paid in kind and in accordance with fixed provisions.

The dynasty which produced Hammurabi lasted till 1530, when it fell under attack from Carchemish (now Jarabulus), a Hittite stronghold on the Euphrates in north Syria. Babylon was sacked. The people called Hittites rose to power from modest beginnings in the Halys River (Kizil Irmak) valley ninety miles east of Ankara, modern capital of Turkey. Physically the Hittites appear on the monuments as a mixture of Indo-Europeans and Armenoids or Alpines. Linguistically their records bear the earliest marks of relationship to Sanskrit and Persian, on the one hand, Greek and Latin on the other. Hittite script took a double form, Babylonian cuneiform and pictographs comparable to Egyptian hieroglyphic.

By 1350 the Hittites had occupied north Syria, wrested from Egypt the Phoenician coast to a point south of Byblus and become the mightiest power in western Asia. Egypt had passed its heyday, and Babylonia was under foreign rule (Kassite). Two weapons of warfare, the horse and the chariot, gave the Hittites an advantage

HITTITE AND EGYPTIAN EMPIRES IN THE MID-FOURTEENTH CENTURY B.C.

over their adversaries. The horse was presumably tamed by Indo-Europeans in the Caspian region and had by this time reached western Asia. The chariot wheel was known since Sumerian days, but the Hittites were the first to employ iron in its manufacture. Southern Syria (Palestine), now under Egyptian suzerainty, became a bone of contention between the two rival powers. The struggle for supremacy in the east Mediterranean area ended in a draw. A treaty signed in 1280 recognized north Syria as Hittite and south Syria as Egyptian. This earliest of international pacts professed to bring "peace and good brotherhood between the contending parties for ever." Other treaties with such wishful thoughts followed.

By 1280 the balance of power in the area had been destroyed. A newly rising Semitic people, the Assyrians, were largely responsible for the destruction of the Hittite empire. The Hittite people slipped into obscurity if not oblivion. It was not until the second decade of the twenthieth century that a Czech scholar succeeded in deciphering their cuneiform inscription. The hieroglyphic script did not yield its secret until the 1940's. With these developments, an exciting event in modern scholarship, the story of a forgotten Near Eastern people was rediscovered.

The elimination of Hittite power and the eclipse of both Babylonia and Egypt left a power vacuum that was soon filled by the Assyrians. Fo centuries these northern kinsmen of the Babylonians had been politically passive, yielding to outside authority. Meantime they developed in their relatively cold mountainous land those traits of hardihood and ruggedness associated with highlanders. Taking full advantage of the situation, they in time built up the greatest military machine of antiquity—prior to that of the Romans—and for five centuries beginning around 1100 they were the leading nation in the Near East.

The Assyrians' culture was largely borrowed from the Babylonian. Their script was the same cuneiform. Their chief god was a sun-deity, Ashur, who gave his name to the first capital (now Sharqat) and subsequently to the country and the people. In

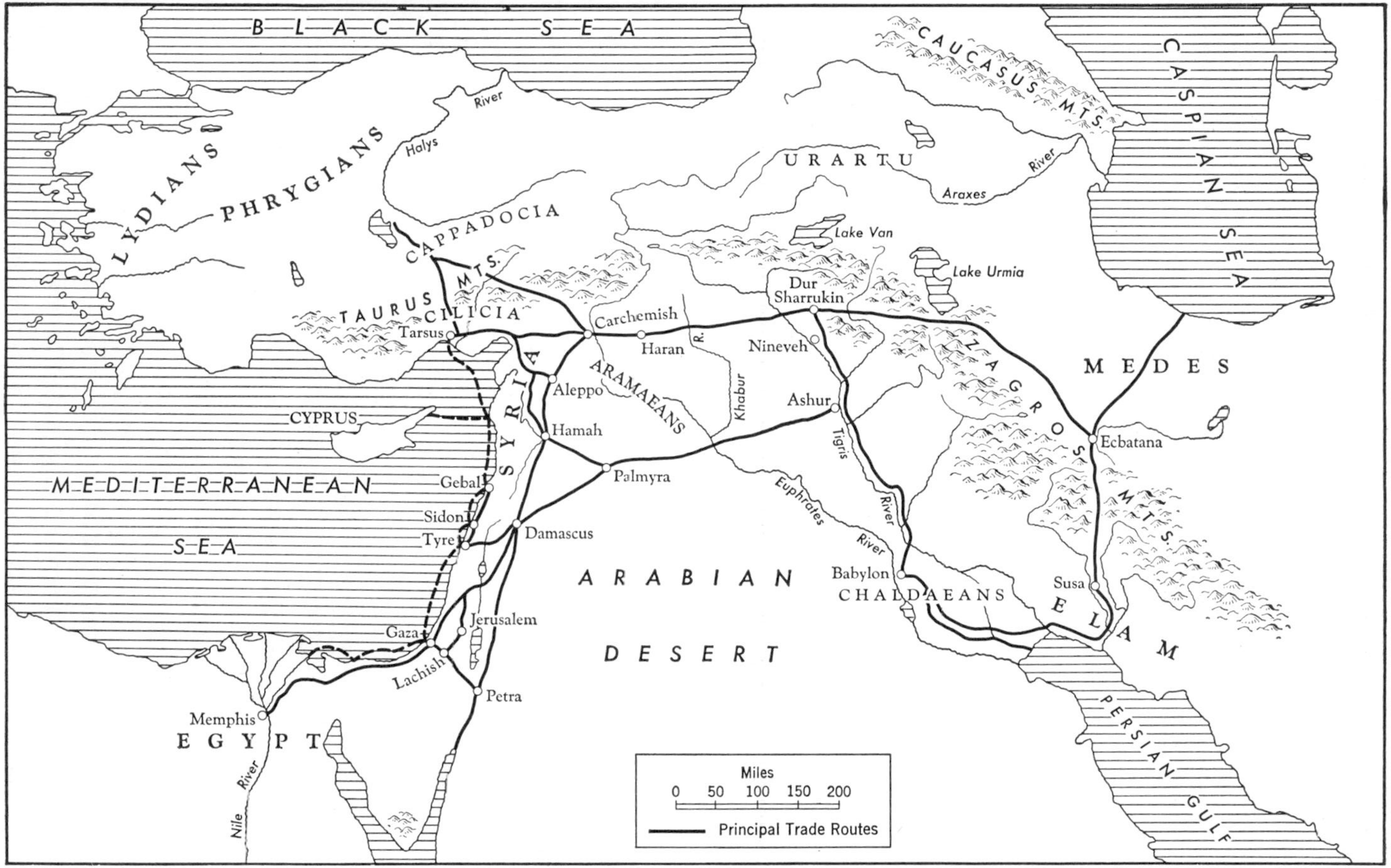

ASSYRIAN EMPIRE

sculpture, architecture, military equipment and political administrations, the Assyrians excelled the Babylonians.

The first essay at empire building was made by Tiglath-pileser I (1116-1093), but it turned out to be abortive. His westward thrust did not result in new acquisitions. The second attempt, however, by Ashur-nasir-pal (884-859), was successful. One after the other of the petty Aramaean states which had risen on ruins of the Hittite empire and stood in the way of Tiglath-pileser yielded to the new warrior king. The Aramaeans belonged to a new Semitic migration from Arabia. Ashur-nasir-pal conquered north Syria and exacted heavy tribute from the Phoenician coastal cities. Peace-loving, prosperous and disunited, those cities were ever ready to purchase immunity from interference with their way of life, based on business and commerce. After Ashur-nasir-pal the westward push became a cardinal point in Assyrian foreign policy. Its aim: the control of sources of copper, silver, iron, stone and lumber, together with the Mediterranean seaports and the international trade routes.

Ashur-nasir-pal's son Shalmaneser III (859-824) faced a formidable coalition headed by Ben-Hadad, Aramaean king of Damascus, and including Ahab, king of Israel, Jundub, an Arabian shaykh, and a number of Phoenician city-states. Jundub is the first Arabic personal name thus far known. On the battlefield of Qarqar (853, in the Orontes valley) Shalmaneser won an indecisive victory. It is not until the reign of Tiglath-pileser III (745-727) that the Assyrian foothold was firmly established. The strongest city, Damascus, was captured (732) and put under a governor from Assyria. Some of its people were deported and replaced by foreigners. By transplanting the would-be troublemakers from a conquered territory and placing it under a non-native ruler, Tiglath-pileser reduced the chances of future uprisings and increased those of full incorporation into the empire. His precedent established a new policy. When Israel's capital, Samaria, submitted (722) after a three-year siege, the flower of its manhood was transported to Assyria and Media and replaced by an alien population.

The consolidation of the empire continued under Sennacherib (705-681). Nineveh on the upper Tigris rose to eminence as the imperial capital of western Asia. Sennacherib's son Esarhaddon dared attack Egypt. In 671 he occupied its delta. In two successive campaigns his successor Ashur-bani-pal (668-626) carried Assyrian arms victoriously into Upper Egypt. The fame of this monarch, however, rests more on his patronage of learning. The library he established in his capital, unearthed by the British in the mid-nineteenth century, provided the world with much of what is known today about Assyrian civilization.

With the conquest of Egypt, Assyria hit the zenith of its power. It stood supreme in the entire Near East. But the fall was precipitous and irrevocable. Fourteen years after Ashur-bani-pal's death, Nineveh found itself under irresistible attack by an army of Medes and Neo-Babylonians. The haughty capital, which had lorded it from the Tigris to the Nile, fell. Nahum's prediction against the "bloody city," "full of lies and robbery," scene of the "rattling of wheels, and of the prancing horses and of the jumping chariots" (Nah. 3:1-2) was literally fulfilled. So utterly wiped out of existence was the city that a Greek general passing by its site two centuries later did not recognize it. A mound now called Kuyunjik, opposite Mosul, hid its secrets for over twenty-four and a half centuries.

The Medes were Indo-Iranians of northwestern Persia. Their leader in the attack on Nineveh was Cyaxares. King Cyaxares' daughter was married to Nabopolassar, the Neo-Babylonian leader. The Neo-Babylonians (Chaldaeans) lived in lower Mesopotamia and were related to the Aramaeans of Syria. Their capital was Babylon.

With the destruction of Nineveh and the decay of Thebes, Babylon once again emerged as the mistress of the Orient. It achieved that position under Nabopolassar's son Nebuchadnezzar II (605-562). When still a crown prince, Nebuchadnezzar crushed the army of Pharaoh Necho at Carchemish. In 586 he destroyed Jerusalem, Judah's capital, and in 572, after one of the longest recorded sieges in history, received the submission of Tyre. The four-century-old Kingdom of Judah ceased to exist. Egypt lost its last chance to stir up revolt among Hebrews and Phoenicians, and its deeply ingrained ambition to dominate western Asia was permanently frustrated.

Nebuchadnezzar rebuilt Babylon, adorned it with new palaces and temples and made it worthy of its imperial status. The "hanging gardens" he built for his Median wife, who is said to have been homesick for her mountainous country, were later counted among the "seven wonders of the world." In his inscriptions, however, he took more pride in recording his digging new irrigation canals and roads. He thereby raised Babylonia to a new level of economic prosperity.

The Neo-Babylonians were to enjoy but a short-term supremacy. Their last king, Nabonidus, began his rule only six years after Nebuchadnezzar ended his. But he left state affairs entirely in the hands of his frivolous son Belshazzar, whose interest centered in food and drink. On his palace wall the writing was clear to all those with vision: "Thy kingdom is divided and gone to the Medes and Persians" (Dan. 5:28). In 539 the Persian army stood around the walls of Babylon and early in the following year fully occupied it. The new star in the political firmament of the East was that of Cyrus the Great (550-529), unifier of Media and Persia and conqueror of western Asia to Lydia (on its western coast). For the first time western Asia from the Aegean to the Egyptian border was brought under one scepter. Herewith Semitic hegemony came to an end, not to rise again till the emergence of Islam in the seventh century after Christ. The Persians were Indo-Iranian in language and Zoroastrian in religion. Pasargadae was maintained as a royal residence, but Susa, more central, became the seat of government.

Cyrus was followed by a series of able warrior rulers. His son Cambyses (529-521) added Egypt and pushed up on the Nile (525). He literally reigned from India into Ethiopia (Esth. 1:1). Darius the Great (521-486) carried on the work of expansion to the Indus. He established new royal residences at Persopolis rivaling, if not surpassing, Nebuchadnezzar's in Babylon. There they stood, a symbol of Persian might and grandeur, until they went up in flames when Alexander the Great burned the city in 330. Other public works of Darius featured a Nile-Red Sea waterway anticipating the Suez Canal. The waterway rendered sea communication between Persia and Egypt possible. The Persian emperor utilized Phoenicians in building a fleet and linked cities with roads. Trade flourished and public security improved. But a revolt among his Ionian (Greek) subjects on the western shore of Asia Minor marked the beginning of a new era in the history of relations between East and West—an era of conflict in which Alexander the Great, Pompey, Saladin down to Napoleon and Allenby played leading roles.

The spark in Ionia ignited a flame across the waters on the Greek mainland. The prolonged conflict between Persians and Greeks was punctuated by such world-renowned battles as those of Marathon (490), Thermopylae (480) and Salamis (off Piraeus, 480). Marathon was lost by Darius, Thermopylae and Salamis by his son Xerxes I (biblical Ahasuerus, 485-465). The last was a naval battle, with the Phoenician fleet forming the core of the Persian navy. Greek story tellers, historians and poets covered the battlefields of victory with honor and glory, raising those who lost their lives thereon to the rank of national and immortal heroes. The issue, according to their interpretation, was Greek liberty and democracy versus Oriental despotism. The fact is that at that time Persian culture was by no means inferior to Greek culture, and Persian religion was certainly superior to Greek religion.

The imperial organization of the state under Darius was unquestionably more centralized, more efficient than any the world had seen. Babylonia and Egypt were placed under direct imperial rule. The rest were divided into provinces (satrapies), each under a Persian governor but allowing the natives a measure of autonomy. The attitude toward native culture was one of tolerance. No imposition of language or religion was attempted. While earlier empires, particularly the Assyrian, dealt at times mercilessly with conquered or rebellious towns and relied mainly on the sword to maintain authority, Persian emperors dealt more humanely with enemies. They displayed unusual concern for the welfare and security of their subjects. They introduced stamped coinage, facilitated communication and organized postal service—all on a scale hitherto unknown. Interstate trade was further enhanced by the general use of Aramaic, the language of the Aramaeans (later, Syrians), as a commercial tongue. By this time the Aramaeans had replaced the Phoenicians as international traders. Aramaic was even used as an official language by the Persian government. Persian emperors reversed the Assyro-Babylonian policy of deporting troublesome elements among their subjects. They allowed Jews to return from Babylon at its conquest, again under Nehemiah (445 B.C., Neh. 2-6) and shortly after that under Ezra (Ezra 5,6).

The empire founded by Cyrus, enlarged and consolidated by Darius, began to show cracks in its structure immediately after the death of Xerxes. Clashes with the Greeks continued. Degeneracy in the royal line, corruption in the court and harem intrigues encouraged ambitious satraps to deal more highhandedly with their subjects. Rebellions broke out in Egypt and in Phoenician cities. In 336 a man was raised to the throne by a eunuch, murderer of his predecessor. The new emperor was Darius III. He lost the empire six years later to an unexpected invader from the west, Alexander the Great.

5

Religion, Science and Literature

In its earliest and simplest form Mesopotamian religion was nature worship. In the course of its development the Sumerians divided the universe into heaven, earth and water, over which presided a triad of deities. The Semitic newcomers built on Sumerian foundations. With the rise of Babylon a Semitic god, Marduk (the young one), styled Bel (lord), rose to power and assumed the position of a national deity. When Nineveh achieved supremacy another Semitic god, Ashur, headed the pantheon. Both Marduk and Ashur were solar deitines. In Ur, whence Hebrew tradition brought Abraham, a moon-god, Sin, stood foremost. Ishtar, the mother-goddess, representing fertility and reproduction, was a general favorite. Following the human family pattern, gods were provided with consorts, given children and a retinue of lesser deities, who presided over minor operations of nature.

To the Mesopotamians, kings were agents of the gods, but to the Egyptians they were gods incarnate. In both lands education was in the hands of priests. But the most important function of priesthood was the correct performance of religious ceremonies, elaborate in ritual, to win the favor or propitiate the deities. Religious festivals normally coincided with the plowing of fields or the reaping of harvests. The unfailing cycle involving the apparent death of vegetation in winter and its reappearance—vivified and refreshed—in spring must have impressed the people of western Asia and Egypt as no other physical phenomenon did. Agriculture was the main sustenance of their lives.

In the New Year festival, the ritual dramatized the death and resurrection of Marduk. As a part of the ritual, passages from the epic of creation were chanted. The Babylonian version, which had a Sumerian original, makes Marduk the author of the present world order; the Assyrian assigns that role to Ashur. Of special interest to us is the striking similarity with the Hebrew version of creation, which, as we know, came later. Both accounts start with a watery chaos, proceed to a division of the world into heaven and earth, and lead to the creation of man as the capstone of the entire structure. In both stories the number seven figures. The Hebrew terminology betrays Babylonian origin. *Tehom*, for example, of Genesis (1:2; 7:11), where it is rendered "deep" and given the meaning of chaos, is Babylonian *tihamat*. The word occurs in its plural form in Proverbs (3:2). The biblical account, however, in its dignity and simplicity excels all other early cosmologies.

Longer and more interesting than the epic of creation is that of Gilgamesh, whose adventurous hero wanders in search of immortality. His hazardous journey takes him through a cedar forest in the west dominated by a frightful god, guarded by a dragon. He kills the dragon and faces an awesome bull sent against him by a goddess whose love-advances he had shunned. With the aid of a companion, Gilgamesh destroys the bull, but on his way back home his companion dies. This sets him on a new venture, the quest of eternal life. On an isolated island he at last meets the only man who with his wife had escaped a devastating flood which the gods had sent to destroy mankind. Forewarned, the Mesopotamian Noah had built a large boat and occupied it with his wife and pairs of all living things. As a reward for preserving life on earth, he received the universally desired gift of eternal life.

Clearly this is the ancestor of the biblical story of the deluge. Any doubt may be dispelled by the similarities of such details as the dimensions of the boat and the ark, the sending out of the dove and the landing atop a mountain. The Hebrew version, however, is more rational and less intricate. It introduces an ethical element and a monotheistic concept entirely lacking in the original. In the Mesopotamian version the sending of the flood was an arbitrary act on the part of the deities.

The Gilgamesh epic was translated early into Hittite, set the pattern for later epics, including that of Homer, and left echoes resounding in the exploits of the Greek Hercules and of the koranic Iskandar (Alexander) dhu-al-Qarnayn (the two-horned, Koran 18:84-98).

Parallelism between Babylonian and Hebrew literatures extends to the legal field. Hammurabi's code, compiled five centuries before the Mosaic, claimed divine origin, as the Mosaic did. In both, the time-honored principle of "eye for eye" and "tooth for tooth" is accepted. The Mesopotamian legislation reflects a more highly advanced society than the Palestinian. Its political, social and economic levels must have been more developed. Hammurabi frees the slave in the fourth year, Moses in the seventh. Both lawgivers make adultery punishable by death. But the Mosaic code strikes an ethical note in the Decalogue that is nowhere matched in ancient codes. No one but Christ has ever been able to improve on the Ten Commandments.

The Egyptian religion was more than one religion. As it evolved it came to embrace vestiges of the most primitive and some of the most highly developed elements. Gods were represented in three forms: animal, human and a combination of both. Of the animals the sacred bull Apis was considered the embodiment of the creator god Ptah and was the one revered most and longest. Pyramid texts and the Book of the Dead mention no less than 1400 deities.

An early god who came near achieving a universal position in the country was Re, who gave his name to the sun. His seat was the ancient capital Heliopolis and his symbol was the sun-ward obelisk. So influential in state affairs did his priests become that they made the Re cult for a time a state cult. With the shift of the capital to Thebes, its patron god Amon, originally a god of fertility and reproduction, rose in esteem. The two deities were gradually compounded, making Amon-Re supreme in the pantheon. The so-called heresy of Ikhnaton, discussed earlier, was essentially an attempt to substitute Aton, another solar deity, for Amon-Re. It indicates how deeply rooted the cult of the sun had become in Egyptian spiritual life.

A hymn ascribed to Ikhnaton shows striking similarity in spirit and wording to Psalm 104, which evidently borrowed from it:

Thou appearest beautifully on the horizon of heaven,
Thou living Aton, the beginning of life!
When thou art risen in the eastern horizon,
Thou hast filled every land with thy beauty.
Thou art gracious, great, glistening and high over every land;
Thy rays encompass the lands to the limit of all that thou hast made.
. . . .
Darkness is a shroud, and the earth is in stillness,
For he who made them rests in the horizon.[1]

In Egypt as in Mesopotamia the celestial family was patterned after the earthly one. The most popular triad was that of Osiris, Isis and Horus. Osiris, originally associated with agriculture and fertility, was presumably of Syro-Lebanese extraction introduced at some early date. The triad he headed comprised his wife-sister Isis and his son Horus. Time came when the happiness of the family was destroyed as a result of an assault on its head by Set. Set murdered Osiris, cut his body into pieces and dumped them into the Nile. His bereaved wife and son set out on a hunt, ending in the discovery of the dismembered body and bringing it back to life. Clearly this is an Egyptian version of the Phoenician Tammuz-Ishtar story. In both cases the dying and rising god symbolizes the annual sequence of the death and vivification of vegetation in a land dependent on agriculture for its livelihood. Thus did Osiris become the center of the cult of immortality, god of the underworld and judge of the dead. Isis became the symbol of the faithful wife and devoted mother, and Horus that of the dutiful child. In Egypt, where the Nile was dependable and the land sheltered against foreign invasion, the heavenly domestic bliss mirrored the generally contented earthly life; whereas in Mesopotamia, where the fitful Euphrates and Tigris often wrought havoc, and the land was exposed to attack from neighboring enemies, life was less secure and more somber.

[1] James B. Pritchard, ed., *Near Eastern Texts* (Princeton, 1950), p. 370.

Egyptian interest in life after death surpassed that of all other peoples of antiquity, the Hebrews included. Life on earth seemed too good to be terminated on death. The unfailing summer rise of the Nile from its bed—a kind of rebirth—and the preservative effect of the dry climate on the dead bodies pointed in the same direction. The preservation of the body became a prerequisite for the preservation of the *ka*, the correspondent of soul. Hence the institution of mummification, one of the longest lived in the history of religion. As a double safeguard Pharaohs resorted to huge pyramids with sealed doors or rock-hewn chambers as burial places. In tombs an adequate supply of food, drink and furniture was essential for the need of the dead, but it could be replaced by statuary and mural paintings of such articles. Herein lay the first impetus to Egyptian representational art. For the guidance of the dead in its perilous journey in its afterlife, mural inscriptions were provided. Instructions could also be inscribed on papyrus and buried with the mummies.

Out of such sepulchral inscriptions grew the Book of the Dead, the chief monument of Egyptian religious literature. In mystical language the book describes the adventures of the soul after death, provides formulas to escape the trials and tribulations of the underworld and discusses in detail the funeral ritual. On the walls of the Egyptian room in the British Museum spreads a richly illustrated papyrus copy of this book. Especially impressive is the judgment scene. The deceased, Ani, enters the hall in a worshipful posture and is followed by his wife. As he proceeds, he makes a negative confession: "I have not stolen"; "I have not told falsehoods"; "I am not a land-grabber"; "I committed no adultery"; "I am not a slayer of man," etc. This is followed by a positive confession: "I am pure"; "I am pure"; "I gave bread to the hungry, water to the thirsty, clothing to the naked and a ferry to him who was without a boat." Each of the forty-two judges, depicted on the walls of the hall, has a moral specialty and can challenge the deceased. Acquitted, Ani, his wife now identified with him, takes his final stand before Osiris. The supreme judge of the dead is enthroned within a shrine, supported by his wife and her sister. The couple is admitted

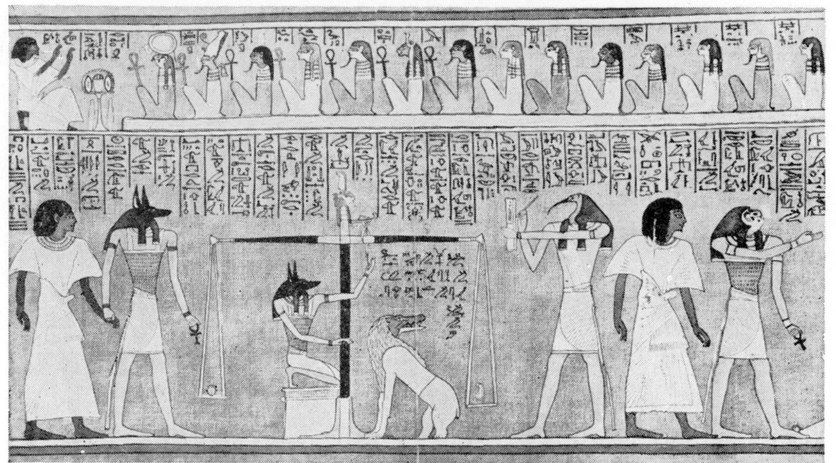

Courtesy of The Bettmann Archive

JUDGMENT SCENE FROM THE BOOK OF THE DEAD

to the fields of blessedness to continue the merry life they led on earth.

What is remarkable about the Egyptian confession of the dead is the note of social behavior it strikes. The traditional concept of sin as failure to observe ceremonial law remained, of course, intact as in Mesopotamia and Iran. But the place given social conduct in Egyptian religion, centuries before the Hebrews or Persians, had no contemporary parallel.

The Persian religion, Zoroastrianism, developed after Judaism and attained a high standard of morality. Zoroaster was a Median reformer, flourished about 600 B.C. and left a record shrouded in myth and legend. The foundations on which he built were undoubtedly those of the Iranian folk beliefs related to Hinduism. The system attributed to the Iranian prophet and reformer passed the pluralistic but fell short of the monotheistic stage. It was a dualism personifying the two opposing principles of good and evil, light and darkness, in two major deities Ahura Mazda (the wise lord, later Ormazd) and his antithesis Ahriman. Ahriman was the counterpart of our Satan. Both deities existed from the beginning of the world; both had creative powers. Mazda was the omniscient, omnipresent, uncreated creator of what is pure and living. As such he is in eternal conflict with his spiritual adversary, Ahriman. It makes it incumbent on the believer to participate in the struggle on the right side. As for the final outcome no doubt is entertained: Mazda will triumph and the good kingdom will be established.

All man's deeds, good and evil, are entered, itemized and checked in a special book. On death the soul is conducted to the "accountant's bridge," leading to the heavenly realm. If the balance of recorded deeds stands on the side of good works, passage is assured; otherwise the deceased is hurled into the hellish realm. The Egyptians had a real balance in which the heart was weighed against an emblem of justice. Islam also had balance and bridge folk beliefs. On the whole the Christian-Moslem ideas of afterlife, with the dependence of its state upon deeds performed on earth, is more akin to ancient Egyptian and Zoroastrian than to Hebrew concepts.

The teachings ascribed to Zoroaster eventually prevailed throughout Iran. They became the state religion. In the seventh Christian century the religion of Muhammad superseded that of Zoroaster. A handful of believers survived in the country. Those extant in and near Bombay are now known as Parsis (Persians).

In Egyptian secular literature the wisdom genre made an early appearance and achieved excellence and prevalence. Egyptian wisdom, in common with the Semitic, aimed at good manners and worldly success. It concerned itself more with "how to win friends and influence people" than with securing a passport to a blessed afterlife. It differed from Greek wisdom, which was mainly philosophical. An early exponent was Ptahhotep (fl. *ca.* 2375), a vizir of the Fifth Dynasty. Ptahhotep addressed maxims to his son, but they were applicable to any schoolboy interested in good conduct.

Magnify not thy heart because of thy knowledge, and fill not thy heart with the thought about it because thou hast knowledge. Hold converse with the ignorant man as well as with the learned. . . . A thousand men seeking what is beautiful [in outside women] are destroyed by them. A man is made a fool of by their shining limbs, but they turn into things that are harder than quartzite sandstone. The pleasure is only for a little moment. . . . If thou wouldst be wise (or, prosperous) establish thyself in a house [get married]. Love thou thy wife in the house wholly and rightly. Fill her belly and clothe her back; oil for anointing is the medicine for her limbs.[1]

In a later sage, Amenemapt (fl. *ca.* 1100 B.C.), Egyptian wisdom writing reached its highest ethical point. Maxims attributed to him must have been used centuries before; revised and polished, they were in vogue for centuries later. Amenemapt counsels against arrogance, snobbery, ill-temper and oppressing the poor. He stresses courtesy, deference, contentment, tolerance and kindness. Egyptian wisdom had a wide vogue outside of its native land. It served as a source for certain Hebrew Proverbs:

> Better is poverty in the hand of God,
> Than riches in the storehouse.
> Better are loaves when the heart is joyous,
> Than riches in unhappiness.
>
> (Cf. Prov. 15:16-17)
>
> Incline thine ears to hear my sayings,
> And apply thine heart to their comprehension.
> For it is a profitable thing to put them in thy heart,
> But woe to him who transgresses them.
>
> (Cf. Prov. 12:17-18)
>
> Fraternise not with the hot-tempered man,
> And press not upon him for conversation.[2]
>
> (Cf. Prov. 22:24)

In storytelling, as in wisdom and religious literature, Egyptians made an early notable contribution. The story of the Two Brothers, dating from Rameside days, has a motif similar to the story of Joseph and Potiphar's wife, but the possibility of borrowing is remote. In the Egyptian story the wife of the elder brother makes advances to the unmarried younger one but he does not respond,

[1] A. E. Wallis Budge, *The Teaching of Amen-em-Apt* (London, 1924), pp. 53 *seq.*
[2] James H. Breasted, *The Dawn of Conscience* (New York, 1933), pp. 372-378.

whereupon she brings false charges against him to her husband. Another story, that of Sinuhe, is an acknowledged masterpiece of world literature. The hero, a high court official, flees the country (*ca.* 1960) for some political reason, works his way through Palestine and settles somewhere between the two Lebanons. There he marries a daughter of a Bedouin chief, identifies himself with the natives and in due course succeeds his father-in-law as the shaykh of the tribe. Later on, however, he feels so homesick as to return to the land of his birth, where he could indulge in the luxury of a bath, sleep in a real bed and escape burial among "sand dwellers."

Sinuhe's narrative gives us the earliest glimpses of life in Palestine and its neighboring land. In its characterization and psychological portrayal it stands unique in its age. Revised and re-edited it was studied in schools for half a millennium. It reminds us of the story of Sinbad in the *Arabian Nights* and, like it, ended as more fiction than history.

An antique body of knowledge which may be called scientific has filtered down into our culture from Babylonian and Egyptian sources. This is especially true in the fields of mathematics and astronomy, medicine and art.

Counting on the fingers of the hand lay at the root of all arithmetical processes. Ten—the number of the two hands' fingers—yielded the basis of the decimal system, which became the Egyptian notation. A multiple of ten, sixty, became the basis of the sexagesimal system; while twelve, a factor of sixty, conditioned the duodecimal system of Mesopotamia. This explains our division of the hour into 60 minutes and the minute into 60 seconds. A multiple of 60 is apparent in the division of the circle into 360 degrees. The degree is again divided into sixty minutes.

Early Babylonians divided the week into seven days, each dedicated to one of the seven movable heavenly bodies. Each one of the bodies was identified with a god. The days of the week were dedicated to the heavenly bodies in the following order: sun, moon, Mars, Mercury, Jupiter, Venus and Saturn. Thus the first day became our Sunday, the second Monday (moonday) and the seventh Saturday (Saturnday). From the Babylonians we also inherited the notion of the zodiac, that imaginary heavenly belt in which were included the paths of the sun, the moon and the principal planets. Babylonian astronomers made consistent observations that culminated in the accurate prediction of lunar and solar eclipses. The father of Greek astronomy was Hipparchus, who was born in Asia Minor about 150 B.C. and used Babylonian observations. After him came Ptolemy, who flourished in Alexandria in the first half of the second Christian century. Ptolemy utilized earlier sources and produced a system of astronomy and geography that was universally accepted until the sixteenth century.

The solar calendar we owe to the Pharaonic Egyptians. In both Egypt and Babylonia the moon was first used for measuring the annual time. But Egyptians took a step further, made the month thirty days and added five feast days at the end of the year. Thus a solar year of 365 days became official about 2000 B.C. It had to wait until Julius Caesar introduced it into Europe. Reformed under Pope Gregory XIII (1583), this is the calendar still in use in the West. It constitutes Egypt's most conspicuous bequest. Another Egyptian astronomical contribution (of Babylonian origin) is the twelve-division of daytime and night. Of this division the faces of our watches and clocks are a constant reminder.

Astronomy played a relatively minor part in the daily life of the Babylonians, but its false counterpart, astrology, played a major one. Astrology's underlying assumption was the existence of a causal relation between man's actions and the god-identified heavenly bodies. The astrologer's function was to determine those relations and foretell future events. He left a noticeable heritage throughout medieval Europe. His descendant can still be seen on the boardwalk of Atlantic City using the same technique—the horoscope.

Disease, according to our Near Eastern man, was caused by demons, and demons could be exorcised by the physician-priest. He would use incantations and magic formulas. Here is a sample incantation to be repeated by the aching person:

Away, away, far away,
Be ashamed, be ashamed! Fly, fly away!
Turn about, go away, far away,
May your evil like the smoke mount to heaven!
. . . .
To my body do not return,
To my body do not approach,
To my body draw not nigh.
My body do not afflict.[1]

In a poem on a clay tablet from Nippur, a helpless bed-ridden sufferer (an arthritic) shares with us his feelings in graphic terms reminiscent of Job:

An evil demon has come out of his (lair);
From yellowish the sickness became white.
It struck my neck and crushed my back.
It bent my high stature like a poplar;
Like a plant of the marsh, I was uprooted, thrown on my back.
. . . .
The house became my prison;
As fetters for my body, my hands were powerless,
As pinions for my person, my feet were stretched out,
My discomfiture was painful, the pain severe.
A strap of many twists has struck me,
A sharply pointed spear pierced me.
All day the pursuer followed me,
At night he granted me no respite whatever,
As though wrenched, my joints were torn apart.[2]

As it developed, medicine added the use of such techniques as massage, poultices and certain herbal remedies. But evidently it was assumed that the filthier and less available the remedy the more efficacious. Mice blood, human urine and excrement figured in prescriptions. An Assyrian medical text offers the following remedy for one afflicted with what we call hemorrhoids: "If a man is sick of anus trouble, and his anus pricks him, pine-turpentine, fir-

[1] Morris K. Jastrow, *The Civilization of Babylonia and Assyria* (Philadelphia, 1915), pp. 245-246.
[2] Jastrow, *op. cit.*, p. 479.

turpentine, opopanax, the husks of barley, in oil or beer, into his anus thou shalt pour, and he shall recover."

In one field, however, surgery, remarkable advance was made. Hammurabi's code punishes a surgeon who blinds a patient when "opening an abscess in his eye [cataract?]" by cutting off his fingers. Egyptian surgeons operated on cysts, boils, carbuncles, wounds and fractures. Mummies show traces of delicate operations involving opening of the skull. Other delicate operations included cataract removal. In Egypt as well as Mesopotamia eye diseases must always have been prevalent due to semi-tropical conditions. The impact of Egyptian medical lore is noticeable not only throughout the Near East but in Greece. Early Greek physicians, Galen, for instance, drew heavily from Egyptian sources.

Mesopotamian art attained its maturity in Assyria. Following the Babylonian precedent Assyrians covered the exterior of temples and palaces with decorative designs, geometrical figures and pictorial representations in animal and floral forms. Concurrently sculpture was promoted. It reached its pinnacle in the imperial palaces of Sargon II, Sennacherib and Ashur-bani-pal. Extant bas-reliefs represent the king in sacred rituals, military campaigns and hunting scenes. The portrayal reveals the artist as possessing not only intimate knowledge of the living body's anatomy, but also ability to convey the impression of pain and terror.

It is Egyptian architectural ruins and artistic remains, rather than scientific legacy, that attract visitors and tourists to the valley of the Nile. In both valleys of the Nile and the Euphrates art had its beginning in religion and remained closely associated with it. The early capital Heliopolis had a craftsman-god in Ptah. In the later capital Thebes (now Karnak) the sanctuary of Amon displays the highest point attained in artistic craftsmanship, not only in Egypt but in antiquity. When in 1923 the rock-hewn tomb of Tutankhamon (d. 1349), restorer of the worship of Amon, was opened the learned world was dazzled with the gorgeous collection of golden beds, couches, chariots and caskets together with garlands of flowers wrought in silver—all in a state of admirable preservation, Egyptian rooms of the leading museums in the West exhibit vases, rings, necklaces, jewel boxes on which eyes of visitors can still feast.

Photograph by Harry Burton, The Metropolitan Museum of Art

TUTANKHAMON STANDING IN HIS CHARIOT CHARGES GAZELLES AND OSTRICHES

In science and literature Persian legacy offered no competition to that of Egypt or Mesopotamia, but in art it did and in certain aspects surpassed. As Indo-Europeans, Iranians have throughout displayed higher esthetic talents than their Semitic neighbors. Their artistic feelings were first expressed in painted pottery of the fourth pre-Christian millennium. They continued through varied media to the present. Copper was used in the mid-second millennium for producing stylized trinkets, mirrors, weapons and horse trapping. Later, bronze was utilized for daggers, diminutive animals, garment pins and votive staves, produced with some decorative intent.

In the Achaemenid period (*ca.* 550-330 B.C.), when Persia was mistress over western Asia and Egypt, Iranian art reached its height. The imperial palaces of Persepolis and Susa begun by Darius the Great (d. 485), completed and embellished by Xerxes and his successors and burned by Alexander the Great symbolized

Courtesy of The Oriental Institute, University of Chicago

A SCULPTURED FRIEZE AT PERSEPOLIS DISPLAYING TRIBUTE-BEARING SUBJECTS OF THE ACHAEMENIDS

Persia as a world empire and embodied its art at its best. Even after the destruction of the empire, Persian art, while adding Greek elements, preserved its decorative quality and value. Mongol conquests introduced new aspects; so did the Moslem one, resulting in exquisite calligraphy, manuscript miniatures, geometric and floral designs on multi-colored rugs and in mural mosaics on mosques and palaces that have not ceased to exercise their fascination on onlookers.

6

Phoenicia and Palestine: Their Contributions

Before Phoenicia and Palestine were so named they formed a part of the land of Canaan. So did Syria. Canaanites were the second major Semitic group after the Assyro-Babylonians of Mesopotamia. They entered the area from the Syro-Arabian desert in the early third millennium. In the thirteenth and twelfth centuries a third major Semitic horde, identified as Aramaeans in Syria and Israelites in Palestine, found its way into these two lands. In the same period "sea peoples" related to Indo-Europeans and called Philistines, occupied the southern coast. They gave their name to Palestine. But Lebanon remained Canaanite. Those of its Canaanites who traded with the Greeks were given by them the name Phoenicians, "purple red," after the color of the cloth which they sold or bartered.

Phoenicians never succeeded in establishing a solid unified state. Their land was narrow, fragmented by mountains and hemmed in between mightier neighbors on three sides. Their political organization took the form of city-states. These were strung along the coast from Ugarit and Aradus in the north through Gubla to Sidon and Tyre. At times a city-state would extend its hegemony to the hinterland and neighboring cities—as did Ugarit in mid-sixteenth century, Gubla in the fourteenth, Sidon in the twelfth to the eleventh and Tyre thereafter—but that was all temporary. Throughout, Phoenician preoccupation remained peaceful: industry, trade, art, religion. When attacked, as they often were, they would usually buy security by paying tribute and pray for partial compensation by an expanded market for their wares. Aradus, Sidon and Tyre consisted of two settlements each, one on the mainland for agriculture and trade, and the other on close-by islets for haven against Egyptian, Assyrian, Neo-Babylonian and other land assaults.

Metallurgy was the first major industry developed by Canaanites. For about nine centuries beginning 2100 they were probably unexcelled in the use of copper and bronze. In quest of tin, for hardening copper into bronze, and of other metals for hardening iron into steel alloy, they undertook long and hazardous journeys into little-known lands.

But it was for their textile industry, particularly in purple-dyed cloth, that Phoenicians became known throughout the world. Tyre and Sidon were the principal centers of this industry and its trade. Their waters abounded in a variety of the murex from which the tiny drops of the precious dye were extracted. So costly were the extraction and processing that only the wealthy could afford the product. Helen of Troy, Cleopatra of Egypt, Jewish high priests and Roman emperors took pride in wearing purple garments. Oriental Church patriarchs and Roman Catholic cardinals perpetuate the tradition. Phoenician trade on an international scale in textiles, metalwork, pottery, glass, timber, wheat and wine gave the country three centuries—beginning around 1000 B.C.—of prosperity unmatched in its history. As late as the early sixth century Phoenician trade was so brisk and impressive that a Hebrew prophet devoted a chapter (Ezek. 27) to its detailed description in graphic terms.

Wherever trade carried Canaanites, there they settled. Their settlements developed into colonies. Colonies were first planted in Egypt, Cilicia and Cyprus, then in Sicily and Sardinia and later in France, Spain and North Africa. All were linked by navigation to the mother cities, particularly Tyre and Sidon. Gades (Cadiz), founded around 1000 B.C. beyond the Pillars of Hercules (later Gibraltar), introduced them into the Atlantic Ocean. From there they evidently reached Cornwall (southwest England) in quest of tin. The discovery of the Atlantic Ocean ranks, together with the development and dissemination of the alphabet and the distribution of Near Eastern material and spiritual cultural elements, among the three greatest Phoenician contributions to human progress.

Tarshish in Spain, Tarsus (Paul's birthplace) in Cilicia, Corinth and other cities in Greece owe their origins to Phoenician enterprise. Europa, daughter of a Phoenician king, legend asserts, gave her name to Europe. A brother of Europa, named Cadmus, introduced the alphabet into the Greek world. But the most distinguished of all Phoenician colonies was Carthage, planted about 814 B.C. in what is today Tunisia. This illustrious daughter of Tyre became a mighty capital of an empire covering what is today Tunisia, Algeria, Morocco and south Spain. It contested supremacy of the sea with emerging Rome and came near achieving it. Its world-renowned general Hannibal crossed the Alps from Spain and for years battled the Romans on their own soil. Defeated in 202 he fled (196) to Tyre and his capital was finally wiped out by an unrelenting enemy.

The Hebrews, we noted above, belonged to the same migration that landed the Aramaeans in what the Greeks later called Syria. The ancestors of the Hebrews must have then spoken Aramaic, which in Palestine was replaced by the local Canaanite dialect, the Hebrew of the Old Testament. Hebrew differed from Phoenician dialectically. Of the many states founded by Aramaeans that of Damascus was the mightiest and best known. It rose toward the end of the eleventh century. The city's richness in water and its location at the head of the caravan route across the desert contributed to its gaining control over the inland trade. Aramaean merchants succeeded the Phoenicians as international traders, especially by land. The kingdom of Damascus reached from the Euphrates to the Yarmuk, a tributary of the Jordan. Between it and the Kingdom of Israel hostility began early and continued for over a century. In 875 B.C. Israel under King Omri became a vassal of Damascus. Omri's successor refused to pay tribute and was attacked in his capital Samaria by Ben Hadad of Damascus (I K. 20:1 *seq.*).

The Hebrews entered the land as nomads, but as they established themselves among the more highly civilized Canaanites they learned how to live in homes, till the land and pursue other ways of settled life. Before the end of the thirteenth century they were joined with a kindred group coming by way of Egypt. En route the leader Moses was initiated to the cult of a north Arabian tribal deity, who became Jehovah of Israel. The deity abode in a tent, practiced vengeance to the point of cruelty and favored sacrifices from the herd. But at the hands of the Hebrew prophets he was radically transformed. Endowed with mercy, righteousness and justice and elevated into a position of universality, he became the one and only God of Jews, Christians and Moslems.

Israel was one of the two states into which the Hebrew Kingdom split after Solomon's death in 923. The other kingdom was that of Judah with Jerusalem as capital. It was Solomon's father David (*ca.* 1004-*ca.* 963) who was the real founder of the Hebrew monarchy. His predecessor Saul (anointed about 1004) was a vassal of the Philistine newcomers into the land who had firmly established themselves along the coast. Hebrew-Philistine rivalry for the possession of the land prompted the rise of the Hebrew monarchy. David occupied Jerusalem, shook off the Philistine yoke and extended his domain in all directions.

Under his son Solomon (*ca.* 963-923) the Hebrew monarchy attained its height in might and prosperity. Prosperity was due mainly to the control of the caravan route that linked Syria and Phoenicia to Arabia and Egypt. Solomon's friend and ally, King Hiram of Tyre, provided the Hebrew monarch with the means for exploiting the mines at the head of today's Gulf of al-Aqabah, constructing a navy and building the great temple and royal palace at Jerusalem. The navy plied the Red Sea exchanging with coastal towns native-produced tin and copper for spices, ivory and jewels. "In his glory" Solomon followed the Oriental monarchical pattern

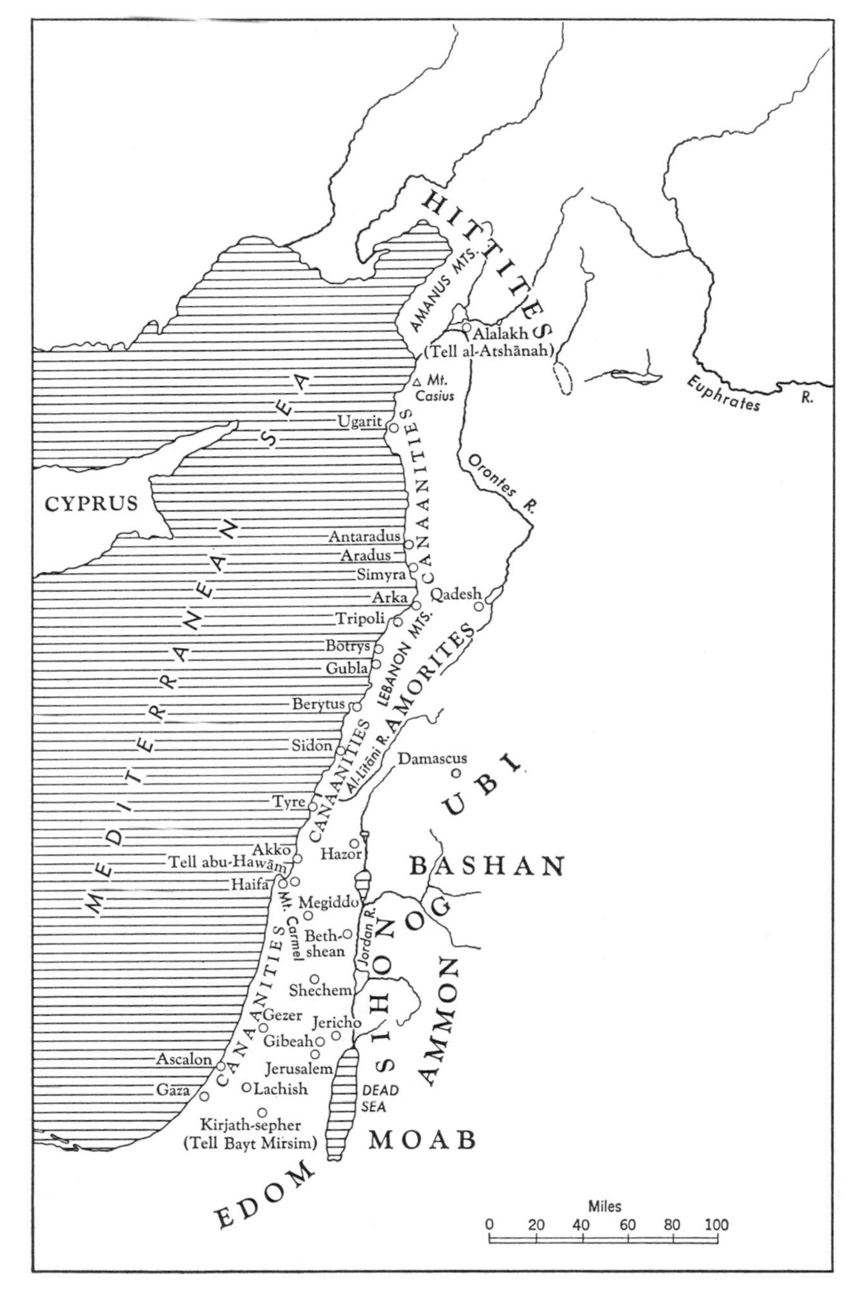

CANAAN BEFORE ISRAEL

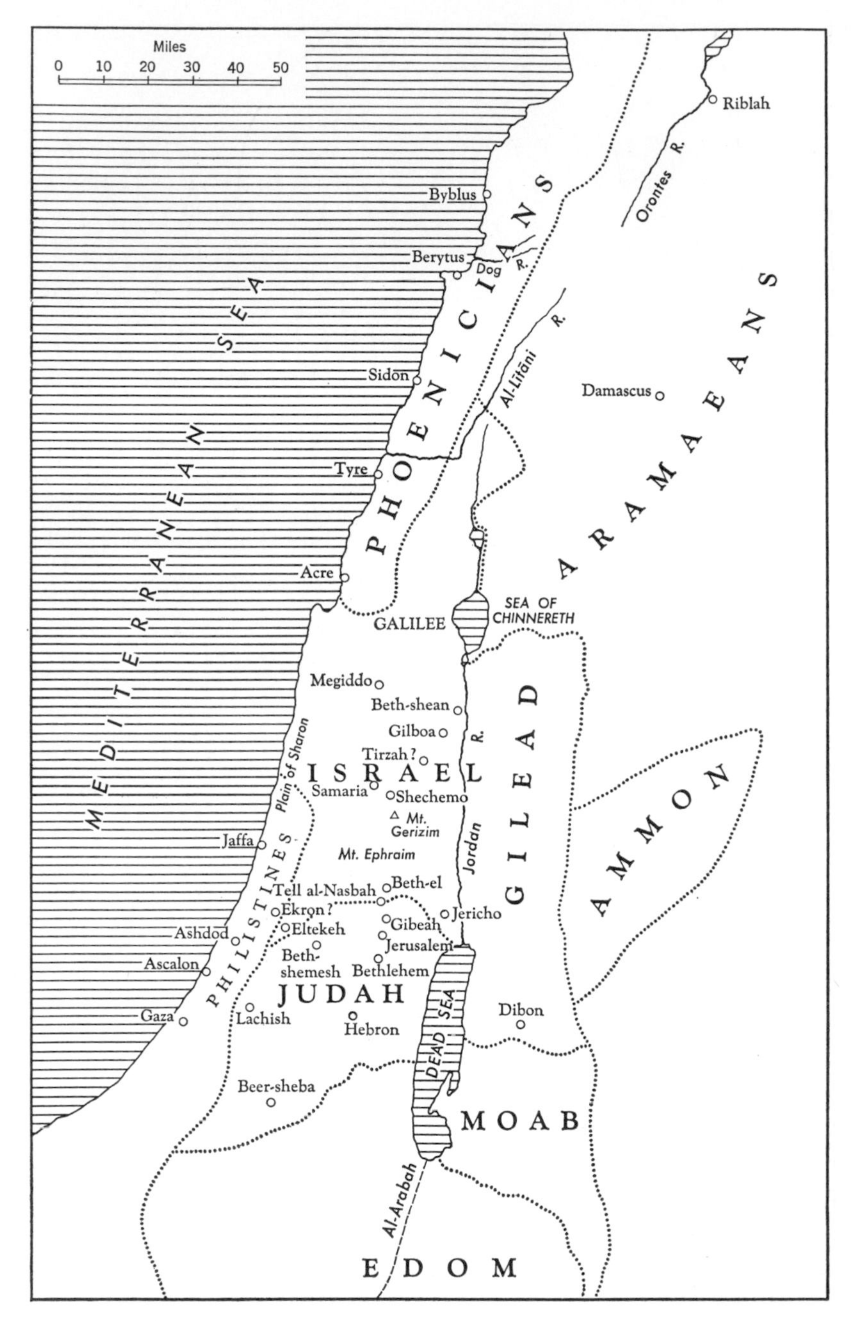

PALESTINE IN THE PERIOD OF THE HEBREW MONARCHIES

in maintaining a harem, living in lavish luxury and ultimately depleting the treasury. On his death the short-lived united kingdom came to an end.

Its two tiny fragments became rivals and at times enemies. Both fell into the complex of political and belligerent developments that plagued the area. In its two-century existence, Israel experienced nine dynastic changes. It was finally destroyed in 722 by the Assyrian Sargon II. The Assyrians, as we learned before, were also responsible for the destruction of Aram. Judah survived till 586, when it fell under the blows of the Neo-Babylonian Nebuchadnezzar.

Aram, Phoenicia, Israel and Judah vanished as political entities but not as cultural influences. As such they continue to form an integral part of the heritage of man.

While the location of Phoenicia and Palestine at the crossroads of the nations and between mighty empires to the north and south was not favorable to political development and stability, it was, nevertheless, favorable to the development of two unique cultures and to the dissemination and transmission of its priceless elements. In several respects our inheritance from these two tiny states surpasses that of all the empires of the ancient Orient which dominated them.

From Phoenicia we received the alphabet, generally considered the most valuable of the boons that country conferred on mankind. It may not be an exaggeration to consider it the greatest invention ever made by man. Out of twenty-two simple, easy-to-write symbols called letters—developed from metamorphosed pictorial signs probably in the fifteenth century—a Byblus man was for the first time in man's long history enabled to convey adequately and effectively whatever thoughts originated in his head, whatever emotions surged in his breast. Phoenician traders passed the magic signs westward to the Greeks (*ca.* 800 B.C.) and eastward to the Aramaeans. The Greeks in turn transmitted them through Latin to other Europeans. The Aramaeans transmitted them to the Hebrews and the Arabs. Herewith Homer's works, the Old and New

Sinaitic	Form represents	South Arabic	Phoenician	Ra's al-Shamrah	Later Greek	Latin	Arabic
[glyph]	ox-head	[glyph]	[glyph]	[glyph]	A	A	ء
[glyph]	house	[glyph]	[glyph]	[glyph]	Β	B	ب
[glyph]		[glyph]	[glyph]	[glyph]	Γ	CG	ج
[glyph]		[glyph]	[glyph]	[glyph]	Δ	D	د
[glyph]	man praying	[glyph]	[glyph]	[glyph]	Ε	E	ﻫ
[glyph]		[glyph]	[glyph]	[glyph]	Ϝ	FV	و
= (?)		[glyph]	[glyph]	[glyph]	Ι	•••	ز
[glyph]	double loop	[glyph]	[glyph]	[glyph]	Η	H	ح
•••		[glyph]	[glyph]	[glyph]	⊗	•••	ط
[glyph]	hand	[glyph]	[glyph]	[glyph]	Ι	I	ي
+		[glyph]	[glyph]	[glyph]	Κ	•••	ك
[glyph]	oxgoad?	[glyph]	[glyph]	[glyph]	Λ	L	ل
[glyph]	water	[glyph]	[glyph]	[glyph]	Μ	M	م
[glyph]	serpent	[glyph]	[glyph]	[glyph]	Ν	N	ن
[glyph]	fish	[glyph]	[glyph]	[glyph]	Ξ	X	•••
[glyph]	eye	o	o o	[glyph]	o	O	ع
[glyph]		[glyph]	[glyph]	[glyph]	Π	P	ف
[glyph]		[glyph]	[glyph]	[glyph]	•••	•••	ص
[glyph]		[glyph]	[glyph]	[glyph]	Ϙ	Q	ق
[glyph]	human head	[glyph]	[glyph]	[glyph]	Ρ	R	ر
[glyph]	bow	[glyph]	w	[glyph]	Σ	S	س ش
+	cross	X	X	[glyph]	T	T	ت

Courtesy of the Macmillan Co., Ltd.

TABLE OF ALPHABETS SHOWING THE DEVELOPMENTS OF LATIN AND ARABIC FROM SINAITIC THROUGH PHOENICIAN

Testament and the Koran were recorded and immortalized. It can be further stated that the ancestry of all alphabetic systems of writing can be traced directly or indirectly to the same Phoenician source.

Ironically those who perfected the earliest system of writing left us but little in the form of literature. Being primarily traders, Phoenicians used their alphabet mainly for business transacations. The writing material was perishable, papyrus. Fortunately, however, certain religious concepts of theirs have survived separately or embedded in Hebrew literature. Canaanite wise sayings and lyric pieces are detectable in the Psalms, Proverbs, Job and Song of Songs. Psalm 29 in its entirety is of Canaanite origin. Hebrew poetical composition followed the Aramaic pattern of parallelism. In the lately discovered Phoenician tablets of Ugarit (Ras al-Shamrah), Baal is "rider of the clouds," and so is Jehovah in Psalm 68:4. Baal's voice is described as "thunder", and so is Jehovah's in Psalm 29:3-5 and Job 37:2-5. Baal slays leviathan, and so does Jehovah (Is. 27:1).

The Canaanite religion, in common with other Semitic systems of belief, was essentially nature worship. Its two central deities were the Father Sky and Mother Earth. The sky god Baal (lord) controlled rain and crops and was propitiated by sacrifices. The mother goddess was Ashtart (Ishtar of Babylonia, Ashtoreth of the Hebrews). Her Phoenician seat was Byblus, where she was known as Baalat (Our Lady of Byblus).

Canaanite religion featured the fertility cult. The cult involved mourning for the periodic death of the vegetation deity by the summer heat, rites for his victory in the underworld over the god of death and finally rejoicing for his revival in spring. The resurrected god, Baal, marries the goddess of fertility, Ishtar, and the earth once more gives birth to green foliage, flowers and fruits. The origins of the cult go back to the Sumerians, who centered it in Tammuz. The Canaanites entitled Tammuz Adhon (lord) and located the Tammuz-Ishtar myth at Byblus and the source of the nearby river called today Nahr Ibrahim. From Byblus the cult passed to Cyprus, Greece and Sicily. Phoenician Adhon became Greek Adonis, and Ishtar was metamorphosed into Aphrodite, whom the Romans identified with Venus. The rite entered Egypt as the worship of Osiris and Isis. Through Ovid and Shakespeare the Adonis-

Venus story reached us. The Semitic name of the goddess has survived in Esther.

The Aramaeans, who succeeded their Phoenician neighbors as the middlemen of the area, achieved more linguistic than political triumphs. Their language became the medium of international commercial communication from India to Ethiopia. Aramaic became for a time also the language of diplomacy and was so used by the Persian Achaeminids. Centuries after the destruction of the Aramaean states their tongue, with local variations, remained the vernacular of the Fertile Crescent. Its triumph over Hebrew made it the one in which Christ communicated his message. Unfortunately the message survived only in its Greek translation.

In art and architecture, metalwork and other industries the Hebrews were on the receiving end of the line. In these fields, together with commerce and politics, they offered little by way of originality. Their genius lay in religion. Their religious literature made them the spiritual leaders and ethical teachers of a large segment of mankind. Its monument, the Old Testament, has remained through the ages a dynamic force in the lives of men and women. From its contents writers, orators, poets, artists have continuously received inspiration and guidance. Its prophetic books raised Jehovah above all Baals and foreign deities. They made him the one and only supreme and universal God, who rejoices in righteousness and ethical conduct—rather than cult—on the part of his worshipers. This exclusive ethical monotheism of Judaism became the essential feature of Christiantiy as well as Islam.

Amos (fl. *ca.* 750), a shepherd from an obscure village in Judah, was the first exponent of theoretical monotheism in the history of thought. He conceived of Jehovah as a god of peoples other than Israelites and as a god of justice (Amos 9:5-7; 5:21-4). Amos was followed by Isaiah, who, at a time that witnessed Samaria's destruction by Sargon II (722) and Jerusalem's siege by Sennacherib (701), envisioned with the eye of faith a new world of peace, one in which wolves would dwell with lambs and leopards with kids

(Is. 10:10; 2:2-4)—a noble vision that refuses to die. Micah (prophesied 730-722) struck the same optimistic note. He expected a new era in which swords would be beaten into plowshares and weapons into pruning hooks (Mic. 4:3).

Like Isaiah and Micah, Jeremiah (prophesied 626-586) was a Messianic prophet. He foresaw a utopia in which full justice would prevail (Jer. 33:5). He advanced religious thinking by representing Jehovah as entering into a new covenant with his people, one involving inwardness and inscribed on human hearts rather than on stones (Jer. 31:31-4; 32:40). In this connection Jeremiah enunciated a new doctrine: individual as against group responsibility. No more shall it be said, "The fathers have eaten a sour grape, and the children's teeth are set on edge," but rather "everyone shall die for his own iniquity" (Jer. 31:31-4; 32:40). The Hebrew concept of justice and social righteousness was summed up by Micah and immortalized in chapter six:

> 6 Wherewith shall I come before the Lord,
> And bow myself before the high God?
> Shall I come before him with burnt offerings,
> With calves of a year old?
>
> 7 Will the Lord be pleased with thousands of rams,
> Or with ten thousands of rivers of oil?
> Shall I give my firstborn for my transgression,
> The fruit of my body for the sin of my soul?
>
> 8 He hath showed thee, O man, what is good;
> And what doth the Lord require of thee,
> But to do justly, and to love mercy,
> And to walk humbly with thy god.
> (Westminster Study Edition)

No such heights in morality and spirituality were attained by any teacher of antiquity, Eastern or Western, until the advent of Christ.

7

Under Alexander and His Successors

The last third of the fourth pre-Christian century marked the end of an era in the Near East and the beginning of another—the Greco-Roman. The new era was to last for a thousand years, starting with the conquest of Alexander the Great and terminating with the rise of Islam. In its cultural action and reaction between East and West it left an imperishable legacy in both.

It all began when in the spring of 334 B.C. a twenty-one-year-old Macedonian at the head of 35,000 fighters crossed the Hellespont (Dardanelles) and launched his campaign. The immediate aim was the liberation of the Greek cities in Asia Minor, for which Greeks and Persians had battled for decades. Not content at its attainment, Alexander pushed on to north Syria. At the narrow pass of Issus, where superiority in numbers could be of no avail, the Macedonians routed (333) a Persian army, three times their number, led by Darius III. The city Iskandarun (Iskandarunah, Alexandretta) commemorates the site and perpetuates the name of the victor. All the area to the south now lay at the feet of the invader. Only Tyre, feeling secure in its insular position and proud of its traditional resistance to inland invaders, dared close its gates in his face. A seven-month siege, however, forced its surrender. Thirty-two thousand of its unhappy population were hanged or sold into slavery. In Palestine Gaza shared the same fate. A lesson had to be taught to future resistants. The way was open to Egypt. Weary of Persian rule, Egyptians were ready to exchange masters. At the northwestern extremity of the Delta were laid the foundations of a city destined to become a radiating center of Hellenic culture and an Oriental successor of Athens. In the subsequent Roman period Alexandria (al-Iskandariyah) ranked next to Rome in intellectual attainments.

The dashing general lost no time. Back through Palestine and inland Syria, he dealt the final blows to the mighty, venerable Persian Empire. Susa, royal residence and flourishing city, opened its treasures. Persepolis, capital of Darius and Xerxes, was given to the flames (331). Xerxes' destruction of the temples of Athens was at last avenged. The ill-starred monarch sought safety in flight but was murdered the following year by one of his own aides. The Macedonian now considered himself the successor of the last Achaemenid emperor. By the right of sword he was.

The path of victory beckoned farther east. Bactra (now Balkh in Afghanistan) was reached. Thence the road led to northwestern India. Not the Hindu enemy but murmuring generals and mutinying soldiers forced retreat (326). When in Babylon, it was time to celebrate, and celebrate the Macedonians did. Nebuchadnezzar's palace provided the perfect scene. Gala banquets, festivities and carousals followed. In their wake the hero fell ill and died. He was 32.

Great as those military exploits of Alexander were in themselves, greater they loom in their cultural consequences. They opened the way to the confrontation, harmonization and final fusion of Greek and Near Eastern ideas and institutions, effecting thereby a pioneering revolution in the world's outlook. In the cultural as in the military field Alexander in person led. He married Darius' daughter, adopted Persian dress and court etiquette and encouraged his officers to do likewise. More effective by way of implementation was the planting of numerous Greek cities by him and his successors all over the area. Before him prophets, sages and philosophers had preached the brotherhood of man and the unity of mankind, but no man of affairs had taken concrete steps toward the realization of the dream.

The hastily assembled, far-flung Alexandrine empire was easier to create than to manage. After a protracted period of struggle for power and scrambling for the largest slice, four states emerged under four of Alexander's generals. Seleucus, the ablest among them, got Syria, a large portion of Asia Minor and eastward to India. This gave him almost all the Asiatic realm. The rest of Asia Minor went to Antigonus, while Antipater acquired Macedonia. Ptolemy, second in ability, received Egypt and contested Palestine and southern Phoenicia with his northern neighbor. Thus was the great horn broken, "and for it came up four notable ones toward the four winds of heaven" (Dan. 8:8).

Seleucus I (312-280) continued Alexander's policy of planting Greek cities for veteran soldiers and for newcomers, whether government officials, businessmen, traders or craftsmen. The new settlements developed into foci radiating Greek language, philosophy and science. Most distinguished among them was Antioch (now Antakiyah) on the Orontes, capital of the Syrian kingdom. The city was so named after the founder's father. Its seaport Seleucia (Saluqiyah)—built by an immediate successor—bore his name. Laodicea (al-Ladhiqiyah, Latakia), farther south on the coast, perpetuates his mother's name. Next to the colonization the establishment of a standard calendar for the entire kingdom was perhaps the most significant Seleucid innovation. The calendar was reckoned from 312 B.C., the year of the establishment of the kingdom. It continued in vogue until the spread of Islam. Called Greek by Syrians and Jews, it is still in limited use.

The kingdom founded by Seleucus reached its zenith under his sixth successor Antiochus III (223-187). By twenty years of incessant fighting, this energetic monarch restored southern Syria, lost to the Ptolemies, as well as northeastern Persia, lost to the Parthians. His triumphs won him the ephithet Great. Not satisfied, Antiochus undertook fresh campaigns into India and western Asia Minor. The last push proved fateful. For the first time it brought the Seleucid power into hostile relations with the rising Roman power. Antiochus' defeat at Magnesia (190) forced him to cede to Rome all his dominion beyond the Taurus and agree to pay a heavy annual tribute. Though enfeebled, Syria under Antiochus IV (175-164) felt still strong enough to strike a fresh blow at its

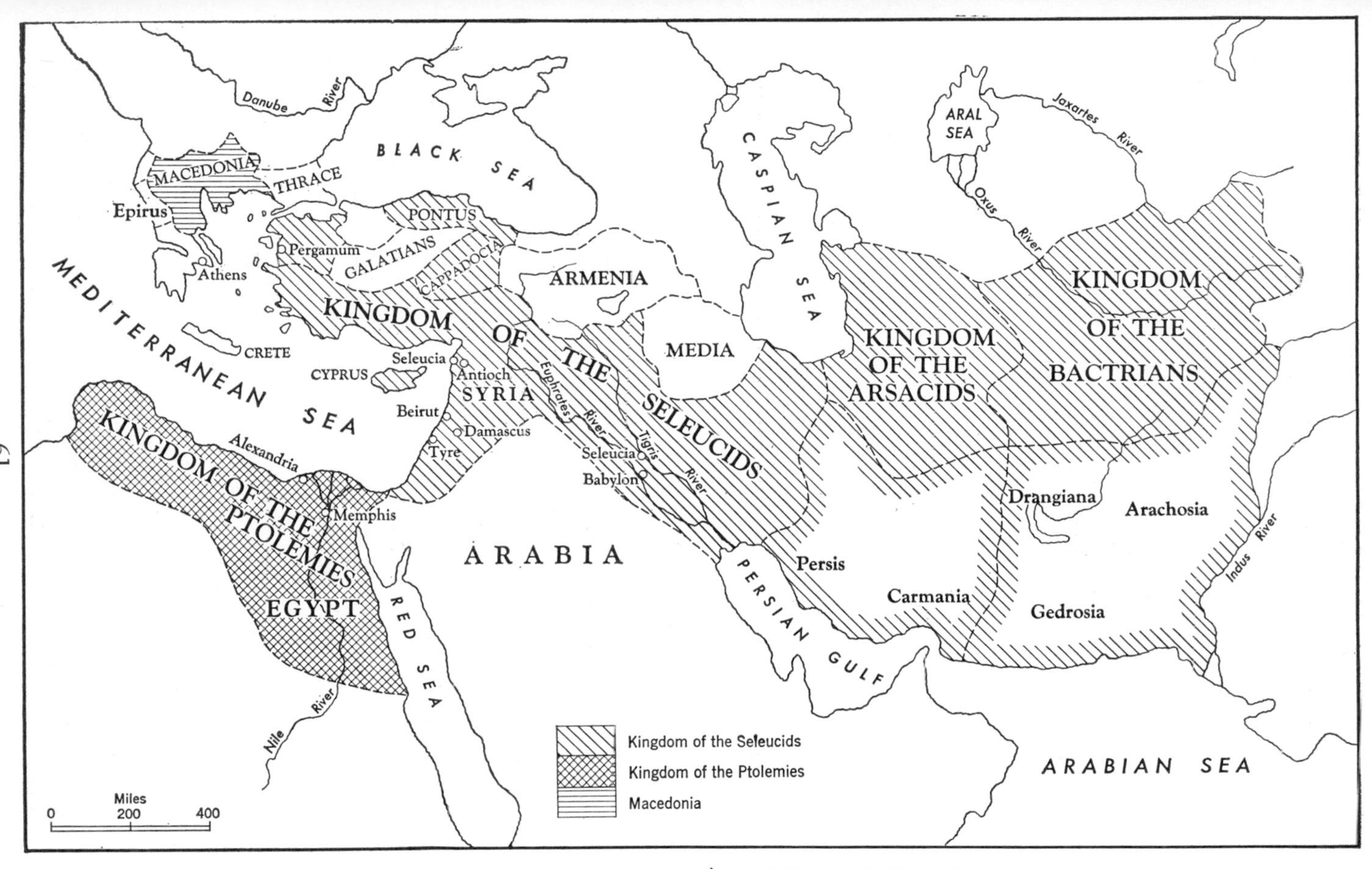

THE KINGDOMS OF ALEXANDER'S SUCCESSORS *ca.* 200 B.C.

southern rival. Egypt was then under a weak debaucher, Ptolemy VI, who suffered a crushing defeat and was himself captured. Lower Egypt was overrun and Alexandria besieged. But under pressure from Rome the Syrian army was withdrawn.

Antiochus was now free to further his house's traditional policy of Hellenizing the East. The desired common denominator was to include a new dimension: religion. To this end the overenthusiastic monarch associated himself with Zeus, already identified with Baal, and proclaimed himself Theos Epiphanes (God Manifest). Polytheistic Syrians could tolerate the innovation, but when he endeavored to identify Baal-Zeus with Jehovah the uncompromisingly monotheistic Jews rose in arms. Led by a hero-rebel named Judas, (surnamed Maccabeus) they scored telling victories over the Syrian army, captured Jerusalem (164) and cleansed its temple from the Baal-Zeus altar, the "abomination" of Daniel (11:31). By 140 B.C. under the Maccabeans the Jewish community had liberated itself entirely from the Syrian yoke. It maintained its independence until the advent of the Romans.

The success of the Maccabean revolt flashed the first warning signal on the precipitous road to the kingdom's disintegration. Bactria and Parthia in the east declared their independence. Asia Minor was annexed by Rome. Arabian tribes began nibbling at southern Syria. The empire that once stretched from the Aegean to India shrank to a local state in north Syria. Even there the Seleucid throne was shaky. The claim of Antiochus XIII (69-65) was acknowledged by Rome but contested by another Seleucid, Philip II (68-64). This Antiochus was the last to wear the royal diadem of the house. The death blow was administered by a dashing, brilliant Roman general, Pompey.

By 67 Pompey had cleared the eastern Mediterranean of its pirates and assumed command of the East. In the following three years he annexed Syria and Palestine; Egypt followed. There Cleopatra, the last of the Ptolemies, ruled, first jointly with her brother-husband, Ptolemy XII, and from 48-30 independently but mostly as a vassal of Rome. In 48 Julius Caesar, Pompey's rival for supreme power, chased after him to Egypt and fell under the charm of its beautiful queen. He returned to Rome the following year as master of the East. On Cleopatra's suicide (30) by poison—not by an asp's bite as legend asserts—the Ptolemaic kingdom was thrown, alongside of its Seleucid sister, on the junk heap of history. Both territories were embraced in the fast-growing Roman Empire.

Seleucids and Ptolemies were no more; but Greek cultural elements, introduced and nurtured by them, remained. The interpenetration of Greek and Semitic civilizations gave birth to a new brand known as Hellenism. For a thousand years Hellenism remained a dominant feature in Near Eastern life. Even later, Islam received a fresh dose of Greek science and philosophy.

The nursery of the new eclectic culture was the score of Greek cities dotting the area. Originally populated by soldiers, traders, scholars and artisans, these cities had their theaters, gymnasiums and forums characteristic of cities back home. This sharply differentiated them from their Semitic neighbors. With the cultural went ethnic integration. The majority of the new settlers depended for wives on native stock. In certain cases colonizers occupied and renamed old towns. Rabbath-Ammon, for example, became Philadelphia, in honor of Ptolemy II Philadelphus (d. 247 B.C.). But it has since reverted to its ancient name in the form of Amman, capital of Jordan.

Antioch in Syria and Alexandria in Egypt stood out as the most influential and enduring centers of Hellenism. So Hellenized was the area around the Syrian capital that it was referred to as the new Macedon. Closely associated with Antioch was Daphne, the site of Apollo's temple, which stood amidst a sacred grove of laurels copiously supplied with water. Daphne was originally the name of a nymph whose beauty so charmed Apollo that he pursued her to this lovely spot, where she was metamorphosed into a laurel. Daphne became the pleasure park for Antiochenes and a center of pilgrimage and licentiousness for Geeeks from the region.

Under the Ptolemies Alexandria grew into one of the most magnificent commercial and cultural capitals in the world. Royal patronage contributed to that end. The city boasted a building which combined the functions of museum, library, academy and translation bureau. It drew scholars from as far as Asia Minor and Rhodes. As the city reflected Greek science and philosophy to the entire East, its lighthouse, the Pharos—one of the world's "seven wonders"—reflected sunrays by day and special lights by night to mariners flocking to its harbor. An Alexandrian librarian, Eratosthenes (*ca.* 276), was the first to mark maps with lines indicating longitude and latitude and one of the first to recognize the roundness of the earth. A mathematician, Euclid, founded (*ca.* 300) a school in Alexandria where he wrote *Elements of Geometry,* which remained until recently the basis of plane and solid geometry.

In Lebanon, Phoenician cities, with a long record of commercial relations with the West, responded heartily to Greek stimuli. Greek became the language of higher learning. A Cyprus-born Phoenician, Zeno (333-261), founded the Stoic school of philosophy, probably the noblest system of the pre-Christian world. In its stress on virtue, ethical living and human brotherhood stoicism was a precursor of Christianity. Throughout its career it maintained close connection with the Semitic concept of life.

Hellenism, it should be noted, was primarily an urban feature. Aspirants for government positions or scholarly and literary careers received their education in Greek and were in varying measures Hellenized. Writing in Greek offered the author an almost worldwide market. But the country folk, isolated and uninterested in higher education, remained relatively unaffected, persisting in their ancestral way of life and in the use of their vernacular, whether Aramaic, Egyptian or Persian. Baalism sustained its Semitic traditions in Syria and Mesopotamia, as Jehovism did in Palestine. It should, moreover, be remembered that Hellenization was a reciprocal operation. Eastern religions, with their rich rituals and exotic mysteries, held special fascination for the sons of the West. Native deities were adopted and Hellenized. Baal, we learned before, became Zeus of the Greeks and Jupiter of the Romans; Tammuz was transformed into Adonis.

Persian participation in the Hellenistic experience was rather limited. Distance from the source, deep-rooted nationalist consciousness and traditional animosity against the Greeks contributed to that result.

At the other end of the spectrum from Persia stood Asia Minor, whose western coast was colonized by Greeks centuries before Alexander's conquest. Here Ephesus, Smyrna and particularly Pergamum (currently Pergama) were leading centers. Though smaller than Antioch or Alexandria, Pergamum lit a Hellenistic torch that burned with brighter and perhaps purer flame. The city with its kingdom flourished for about a century beginning 260 B.C. Its name is echoed in our word parchment, next to papyrus the most important writing material. Under the Romans the city became capital of the extensive province of Asia and remained a stronghold of heathenism. Hence its characterization as Satan's seat in Revelations (2:13).

Hellenism had not only political and cultural but also economic aspects. Under it the Near East enjoyed a measure of uniformity based on common speech, analogous laws, similar coinage and identical calendar—all of which facilitated business transactions to an extent hitherto unknown. Then there were the improved means of transport and communication. Syrian highways were guarded by chains of colonies some with fortresses and garrisons, providing safety and resting places for caravans. Petra was such a caravan city on the Arabian route. Palmyra was another on the Mesopotamian route. Along these highways passed fruits, cereals, oil, wine, purple, glass, slaves, minerals, precious stones, pepper, cinnamon and other semi-tropical porducts. From Syrian and Egyptian ports west-bound ships carried merchandise to Greece and Italy.

In this international exchange of products, southwestern Arabia (Yemen) played a unique role. The area produced frankincense, myrrh, cinnamon and other spices highly prized in the northern as well as western markets. For these products it could draw on its neighbors, India and eastern Africa. To the Romans it became known as Arabia Felix, and happy it certainly was thanks to its climate and prosperity. For centuries its people served in the southern seas as the Phoenicians did in the Mediterranean. Of the South Arabians, the Sabaeans were the best known. Their Queen of Sheba, folklore asserts, visited Solomon. Their capital Marib, east of the modern capital Sana, possessed a dam which, judged by its stupendous ruins, must have been a rare hydraulic feat of antiquity.

The curve of South Arabian prosperity continued upward until the Christian era. The entrance of Roman-Egyptian shipping into the Indian Ocean sounded its knell. Meantime Syria, Lebanon, Egypt and other neighboring lands had fallen under the paws of the Roman wolf. A new chapter in the history of the Near East was opening.

8

Under the Roman Caesars

The Roman age, which was inaugurated by Augustus Caesar (27 B.C.-A.D. 14), was in several respects a continuation and development of the Hellenistic. The Near East, Persia excluded, found itself for the first time in its history part of a political unit with limits reaching from the Atlantic in the west, the Rhine, Danube and Black Sea in the north, to the Euphrates in the east and the African Sahara in the south. No such conglomeration of peoples, languages, religions and cultures under one scepter had the world ever seen before. Roman Caesars achieved a measure of success far beyond that of Macedonian generals and translated into actuality the dream of Phoenician-Greek philosophers.

The policy of unification, consolidation and defense, initiated by Augustus, was continued by his successors. Even before Augustus the practice of conferring Roman citizenship upon provincials as a reward for signal service had begun. Such citizenship carried legal rights and priviliges as well as social distinction. Paul challenged the right of a Roman officer in Jerusalem to scourge him, a Roman citizen (Acts 22:25). The extension of citizenship reached its climax under Caracalla (211-217) of the Syro-Lebanese dynasty in Rome, who conferred the franchise on all freeborn men in the realm.

With the assimilating influence of common nationality went that of social and economic intercourse. For such intercourse, safe and easy means of communication was essential. This was a cardinal point of Roman policy. Italian engineers built bridges, widened and paved old roads, and opened new ones, linking all parts of the far-flung empire. The postal service inaugurated by Emperor Augustus for imperial messages could then be more widely used.

Traders and travelers were provided with maps and road books; they also had available lodging facilities. Roman armies saw that land routes were kept free from robbers, as the fleet kept the Mediterranean safe against pirates. Within the provinces Roman governors endeavored to maintain peace, stability and order. The common market for which Western Europe is now striving may then be said to have been attained. It all added to the attainment of an unprecedented measure of general prosperity and welfare in which the Near East shared.

With the growth of a wealthy class of businessmen and landowners went urbanization. In urban communities linguistic distinctions tend to decrease and the fusion of cultures to increase. Roads made possible the free exchange not only of commodities, but of ideas. Latin culture, after all, was in essence a version of Greek culture, which had already become fused with that of the East.

Roman Asia Minor had no difficulty in adapting itself to the new order. Its western Greek-populated coast was incorporated into the Roman realm in the second pre-Christian century, the rest of the extensive peninsula in the second. Italian businessmen, soldiers and government officials, of course, introduced Latin. But Greek remained the literary, commercial and to a considerable extent the legal language. The western cities, including Ephesus, Sardis, Smyrna, and headed by the capital Pergamum, formed the main outlets for the hinterland and the connecting link with Greece and Italy. Ephesus acquired additional fame for its shrine of the "great Diana of the Ephesians" (Acts 19:28, 34), the mother goddess of Asia Minor. Her Greek counterpart, Artemis, had her principal shrine at the capital city. The mother goddess was also known as Cybele and had a renowned temple at Sardis, once capital of Lydia and seat of the proverbially rich Croesus. What remains of the temple testifies to its past grandeur. The city became one of the "seven churches" of Asia Minor cited in the Revelations (3:1).

Christianity was introduced to the country in the mid-first century and evidently made rapid progress in certain cities. In his first missionary journey Paul penetrated inland into Galatia, whence the first specimen of his preaching has been preserved (Acts 13:16-41). In his third journey the great missionary to the gentiles reached Ephesus and lingered there for more than two years (Acts 19:1; 8:10). This city was the first of "seven churches which are in Asia" to which John addressed his Revelations (1:4, 11).

The Roman province of Syria, which included Lebanon and Palestine, was put under a proconsul with authority to levy troops and taxes and engage in war. Next to Gaul its governorship was the one most coveted. Because of its strategic location Syria was considered a focal point of Roman power in the whole area, including Armenia, Mesopotamia, Arabia and Persia. But its governor was not able to exercise direct effective rule beyond the capital Antioch and its surrounding district. The rest was wisely left under native rulers with a thin Hellenistic veneer. Outstanding among these rulers were the client kings of Judaea and Nabataea. For protection against foreign enemies and unruly Arabian tribes a chain of military posts was established along the eastern border and the fringe of the desert. For guarding against internal disorder and civil disturbance adequate force was always on hand. But equality before the law and participation in a fuller life perhaps served equally as a deterrent.

Under Pax Romana the Syrian province raised itself from the depth of the depression into which it had sunk at the disintegration of the Seleucid kingdom and achieved a new record of prosperity. Its population probably reached six million. Remains of walls and aqueducts mark sites of towns on the banks of the Orontes, east of Aleppo and Hims and along the frontiers of the Syrian Desert, in all of which only barrenness currently rules. Syrian merchants spread themselves over Europe as far as Gaul and Spain. "Syrian" was then used as a linguistic term for all those who used Syriac (Aramaic) and including Lebanese, Palestinians and Mesopotamians. Their activity embraced the East as well as the West. Syrian merchants were successors of the Phoenicians and predecessors of the Venetians and Genoese.

Four Syrian cities under Roman rule achieved high distinction and claim our special interest: Antioch, Baalbak, Beirut and Jerusalem.

In fame, splendor and luxury the capital city, Antioch, yielded only to the imperial one; in population it vied with Alexandria for second place in the empire. Estimates make its inhabitants half a million. With its suburb and consecrated park Daphne, it attracted pilgrims and pleasure-seekers from near and far. Julius Caesar enriched Antioch with a theater; Caracalla raised its status to that of a colony. The four-mile road connecting it with Daphne was bordered by gardens, fountains and villas providing appropriate framework for the gay festive processions that periodically moved between the two towns. Daphne enclosed a cluster of shady gardens, with flowing waters, towering cypresses and beautiful laurel trees. Dedicated to Apollo, the laurels were protected by law against cutting. Daphne housed renowned oracles consulted even by emperors. It was the site of the Daphnian festival comprising games, dances, dramatic performances, chariot racing, gladiatorial contests and sexual indulgences.

Baalbak, as indicated by the name, was originally dedicated to the chief deity Baal, who guarded the fertile plain stretching between the two Lebanons. The Seleucids identified the Semitic god with the sun, renaming the city Heliopolis (city of the sun). The Romans retained the Greek name of the city but Latinized the deity into Jupiter Heliopolitanus. Augustus made Heliopolis a colony. But the city remained less Greek than Antioch, less Roman than Beirut and more Semitic than both.

The elaborate construction, ornamentation and expansion of the temple to majestic dimensions were completed under Caracalla (211-217) and his successors of the Syro-Lebanese dynasty. Caracalla's mother, Julia Domna, was the talented and beautiful daughter of a high priest at Hims (Emesa). She had met her husband Septimius Severus (193-211) when he was commander of a legion stationed in Syria. The Syrian queen gloried in her title Augusta. She collaborated with her imperial husband in the conduct of state affairs and continued to wield power after his death. For counselor she invited an eminent professor of law at Beirut named Papinian, who was related to her. Papinian was succeeded at Rome by an equally distinguished Beirut professor, Ulpian. Ulpian served under Alexander Severus (223-235), the last and best of the dynasty, who was born at Arqah (Arka), north Lebanon. The outstanding contribution these two imperial advisers made to Roman law will be mentioned later.

The Heliopolitan temple area of 300 by 200 yards, exceeds that of any cathedral of medieval Christendom and is surpassed by only St. Peter's of Rome and a few other modern ones. Within the area lie the ruins of the older and larger temple, that of Jupiter, and of the smaller but more ornamented temple of his consort Atargatis (Ashtart). The Atargatis temple is commonly attributed to Bacchus. Of Jupiter's columns only six still proudly lift their heads erect, defying earthquakes and ravages of time and beckoning a welcome to all visitors miles away. Each column consists of three blocks and rises to a height of sixty-two feet, displaying a diameter of over seven feet. The massiveness of the blocks in the columns and in the walls, the spaciousness of the area, the wealth of detail in ornamentation and the delicate figure work in the friezes make of Baalbak an international magnet of tourism. Even Rome can boast no parallel.

If Baalbak gloried in its religious eminence, Beirut (or Berytus, to use its Latin name), gloried in its intellectual attainments. In this respect Beirut stood supreme in the Near East, parting company with its commercial past. The city was honored early when Augustus Caesar made it a colony and named it Colonia Julia Augusta Felix after his daughter; but what gave it unique distinction was a Roman school of law. Founded by Septimius Severus (d. 211), the school flourished until the mid-sixth century. In the provinces probably no school excelled it other than that of Athens. It made of this Lebanese city a mecca for some of the best minds of the area, just as the American University and the Jesuit University do today.

The two professors who shed luster on Beirut as a center of learning, Papinian and Ulpian, were born one in Hims and the other in Tyre. Of Papinian's legal writings, 595 were incorporated in Justinian's *Digest*, of which no less than a third was extracted from Ulpian's writings. In recognition Emperor Justinian (d. 565), whose name the Code bears, styled Berytus "the mother and the nurse of the laws." Laws are considered the greatest and most enduring legacy of the Roman Empire.

Jerusalem was the capital of Roman Palestine, known to its people as Judaea. Under Herod the Great, the kingdom of Judaea attained its greatest territorial extent. Herod succeeded his father, an Edomite (Idumaean) kinglet appointed by Pompey. The Edomites were Judaized Arabians. Herod refortified Jerusalem and rebuilt its temple on a magnificent scale. He also promoted agriculture and industry in his realm. The Herodian temple was the one known to Jesus. On the coast Herod rebuilt what became the port of Roman Palestine and named it Caesarea in honor of his patron Augustus. This and similar acts aroused his subjects to open rebellion against him on the ground that he favored Hellenism and promoted Romanism at the expense of Judaism. Of all Near Easterners the Jews were the least amenable to Roman rule. As the "chosen people of God" and of the "seed of Abraham," Jews resisted all attempts at integration or assimilation and insisted on maintaining their own identity. Theirs was an exclusive society. Echoes of the repressive measures taken by the king may be detected in the "massacre of the innocents" reported by Matthew (2:13-16). After a thirty-three-year rule Herod died in 4 B.C. (two years after the birth of Christ in 6 B.C., according to scholarly reconstruction).

Two caravan cities in the Roman province of Syria are worthy of special consideration: Petra and Palmyra.

Petra, capital of Nabataea, provided the most convenient halting station for caravans on the Hejaz-Palestine route. Originally north Arabian tribesmen, the Nabataeans, as evidenced by their inscriptions, spoke an Aramaic dialect. Caravanceers found in Petra a spring abundant in fresh water and in its rock-hewn lodgings ample protection against Bedouin raids. There they could relay their camels and resume their journeys originating in the spice-producing lands of South Arabia and terminating in Mediterranean ports or inland cities. Thence they returned laden with textiles, grains, vessels and other products of the northern area. For two centuries before and one after Christ, Petra flourished as a focal point on that international trade route. Its kingdom at its height embraced north Arabia, Palestine and southeastern Syria. It was an ethnarch of the Nabataean king Harithath IV (Aretas, 9 B.C.-A.D. 40) who tried to arrest Paul in Damascus (2 Cor. 11:32). The kingdom was held in vassalage by Rome, though its people had once repulsed an attack by Pompey. They gradually succumbed to the lure of Hellenism, the dominant culture of the day, and finally found themselves in the embrace of Rome.

Their capital then took on the aspects of a Hellenized town with theaters and temples in Greco-Roman style, but their kings remained semi-independent. Such political status became intolerable to Rome when poised for a match with its only remaining rival in the east, Persia. In accordance with Trajan's orders the Roman legate in Syria in 106 captured Petra and destroyed it. The picturesque, opulent and "rose-red city half as old as time" was pushed into the limbo of history. Its local name, Wadi Musa (Moses' valley), perpetuates the memory of an earlier historic event.

Petra's mantle fell on Palmyra. Like its predecessor Palmyra owed its rise to a copious spring of not as good but drinkable water and to its location on west-to-east trans-desert trade route. In common with the Nabataeans the Palmyrenes originated in an Arabian tribe, became Aramaicized in speech and Hellenized in culture. Trajan incorporated the mid-desert caravan city in the Provincia Arabia he created on the destruction of Petra. Under Roman aegis Palmyra prospered economically and gained politically. In 260 its ruler Udaynath (Odenathus) received a title that recognized him as virtual vice-emperor of the eastern part of the empire. This was in recognition of loyalty expressed in his leading a Syro-Arabian army to rescue Emperor Valerian, who after a battle in north Syria was shamefully captured by his Persian adversary.

On Udaynath's death (*ca.* 266) his widow Zenobia held the reins of authority in the name of their minor son. An able and audacious woman, the queen modeled her court after that of the Persian emperors but employed as counselor a Greek philosopher who taught her Greek. Taking advantage of the enfeebled imperial condition in Rome, she extended her authority beyond Syria and north Arabia into Egypt, where she established a garrison in Alexandria, and into Anatolia, where her troops reached Ankara (Ancyra). By 272, however, Rome had recovered from its humiliation at the Persian hands and from its harassment by its western enemies. Aurelian in person led his legions to victory through Anatolia, north Syria and ultimately to Zenobia's capital. The unhappy queen expected but received no aid from Persia. She sought safety by flight on a dromedary by night. Pursuing cavalry overtook her just before she could cross the Euphrates. The proud queen of the East, loaded with jewels, was led (274) by golden chains to grace the triumphal entry of the Roman emperor into his capital. Palmyra was subsequently destroyed and its inhabitants put to the sword. Only the Bel temple was spared to house in later days a miserable Moslem village bearing an Arabic form, Tadmur, of the ancient Semitic name.

Outside the temple extend long colonnades, high arches and other vivid but mute reminders of what was once an affluent and influential metropolis. In the 1240-yard avenue of columns, 375 remain, each about 55 feet high. The granite material of some indicates Egyptian origin. Statues that once decorated the colonnade commemorating distinguished Palmyrene citizens may be seen today in European and American museums.

By the end of the third century the Roman eagle had spread its wing eastward as far as the Euphrates. Beyond that lay Persia, proud in its tradition of independence, conscious of its might and defiant. Those were the same forces that kept it relatively alienated from Hellenism, which had engulfed the area. The gap between Persia and its neighbors was further widened as Christianity spread, taking a westward course.

9

Christianity on the March

Christianity was a Semitic religion born in the Near East but nurtured at the crossroads of the Greco-Roman world. From this Hellenized area it made its way westward to achieve in Europe its greatest triumphs. To that end it had incorporated into itself certain features that made it acceptable. Thereby it transcended its Near Eastern origins and lifted itself to an international level. The process, effectively started by Paul, a Hellenized Jew, was continued by Greek- and Latin-writing Fathers of the Church in Alexandria and other cities of Asia Minor and North Africa.

Progress was painfully slow and success uncertain. Throughout the first century the new religion must have looked like one of those many Eastern cults mushrooming from time to time in the area. Not until the second century did it offer a challenge to the older faiths. Believers in many gods were, by the nature of that belief, tolerant, compromising and non-aggressive. But believers in one God and adherents of a religion considered by them the only true one were different. They could not very well participate in official religious festivals, offer sacrifice to another deity or bow down in worship before a Caesar. Imbued with missionary zeal, they were intent upon converting the whole world. Theirs was not a policy of coexistence. Whoever was not with them was against them. A clash with the official religion was inevitable.

The so-called persecution of Nero, which began in A.D. 64, had no religious motivation. Christians were conveniently made the scapegoat of an accidental conflagration that consumed the center of the capital. Paul, who died in Rome in 67, was supposedly a victim of the Neronian decree. More serious was Trajan's decree in

112. It made traitors of Christians unwilling to pay homage to the gods of the state. Actuated by local or personal motives provincial governors took advantage of the opportunity to impose upon their Christian subjects all kinds of penalties. Valerian (257) went further, forbidding all Christian gatherings. The list of martyrs "whose blood was the seed of the Church" mounted higher under Diocletian in 303. Under pressure from heathen priests aware of the threat offered by the new religion, that emperor—whose wife and daughter were presumably Christians—issued a devastating edict ordering churches razed, books burned and civil as well as military officials dismissed. Government officials must also have felt the competition offered by Christians and put pressure on the emperor. For ten years persecution raged in the Near East with unabated fury. It spread into the remotest provinces, where governors again exploited the imperial edict for their selfish purposes. New means of torture were devised. In north Syria, we are told by church historians, men were roasted on gridirons and women driven to commit suicide to escape rape. Palestinian martyrs were given to beasts. In Arabia Christians were butchered by the ax. A bishop in Asia Minor named Nicholas was tortured to death. His name, Saint Nicholas, was transformed into our Santa Claus. The custom of giving presents on the eve of his feast was later transferred to Christmas Day. Tradition asserts that the custom originated in his stealthy bestowal of dowries on three daughters of an impoverished parishioner who was on the point of giving them up to a life of shame. Imperial executioners in Rome erected a triumphal column commemorating the extermination of the "Christian name and superstition."

But, as often happens, ruthlessness overreached itself. Sensitive non-Christians were shocked. Before persecution was over the religion of Christ was already on the way to becoming not only a tolerated but a favored one. For this it had Constantine the Great (306-337) to thank. He opened the way to its becoming the official religion.

While the first three centuries were punctuated with official persecution of Christians, Christian philosophy was establishing good rapport with the two prevailing Greco-Roman philosophies: Stoicism and Neo-Platonism. Christianity had to be Romanized before it could Christianize the Romans. Both Stoicism and Neo-Platonism represented syncretistic systems of Western and Oriental thoughts. The founders and leading opponents were Hellenized Orientals. A Phoenician, Zeno, we learned before, laid the basis of Stoicism. Another Phoenician, Porphyry ("purple-clad," d. *ca.* 305) was a founder of Neo-Platonism. His Semitic name was Melik (king). Porphyry had an Egyptian-born teacher and a Syrian pupil, both of whom contributed to the formulation and propagation of the system. The process of reconciling Christian and Stoic philosophies involved give-and-take. It was inaugurated in Paul's Epistles with their thesis on human nature and the analysis of the body into earthly or natural, and heavenly or spiritual.

Neo-Platonism endeavored to reconcile both Plato and Aristotle with Semitic thought. It developed the dualistic theory of "idea" and "matter" and made the physical world an emanation of the immanent divinity, the "one," from whom human souls are arisen and with whom they may be reunited. This Neo-Platonic distinction between the world of tangibles that is changeable, transient, and the world of ideas that is stable, eternal, became a feature of Christian doctrine. It set matter apart from space, the body apart from the soul. It made the world to the medieval Christian a "vale of tears" leading to the next world. Among the Jewish philosophers Philo of Alexandria (*ca.* 20 B.C.-A.D. 40) accepted the dualistic doctrine of man, elaborated on it and passed it to his people. It made of the body a prison of the soul, from which it seeks to return to God. From Christians and Jews the concept passed on to Moslems, particularly the Sufis among them.

The Christian system was fortunate in inheriting both Stoic and Neo-Platonic ideas and therewith attracting some of the most brilliant Hellenistic minds. By the early third century the intellectual world center had shifted from Rome and Athens to Alexandria. Its philosophical leadership was provided by Hellenized Anatolians, Syrians, Egyptians and other Orientals. The founder of the Alexandrian school of theology was Clement, who had a pagan background and studied Greek philosophy. Clement headed the catechetical school there from 190 to 203 and endeavored to harmonize the best in antique culture with Christian thought. His pupil and better-known successor, Origen (d. 253), was born in Egypt to a pagan family. He made extensive use of allegorical interpretation of the Bible. Another Egyptian-born Greek Father of the Church was Athanasius (d. 336), a stalwart opponent of paganism and heresy. Athanasius became known as father of orthodoxy mainly because of the fight he directed against Arianism. Arius (d. 336) was a Greek ecclesiastic who taught that Christ was a created being and not God in the full sense. His theology was condemned at Nicaea (325), where Athanasius figured in the formulation of the Nicene Creed, featuring the Trinity. The Trinity doctrine may be considered a contribution of the Alexandrian catechetical school. The Unitarians of today are heirs of Arian Christology.

A work ascribed to Athanasius sketches the life of an Egyptian-born contemporary hermit, Anthony. Anthony spent twenty years in the desert where he gathered a circle of disciples to become the first colony of ascetics. Ascetic colonies grew into monastic orders. They spread from Egypt into Palestine and throughout Christendom.

While the Fathers of the Greek Church in Alexandria were enriching Christian doctrine with philosophic thoughts, Fathers of the Latin Church in North Africa were introducing into church government and administration Roman legal ideas and juridical concepts. First among these was Tertullian (d. *ca.* 230), a Carthaginian practitioner of law who embraced Christianity at the age of thirty. His pupil and fellow-Carthaginian, Cyprian, who also pagan-born (*ca.* 200). Cyprian occupied the bishopric of his native city, where he was decapitated during Valerian's persecution.

Towering above all Latin—if not all Church—Fathers stands the gigantic figure of Augustine. Born west of Carthage (354), Augustine was converted at the age of thirty-three after having been a votary of Manichaeism (a Persian religion posing a duality of light and darkness) and Neo-Platonism. Mithras was the god of light, whose feast celebrated on December 25—when the victory of light over darkness began to become apparent in the lengthening of the day—probably determined our date of Christmas. From 394 to 430, when he died, Augustine held the bishopric of Hippo; like Carthage, Hippo was a Phoenician colony. His sermons and pastoral letters have continued to influence Christian thought. Of his works the *Confessions* is an interesting autobiographical sketch, and the *City of God* envisages the Church as a new empire rising over the ruins of old Rome, but one that has existed from the beginning of time. All these early Church Fathers became known not only for their learning but for their sanctity, and their names are usually prefixed with "saint."

The medieval Christian Church became the institution embodying the Hebrew and Christian heritage of Jerusalem as well as that of Athens, through Alexandria, and of Rome, through Carthage and Hippo. From the Greek source flowed the love of learning with stress on intellect and mind. The church became the depository of knowledge for the Christian society. From the Roman source flowed the principles of organizing human society and regulating it with law involving order and discipline. Our canon law inherited Roman law. In a sense, therefore, the medieval Christian Church stepped into the shoes of the Roman Empire and the pope developed into an emperor.

10

In Byzantine Days

Two history-making achievements entitled Constantine (joint emperor 306, sole emperor 324-337) to greatness: raising Christianity to an official state religion and founding Constantinople. The site of the new city was an old Greek colony named Byzantium. For a millennium Constantinople served as capital of the Byzantine Empire, and for half a millennium as seat of the Ottoman Empire. Today it is known as Istanbul. Its unique situation on a hilly promontory, separated from the Asian coast by the narrow Bosporus, gave the city of Constantine command of the gateways to two continents and entrances to two seas. The influence it was able to exercise on human affairs was comparable to that of Rome, Athens and Baghdad. For a time Rome and Constantinople shared imperial honors, one in the western and the other in the eastern half of the empire. But as the old Rome on the Tiber declined, the new Rome on the Bosporus rose. When in 476 the Western Roman Empire collapsed and its "eternal city" fell, Constantinople became the sole representative of imperial power. In two respects the Eastern Roman Empire differed from the Western: It was Greek in language and Christian in religion. It was more imbued with Hellenistic concepts and Oriental ideas. In it the provinces of western Asia played the leading role.

For centuries Eastern Roman, or Byzantine, power was based in Asia Minor. Asia Minor was by then largely Hellenized. Syria remained Semitic, Egypt Hamitic. Syrian Christianity was considered schismatic, if not heretic. So was Egyptian Christianity. But the Christianity of Asia Minor was orthodox, the official form. In its language and ritual the Syrian Church differed from the Byzantine. The language was Aramaic (Syriac). Its liturgy may not date back, as asserted by tradition, to St. James, brother (cousin?) of Christ, but it undoubtedly antedates both the Greek and Latin liturgies. In Syria Christianity took the form of Nestorianism and later of Monophysitism, the two greatest schisms in the Eastern Church. Both of these schisms served as an outlet for the political separatist movement of the people.

Nestorianism maintained that in Christ a divine person (the Logos) and a human person were joined in perfect harmony of action but not in the unity of a single individual. The author of the doctrine, Nestorius, was born in Cilicia and occupied the Constantinople patriarchate from 428 to 431, when the council of Ephesus condemned his views. Monophysitism (from two Greek words meaning "one nature") taught that the divine and the human in Christ constituted but one composite nature. Egypt followed Syria in its Christology. In the fourth century it was seriously disturbed by Arianism, and in the fifth century it accepted the Monophysite doctrine condemned by the council of Chalcedon (451). This council, which also condemned Nestorianism, formulated the doctrine of the two perfect and indivisible, but separate, natures of Christ still considered orthodox by Roman Catholics, Greek Orthodox and Protestants. In Egypt as in Syria hostility to the central government at Constantinople encouraged ecclesiastical separatism.

Alienation between Byzantium and its Syrian and Egyptian provinces was not due only to theological, but to political and economic causes also. Byzantine emperors were more autocratic in their administration, more oppressive in their taxation and in certain respects less tolerant in their religious treatment than their Roman predecessors. True, Syriac-speaking merchants maintained their hold on the eastern Mediterranean trade, and Egyptian farmers continued to supply the empire with its granary, but such was the scale of taxation that both parties complained. Besides, Syria's position athwart the path of Persian armies, as they battled with their Byzantine enemy, subjected its economy to extraordinary strains. Egypt was subjected to only one Persian invasion

(616-618) when it was occupied for ten years, but the country suffered from recurring plagues. The taste it got of Persian rule was evidently more agreeable than the Byzantine.

Perso-Byzantine relations were more strained than Perso-Roman relations. Persia was then under an energetic nationalistic, aggressive dynasty, the Sasanid (226-651). The Sasanids offered a serious challenge to Byzantines and on at least two occasions came near driving the enemy out of western Asia and restoring the empire of Darius I. Shapur I (240-272) invaded Mesopotamia, occupied north Syria, took Valerian as a captive (260) and penetrated through Asia Minor as far as Caesarea in Cappadocia. The day was saved for the Byzantines, it may be recalled, by the swift action of the Palmyrene prince Odenathus. More serious was the westward thrust by Khosrau I (Chosroes, 531-579), the most distinguished member of the dynasty. Khosrau's troops forced their way into Syria, sacked Antioch and finally reached the Black Sea. With difficulty did Justinian succeed in buying at a high price a fifty-year peace treaty (562). The treaty marked the definitive wane of Byzantine influence in the Near East.

But the Khosrau-Justinian treaty brought no more peace than others of its kind. Khosrau's grandson, Khosrau II (589-628), conducted a campaign (605) which ravaged north Syria, captured Caesarea in Asia Minor and reached Chalcedon (Scutari, Uskudar), across from Constantinople. A later campaign (611-617) resulted in the sack of Jersualem and the carrying of the "true cross" to Ctesiphon. This was the campaign in which Egypt was subjugated. But at last Khosrau found a match in Heraclius (610-641). Heraclius rolled back the Persian tide, restored Roman Mesopotamia, Syria and Egypt and was hailed savior of the empire. In 630 he entered Jersualem triumphantly and amid great rejoicing returned the holy cross. But the new Byzantine hold on its Near East domain was destined to be temporary. In the area Byzantines and Persians had battled one another to a standstill, giving a new power—Islam—its chance. This will be the subject of the next chapter.

The Byzantine was predominantly an ecclesiastical age. The church was its greatest institution. Church buildings, monasteries and shrines multiplied. Saints were its heroes. Priests, bishops, monks and anchorites played a more effective role in society than scholars and poets. It was a time in which faith in secular institutions and confidence in rational and intellectual processes were badly shaken. Monasticism became a favored way of life. It was a development, we learned before, of asceticism, first practiced in Egypt. The ideals of celibacy, poverty and obedience found ready response throughout the area.

Edessa in north Syria flourished as the intellectual center of the East Syrian Church. The church proudly claimed Apostolic origins and developed its own ritual. It certainly antedated Nestorius, but since it refused to anathematize him it became known as Nestorian. From Edessa its communion spread into Persia, where it became centered. The intellectual products of the Edessan school were enriched by translations from Greek. When Emperor Zeno in 489 destroyed the Edessan school its professors moved eastward to Nisibis (Nisibin) and carried on their work, including translation. The church was imbued with evangelistic zeal as attested by its penetration as far as China. Names and labors of sixty-seven of its missionaries, who arrived there in 635, have been preserved on a monument. Thereby Syriac characters were introduced and adapted to Chinese use. Southward other missionaries established the church on the west coast of India that now bears the name of Saint Thomas.

The Western Syrian Church was Monophysite in its theology and remained centered in Syria. Though less aggressive than its eastern sister, it had enough vitality to spread its Christology to Armenia, whose church is known as Gregorian, and to Egypt, where the church is called Coptic. After the sixth century the Western Church became known as Jacobite, after Jacob Baradaeus, bishop of Edessa (543-578). Its adherents, however, prefer the name Orthodox or Old Syrians.

Besides these two Syriac-using churches there was in Syria a small body of Christians, centered in Antioch, which used Greek and accepted the Christology formulated at the council of Chalcedon. This was the Orthodox Church. Oriented toward Constantinople, the communion enjoyed imperial protection and became known as Melkite (royalist). Strangely, the term Melkite is used today for that fragment which, under Roman Catholic missionary influence in the eighteenth century, split to follow Rome. Both Greek Catholic (Melkite) and Greek Orthodox Churches still use Greek in their liturgy. The liturgy is ascribed to St. Basil (d. 379), bishop of Caesarea of Cappadocia, and revised by St. John Chrysostom, patriarch of Constantinople (398-404). The epithet ("golden mouthed") was given because of his eloquence in denouncing laxity in morals and luxury in living.

In the non-Christian intellectual field the professors of the law school at Beirut continued to make their distinguished contributions. When in 533 Justinian the Great decided to compile and annotate that body of Roman law considered the most important of all monuments of jurisprudence, he turned to Beirut, whence he summoned a professor, Dorotheus, to be its editor. Dorotheus moved to Constantinople, where he labored for years to preserve for future generations the legal contribution of the past, including those of his two Beirut predecessors—Papinian and Ulpian—cited above.

Other original contributions of Byzantine civilization relate to art and architecture. In the fourth to the sixth centuries diverse elements of Greek, Roman, Hellenistic and Eastern origins blended to produce a distinct artistic expression. It prevailed for centuries and left specimens in the area between Armenia and Italy, including some of the grandest monuments of medieval times. Places of worship embodied the finest in architecture.

Byzantine art was primarily Christian. Christian art was cradled in Syria. There the church drew upon the synagogue for structure and symbolism. The early representations of Christ are reminiscent of Moses. Figures of the Apostles follow those of the Old Testament patriarchs. Eastern Syrian sculptors specialized in columns, capitals, architectural ornaments, wood and ivory carving, book covers and reliquaries. From sixth century Syria came some of the best silver vessels used in church services, including chalices and plates decorated with religious scenes. The way was thus paved for Christian medieval art. Present-day museums display with pride specimens of illuminated and illustrated Eastern Christian manuscripts, and of decorated wood and ivory carvings of crosses and saints.

Egyptian Christian craftsmen also worked on carvings—which display a wealth of decorative motive—and excelled in woolen textile decoration, all of which have merged into Islamic art. Mesopotamians produced some of the earliest illuminated Gospel manuscripts. Especially striking are those in gold and silver letters on purple-stained parchment.

Byzantine architecture began with Constantine the Great. His architects pioneered in the construction of places of worship. Before long, churches, chapels, basilicas and monasteries dotted the entire area. Ephesus, Antioch and Alexandria developed famous schools of architecture and minor arts. From Constantine's days we have remains in the Holy Sepulcher, dedicated in 336. The original building, constructed in the form of a rotunda, survives in shape in the existing complex structure. Other remains are in the Church of the Nativity with its five naves, apse and apsidal transepts. These two churches are the holiest shrines in Christendom.

From one of the earliest and largest monasteries, that of Saint Simeon (d. 459) east of Antioch, we have a part of the sixty-foot pillar atop which the Syrian ascetic reportedly perched for the last thirty years of his life. The pillar stands today amidst the ruins of the monastery. From his aerial seat Simeon taught, preached and won converts, The first and most notable of pillar-saints (stylites), Simeon had disciples who practiced his way of living as late as the fifteenth century.

Under Justinian the Great the Byzantine style of architecture and decoration reached its first golden age. Its masterpiece was

Saint Sophia ("divine wisdom"). In this cathedral, completed in 537 at an estimated cost of $75,000,000, East Syrian art is manifest at its best. When the Ottoman Turks captured Constantinople, they converted the church into a mosque, plastering the figure mosaics on the walls. Mustafa Kemal permitted the murals to be uncovered and turned the mosque into a museum.

Courtesy of Arab Information Center

THE CHURCH OF THE HOLY SEPULCHER BEARING REMAINS FROM CONSTANTINE'S TIME

With the extinction of Byzantine art, after a thousand-year life, an appreciable legacy was left in the East as well as in the West. Modern European and Islamic art are its beneficiaries.

Persia remained outside the pale of Christianity. The Christian (Nestorian) minority there constituted no problem. It was accorded full tolerance. The Sasanids deliberately resumed the old Achaemenid tradition and reactivated Zoroastrianism, with emphasis on the god of light, Mazda, making Mazdaism the state religion. They generally reacted against Greek and Hellenistic influences. Christian Persians, however, maintained their contact with Greek thought. In 555 Khosrau I established at Jundi-Shapur a school of medicine and philosophy under Christian professors whose science was based on the Greek tradition. Syriac was the language of instruction. The native tongue was Pahlawi (Middle Persian), a descendant of Old Persian (but written in Aramaic characters), and parent of modern Persian, written in Arabic characters and rich in Arabic and Islamic terms.

An offshoot of Mazdaism, Manichaeism, reached the West through North Africa. Its founder was Mani (216-276), who claimed to have received a divine revelation making him the final prophet of God. Mani aimed at a synthetic universal religion to be achieved by harmonizing and blending Zoroastrian and Christian thought. But the interpretation he gave the Gospels was gnostic. Gnosis (knowledge) involved initiation and the imparting of special knowledge for the emancipation of the individual from the dominance of matter. Though the master was put to death by crucifixion, the disciples carried his doctrine into distant lands. St. Augustine, we learned, was for years an adherent of Manichaeism. Another offshoot of Mazdaism was Mithraism, which had wider vogue in the West. Mithras was another name for the god of light, later of the sun. His cult was introduced into Europe from Persian Asia Minor after its Roman occupation. It was a mystery cult, with elaborate rituals involving initiation and assuming that only those thus treated possessed something essential that cannot be explained. It made of its devotees a secret society. Mithras was represented as a warrior and held special appeal to Roman soldiers. A Roman emperor was initiated to its mysteries.

In art and architecture, as evidenced by their remains, Sasanid Persia continued to manifest reaction against Greek influences and dependence on the local Parthian tradition. Specimens of metalwork, carpets and textiles display progress. But in ceramics no distinction was achieved. The architects of the period are credited with the development of the arch on a high scale and its early use as a unit of construction. More importantly, they were able to construct the cupola or squinches over a square room. Sasanid palaces featured barrel-vaulted halls used as main entrances or audience chambers. The most distinguished among the royal palaces is that of Persepolis with a grand vault 90 feet high, 75 feet wide and 150 feet deep. Known as Taq-i-Kisra (Khosrau's arch), it was probably built by Shapur I (d. 272) and was used as a ceremonial room and for state audiences. The Moslem conquerors viewed this vaulted building with awe, and their chroniclers recorded its capture with special pride.

11

The Arabian Prophet

The rise of Islam in the mid-seventh century more than ended the thousand-year-old Greco-Roman era. It marked the sunset of ancient times for the Near East and the dawn of the medieval age. It introduced a new religion, ordained to supplant the native religions; a new tongue—Arabic—destined to displace all local ones; and a new culture, itself a synthesis of earlier cultures.

It all began with the birth in 570 of an unheralded child in a hitherto little-known land called Hejaz. The child's name, Muhammad (highly praised), is probably now given to more children than any other name. The name of Mecca, where he was born and which is visited annually by hundreds of thousands of believers, can now be used as a common noun denoting a place sought by crowds for pilgrimage. His migration in 622 to Medina, where he died in 632, gave us the word hegira (*hijrah*), meaning exodus, flight. The year 622 became the starting point of the Moslem calendar, used today by his followers everywhere.

Islam (surrender, to God's will), the religion Muhammad founded, claims currently about 440,000,000 adherents representing all races and living under all climates. The book (Koran, reading, recitation) he, considered illiterate by Moslems, produced is to them the embodiment of all religion, philosophy and science. The Koran was more than revealed. It was dictated verbatim by God, through Gabriel. Dictated in Arabic, it should be so used. It made Muhammad the messenger of God, the last and greatest of all prophets. His dispensation more than supplemented earlier ones. His association with the Koran, according to the learned system, constituted his only miracle.

But Muhammad was more than a religious leader, more than a prophet. He called forth a nation, the Arab nation, represented today by 80,000,000 from Morocco to Iraq. That nation had no national consciousness before. Muhammad laid the basis of an empire (the caliphate) that lasted for centuries and at its prime extended from France and Spain through North Africa into central Asia. No such empire existed before or after. Through this empire for centuries Islamic culture, expressed through Arabic, shone with greater brilliancy than any other culture.

The Arabian Prophet built solidly on earlier Semitic foundations. He considered his dispensation a culmination of earlier ones. Most of the so-styled prophets of the Koran are Old Testament, particularly Pentateuch, characters. They include Adam, Noah, Moses, Abraham, Isaac, Joseph, Jonah, Elijah, but not Amos, Isaiah, Jeremiah and similar prophets. Abraham was particularly favored. He was Muhammad's ideal predecessor. It was he who built the Kaaba, Islam's most sacred shrine. Surah (Koranic chapter) fourteen is dedicated to him. The stories of creation, the flood, the destruction of Sodom echo the Hebraic versions, but are told in brief and for the purpose of teaching a lesson. Of the New Testament characters the Koran recognizes only Zachariah, John the Baptist, Jesus and Mary. Paul was unknown. Jesus was also an esteemed predecessor of Muhammad. His virgin birth is accepted, as are his miracles, which began in the cradle. But his crucifixion is disclaimed. That puts Jesus—in theory—a couple of notches above Muhammad.

First and most important of Islamic dogmas relates to the oneness of God (Allah), emphasizing and refining the Judaeo-Christian concept. It is expressed in the euphoneous formula: *La ilaha illa-l-Lah* (No God whatsoever but God). (See medallion on title page). It is one of the most oft-repeated religious phrases in Arabic. It is used for a child when born, accompanies him through life and follows him as he is being carried to his grave. The dogma found its most poignant expression in surah 112:

Say: He is God, the one
God, the everlasting.
He beggeth not, nor is He begotten.
And there is none equal unto Him.

Closely associated with the first is the second dogma, declaring the prophethood of Muhammad: *Muhammadun rasul-l-Lah* (Muhammad is the Messenger of God). (See medallion on title page). This, it should be noted, does not make of Muhammad more than a human ordained by God to deliver a message. Moslems pride themselves on being the only Unitarians and object to being called Muhammadans, following the example of Christians, who consider Christ divine. In folk religion, however, God's Messenger is invested with divine aura. So transcendent and infinite was the koranic God that the finite believer had to posit a semi-divine human in between. The third article of belief makes the Koran the word of God, word in the literal sense. The Koran enshrines the final and most complete revelation. It embraces the entire message communicated to the Prophet. The finality of Muhammad's message gives his religion a dinstinctive feature and raises him above Abraham, Moses and Christ.

Belief in angels ranks next. Angels form a hierarchy headed by Gabriel, bearer of the revelation. The last dogma asserts the reality of life after death. That life involves the resurrection of the body and entails reward for the righteous and punishment for the wicked. Both reward and punishment in the Koran are expressed in physical, material terms. Some of the most impressive surahs deal with eschatology. The delights of heaven and the horrors of hell partake of the same nature as those on earth. They were all anticipated by Syrian Christian Fathers.

Islamic acts of devotion or worship, also called the pillars of faith, include profession of faith, prayer, fasting, alms and pilgrimage. They all reflect Jewish and Christian practices. Profession implies the open declaration of the unity of God and the messengership of Muhammad. Belief is not enough. It should be publicly professed. This profession is of such importance that once a new convert makes it, he is to all intents and purposes a Moslem. The double-formula professing God's unity and Muhammad's messengership is repeated by the muezzin thrice in each of the five prescribed daily prayers. At the muezzin's call the believer should observe his ritual prayer. He should go through the ritual ablution, turn his face toward Mecca and follow a prescribed pattern of bodily posture, genuflexions and prostrations, while repeating certain formulas. In each of the five prayers the opening chapter of the Koran is repeated four times, making it perhaps the most-often used prayer ever devised:

> In the name of God, the merciful, the compassionate.
> Praise be to God, lord of the universe,
> the merciful, the compassionate,
> ruler on the day of judgment.
> Thee alone we worship; Thee alone we ask for aid.
> Guide us in the straight path,
> the path of those whom Thou has favored,
> not of those against whom Thou art wrathful,
> nor of those who go astray.

Aside from these ritual prayers there are, of course, private ones which an individual can offer at his own initiative. These are spontaneous and unceremonial.

The third major duty, fasting, is enjoined from dawn till sunset throughout the lunar month of Ramadan. Its Semitic antecedents are recorded in the Bible, where both Moses and Christ fasted forty days. In Islam fasting involves strict abstinence from food, drink, smoking and conjugal relations.

Almsgiving is associated in the Koran with prayer and ordained as a manifestation of piety. Its Semitic background is the tithe. South Arabians could not market their spices without offering a tithe to their gods. In the Moslem state almsgiving developed into a regular tax on personal property, farm products and merchandise. Collected by government officials, it was used for building mosques, undertaking public works and supporting the needy among the believers. In most Moslem lands today it is a voluntary but meritorious act left to the conscience of the faithful.

In pilgrimage Islam entered upon its richest heritage from Arabian heathenism. Thereby it deviated markedly from the practices of its two monotheistic sisters. The heathen ceremonies—involving circumambulating the Kaaba, kissing the Black Stone, drinking from Zamzam well, throwing stones at Satan and finally offering sheep or goat sacrifices—were all adopted, given new meaning and Islamized. The Koran makes it incumbent on all able-bodied believers who can afford it to undertake the holy pilgrimage (*hajj*) once in a lifetime. This should be performed at a stated date in the month of dhu-al-Hijjah, and the pilgrim should follow the prescribed elaborate ceremony. Other personal visits to Mecca could, of course, be made, but these are less meritorious.

Aside from its value in spiritual terms, pilgrimage has through the ages supplied the Moslem society with a renewed sense of solidarity and a reactivated consciousness of the bond of unity that makes of the community a religious fraternity. No other religion provides such an opportunity for spiritual inspiration, social intercourse and intellectual cross-fertilization. On the soil of Mecca, hallowed by association, Arabs, Persians, Turks, Pakistanis, Indonesians; black, white and yellow; rich and poor; male and female; old and young, pray together, share the same ceremonial experience and exchange Arabic greetings commonly understood. For propagandists, advocates of new sects and sowers of seeds of new schools of thought, Mecca at the pilgrimage time has been a paradise. In modern times Wahhabi doctrines from there found their way into North Africa.

True, Islam—like all other religions—drew upon earlier sources, but it adapted what it adopted and itself developed into a distinct entity. After all, a religion is more than a collection of beliefs, practices and institutions. It is a form of spiritual energy sparked by some one personality and developed into a living organism. The divine spark normally hits one individual. From him the radiation passes into those nearest to him and thence into the masses. As the raw material passed through Muhammad's personality, it acquired new meaning. More than that, it was energized, nationalized and Arabicized to grip and hold the massive audience as it did.

In more than one field of endeavor Muhammad's originality was manifest. His was the first attempt in Arabia at a social organization based on religion rather than blood. All within his new community, regardless of tribal organization and tribal loyalties, were now brethren—at least in principle. In the course of his last pilgrimage before death, Muhammad declared: "Know ye, that every Moslem is a brother unto every other Moslem and that ye are now one Brotherhood. It is not, therefore, legitimate for any one of you to appropriate unto himself anything belonging to his brother unless it is willingly given him by that brother." Thus by one stroke the most vital bond of Arabian tribal kinship was severed and replaced by a new bond, that of faith. The religious brotherhood was to have no priestly hierarchy, no central authority, no sacraments. The leader in prayer, a layman, was also to be military commander in time of war. The Prophet himself commanded his followers on many a battlefield in and around Medina. Brothers in peace, defenders of one another in war, the believers were to present a common front against the world of unbelievers. More than that, it was their religious obligation to persist in pushing back the wall separating the two worlds. All wars were then holy wars (sing: *jihad,* Koran 2:186-190), and death on the battlefield was martyrdom, assuring the victim entry into Paradise and the enjoyment of special privileges therein.

12

Islam on the March

At Muhammad's death in 632, the Arabian peninsula was still outside the fold of Islam, Arabic chronicles notwithstanding. Even in Hejaz, Mecca's complete conquest was not achieved till two years before his death. Outside of Arabia only two raids had been made, affecting settlements in southern Palestine. The first major task confronting Muhammad's successor (caliph, *khalifah*) abu-Bakr (632-634), was to extend Islamic control to the southern and eastern parts of the peninsula. Abu-Bakr was an aged relative, early convert and close associate of the Prophet. His seat was Medina. As caliph he succeeded Muhammad in all his functions except prophecy. In dealing with non-Moslem Arabians abu-Bakr was adamant. Arabia had to conquer itself before it could conquer the world. It had to be Islamized before it could Islamize others.

A series of brilliant campaigns, conducted mainly by Khalid ibn-al-Walid, netted the bulk of the peninsula. Khalid was a young Qurayshite, newly converted and destined to become the "sword of Allah." The military momentum thus generated on the domestic battlefield had to seek outlets. Fighting among Moslems was prohibited; even raiding, a favorite pastime in Bedouin life since the beginning of time, was now frowned upon. Syria and Iraq offered the easiest access. Soon two columns were on the march. The Iraq one, under Khalid, was scoring against the Perisans, but the other in Syria was hard pressed by the Byzantines. On orders from abu-Bakr, Khalid halted his advance and rushed to the aid of his coreligionists to the west. His perilous crossing of a five-hundred-mile waterless desert in eighteen days became a saga in Arab military annals. With dramatic suddenness he appeared on the scene and before long (July 634) effected junction with the Arabian forces operating in southeastern Syria. In the following year the Byzantine provincial capital Damascus, future Umayyad capital, was subjected to a six-month siege. It surrendered. Treachery on the part of certain officials, headed by the grandfather of St. John of Damascus, played a part in the conquest. But the decisive victory was still to come.

On the banks of the Yarmuk, Jordan's chief tributary, 25,000 Arabians under Khalid encountered a Byzantine army of twice their size. It was a motley host of Byzantines, Syro-Arabs, Armenians and other mercenaries led by a brother of Emperor Heraclius, who was himself in Syria. The day was an excessively hot August 20, 636, clouded by blinding wind-blown dust. Arabians could manage dust storms, but to the Byzantines it was a new experience. Many of them were relentlessly slaughtered; some were hurled into the river; only few escaped. Chants of priests and parades of icons and crosses were of no avail. The fate of the country was sealed. "Farewell, O Syria," were the parting words of Heraclius, "and what an excellent country this is for the enemy." Syria headed the list of countries to build up the Arab empire. It served as a base for operations against Armenia and upper Mesopotamia. Its conquest also facilitated the conquest of Egypt, the second Byzantine province to fall into Arabian hands.

The hero of the Egyptian adventure was another Qurayshite, Amr ibn-al-As, who had led a contingent in the Syrian war. Amr had been a caravaneer on the Hejaz-Egypt route, the only credential he could offer the caliph as he sought permission for the undertaking. The caliph was then Umar ibn-al-Khattab (634-644), father-in-law of the Prophet and after him the greatest figure in early Islam. The conquests accomplished during his caliphate, beginning with that of Syria, make him the founder of the Arab empire. Umar granted Amr the requested permission hesitatingly and conditionally. At the head of some 4000 troops, greatly augmented later, the Arabian general followed from southern Palestine the same coastal road trod by numberless warriors before and after him. The first major encounter with the enemy was at the fortress of Babylon (Babilyun, on the site of Cairo) early in 640. The Byzantine governor was offered the usual three choices: Islam, tribute or the sword. He, who was also patriarch of Alexandria, would not even consider the first two. The Moslem battle cry: *Allahu akbar* (God is greatest) rose, echoed and resounded first outside the fortress walls, then inside. The only serious roadblock on the way to Alexandria was removed.

The nine-hundred-year-old capital, with its reputedly impregnable walls, 50,000-garrison and harbor-based fleet, was the second strongest city in the empire. Its architectural monuments, going back through Byzantine, Roman and Ptolemaic to Pharaonic days, made it without a peer. Early one summer day in 642 a desert horde of 20,000, with no siege or other special military equipment, stood outside the walls ready to attack the city. It was clearly a case of audacity born of ignorance, but it worked. The city's garrison capitulated. "I have captured a city," was the laconic report of Amr to Umar, "from the description of which I refrain. Suffice it to say I have seized therein 4000 villas with 4000 baths, 40,000 poll-tax-paying Jews and 400 royal places of entertainment." The caliph treated his general's messenger to bread and dates. He held a thanksgiving service in the Prophet's mosque, where *Allahu akbar* again reverberated. Egypt, granary of Byzantium and Rome, was now incorporated in the rising Arab empire. Moreover, it served as a springboard for expansion through North Africa and thence to Sicily and Spain. Native Egyptians shed no more tears than the Syrians did, and for the same reason. It was a case of changing an oppressive hated master for one expected to be less disagreeable.

In the meantime, all was not quiet on the eastern front. There stood Persia, for centuries the mightiest and only independent country of the Near East. On his departure Khalid was succeeded by Sad ibn-abi-Waqqas, a companion of the Prophet. With reinforced troops Sad operated successfully first in Iraq. In June 637 he routed the Persian army at the decisive battle of al-Qadisiyah. He thereupon crossed the Tigris and dashed with energy and determination against the Sasanid capital Ctesiphon, twenty miles southeast of Baghdad. Ctesiphon, bisected by the Tigris, was given by the Arabs the name Madain (the cities). Sad found the city abandoned by its demoralized garrison and by the young monarch Yazdagird III. In a few more years the entire country was overrun and consolidated. The booty dazzled the eyes of the victors and exercised the unbridled imagination of the chroniclers. Its estimated value, we are assured, was nine billion silver pieces. Certain warriors were willing to exchange gold pieces, unfamiliar to them, for silver ones. Other's taking it for salt, used camphor for cooking. A soldier offered an aristocratic maid, included in his share of booty, for a thousand silver pieces and confessed later he never knew there was a higher number.

In 651 the fugitive monarch fell victim to the greed of one of his men coveting the crown jewels. Therewith the twelve-century-old empire—interrupted only once by the Alexandrine conquest—came to an end, not to rise again for eight more centuries. And when it rose, it was no more a version of the old.

Thus in a score of years was the entire map of the Near East utterly changed. At Muhammad's death (632) two world powers, the Byzantine and the Persian, dominated the whole territory. North Arabians had not yet stepped within the threshold of history. They had played no national or international role. By 651 those sons of a desert land had stripped the Byzantine Empire of its fairest western Asian possessions and utterly demolished the Persian Empire. In the process, they undoubtedly lost battles and suffered setbacks, but what interests us is the net result.

Arab chroniclers had an easy explanation for this historical phenomenon: It was all the work of Allah. What triumphed, they assure us, was Islam the religion. In this they followed the Providential interpretation of history offered in the Old Testament for the Hebrew conquests and accepted by Christian writers. As a matter of fact what had triumphed thus far was not Islam the religion but Islam the state, not Muhammadanism but Arabianism. This seventh century outburst from an overpopulated, impoverished peninsula in quest of a fuller life in the Fertile Crescent had been preceded by similar ones which gave us the Semites there. The only difference was that at this time religion was a factor. It provided the spark that ignited the nationalist powder keg. The religious conquest followed the nationalist. It proceeded at a slower pace. Some two centuries had to elapse before Iraq and Egypt were largely Islamized. Syria did not assume its Moslem character until the latter part of the Crusades. As for Mount Lebanon, it has maintained its Christian character to the present.

If the first to triumph was Islam the state and the second Islam the religion, the third was Islam the culture. Islamic culture was expressed through the medium of the Arabic tongue. The victory of Arabic over the native languages was conditioned by the progress of Islam the religion. Even where the vernacular survived, as in Persia, Arabic was accepted as the religious language, in which ritual prayer was recited, and the lingua franca, in which writers communicated their thoughts. It should be remembered in this connection that the so-called Islamic culture was Islamic in the sense that it developed and flourished under Moslem aegis. In reality it was basically a synthesis of ancient Semitic—particularly Judaeo-Christian—elements with a veneer of Greco-Roman elements.

Driven half-blindly from a crowded inhospitable habitat, imbued with the will to conquer, fired by a new faith and emboldened by its promise of Paradise to him who falls in the "path of Allah," Moslem Arabians swept unchecked through the area. To them Byzantines and Persians must have looked effeminate. Both powers had become anemic through generations of strife. The newcomers could count on the cooperation of long-domesticated Arabian tribes on the Syro-Iraqi frontier. To the Monophysite Syrians and Egyptians, as well as to Iraqi and Persian Nestorians, all of whom harbored hostility towards official Byzantine Christianity, Islam may have looked like a new Christian sect. As Semites, Syrians and Iraqis must have sensed that the invaders were closer of kin than the Byzantine masters. To some extent the Egyptian Hamites shared this feeling. For a millennium these nationalities had been submerged under Western domination. In the conquest of Islam they vaguely saw a promise of self-reassertion.

But conquest is one thing, and administration another. How to administer such a hastily assembled, heterogeneously populated empire whose conquerors were on a lower level of culture than those conquered presented a Herculean task. The simplest procedure was to keep the Byzantine administrative framework in Syria and Egypt, and the Sasanid governmental machinery in Iraq and Persia. This the Arabian Moslems did. The pre-conquest functionaries and bureaucrats were not dismissed—not yet. The bulk of the natives were also left in the pursuit of their usual professions and of agriculture. Those among them of the Christian and Jewish faiths were accorded a privileged status, that of dhimmis (covenant-protected), but subject to special tribute. So long as they behaved and paid, they were not to be molested. Polytheists, however, had in theory only two choices: Islam or the sword. But in practice they were tolerated. There were too many heads for the sword of Islam to cut off. Slaves and prisoners of war stood at the bottom of the sociopolitical ladder. Moslem Arabians stood at the top. There they maintained—rather tried to maintain—themselves as a religio-military community, distinct and self-perpetuating. But the entire system was not to last, as we shall see in due course.

13

The Caliphal Empire

The caliphal empire had its first seat in Medina, burial place of the Prophet. Four caliphs ruled there: abu-Bakr (632-634), Umar ibn-al-Khattab (634-644), Uthman ibn-Affan (644-656) and Ali ibn-abi-Talib (656-661). All four were of the Quraysh tribe; the first two were Muhammad's fathers-in-law and the last was his first cousin and husband of his only daughter Fatimah. These three were early converts and close associates of the Prophet in his career; but Uthman belonged to the aristocratic branch, the last to acknowledge Muhammad's prophethood. Umar was the strongest, Uthman the weakest and Ali the most devout. The Medinese caliphate was purely Arabian, patriarchal and unsophisticated. The head of the state behaved like a tribal shaykh—the only pattern he could follow—rather than a monarch. Kinship to and association with the Prophet, seniority in the adoption of the new faith and in age (except in Ali's case) were determining factors in the election to the high office—if it could be called election. Of the four, only abu-Bakr met a natural death. The period was styled Orthodox because the caliphs were supposedly still so awed by the deceased leader's personality and inspired by his influence as to conduct state affairs as if he himself were conducting them. It was a formative period, rich in events of lasting effects.

First among these events was the laying of the empire's foundations. Arab historians, the earliest of whom wrote a century and a half after the events, report them as if these early caliphs had worked out deliberate plans for the conquests, the administration of the empire and the treatment of the conquered peoples. The fact is that systematic campaigning and the creation of an empire were due less to design and more to the logic of natural development. Generals and caliphs built better than they knew.

Umar, whom tradition credits with instituting the empire, organizing the provincial governments, creating the state register and the judicial system, had to his credit designating the date of Muhammad's migration (*hijrah*) to Medina (622) as the beginning of the Moslem era. The Moslem year, it should be remembered, is lunar. To Uthman goes the honor of the final committal of the "word of God" into writing. The compilation of the material and its canonization established once for all the text of the Koran. The mother copy was installed in Medina. A copy was sent to each of the military camps in Basra, Kufa (Iraq) and Damascus. All earlier copies were ordered destroyed. All texts in use today are presumed exact copies of the Medinese codex. This codex reportedly was preserved there, to the first World War, when the Turks took it and gave it to their German allies.

Uthman's reign was marred by the first civil disturbances in Islam. It ended with the earliest shedding of caliphal blood by Moslem hands. The disaffection began in Iraq and Egypt, where officers and troops reacted against the trend toward centralization in control on the part of Medina. The caliph was charged with nepotism for sending his relatives to the provinces as governors. At home a party had risen which firmly believed that Ali had the prior claim to the caliphate, even from the outset. Such an important office, they argued, could not very well be left to the determination of an electorate. Ali, they asserted, was divinely designated to be Muhammad's successor and it was so announced by Muhammad. This divine right should, moreover, be passed on from Ali to his sons, the only progeny of the Prophet. Uprisings broke out and spread. In 656 a band led by a son of abu-Bakr broke into the caliph's chamber and killed him while he was reading the copy of the Koran he had ordered compiled. While Ali was not blamed for the act, it was maintained he could have stopped it. Ali succeeded to the caliphate. The Alid party developed into a sect. In Islam the line of demarcation between politics and religion is thinly drawn. The unity of Islam was early shattered and forever destroyed. The split into Shiites (partisans, of Ali) and Sunnites (orthodox) has persisted to the present.

No sooner had the new caliph established himself firmly than he encountered a formidable rival in one of his governors, Mu'awiyah. Mu'awiyah was a kinsman of the murdered caliph and had taken part in the conquest of Syria, which he now governed. Ambitious, shrewd and resourceful, he exhibited in his capital's mosque the "martyred" caliph's blood-stained shirt together with the chopped-off fingers of his wife who tried to defend him. He thereby challenged Ali to apprehend and punish the assassins or accept the role of an accomplice. The Syrians rallied behind their governor, Iraqis and Hejazis behind Ali. To the Arabians the Prophet's son-in-law was more nationalistic, more puritanical and more entitled to the caliphal seat. The Iraqis had one other reason for favoring Ali: He had made Kufa a second place of residence. This city became a hotbed of Shiism.

Civil war, the first in Islam, was inevitable. In July 657 the two opposing parties, mostly Iraqis and Syrians, met on the plain of Siffin on the western bank of the Euphrates. After skirmishing the forces joined in combat. As the tide of victory turned in favor of the Alids, copies of the Koran were hoisted on Syrian lances high in the air. The gesture was interpreted as an appeal from the decision by arms to one by the word of God. God was to be the arbitrator—whatever that might mean. The ruse, contrived by Mu'awiyah's ally from Egypt, Amr ibn-al-As, worked. Hostilities ceased. Mu'awiyah appointed Amr to represent him at the arbitration session. Ali appointed an aged theologian who was no match to his wily opposite number. What actually transpired at the session is not clear, but one fact emerged clear: By submitting his case to arbitration Ali lowered himself to a pretender's position and raised his opponent to the caliphal level. Until then Syria's governor had carefully refrained from professing any caliphal aspirations. He knew that Ali had the prior claim. Amr now took his place with Mu'awiyah among the four geniuses in early Islam.

As caliph, Ali continued to lose ground. A large body of followers defected and rose up in arms. Early one day in January 661, as the caliph was on his way to the mosque at Kufa, one of them struck him on the forehead with a poisoned sabre. The first martyr of Shiism was buried nearby. Mashhad (the shrine of) Ali at Najaf became to his followers as sacred as Muhammad's burial place in Medina—if not more sacred. It is still annually visited by thousands of pilgrims.

Ali dead became more effective than Ali alive. He was elevated to the position of a patron saint of Shiism. Extremists made him vicegerent of God on earth, endowing him with a divine halo. To Moslems in general he lived in history as the paragon of Arab nobility and chivalry. Tradition endowed him with superior wisdom and fathered on him, Solomon-like, numberless sayings and anecdotes.

On Ali's death Mu'awiyah was proclaimed caliph by his followers, but these were now mostly Syrians. Iraq, permeated with Shiism, proclaimed Ali's eldest son, Hasan, the legitimate successor. Conservative Hejaz looked with favor upon the choice. To them the Islam of Mu'awiyah and his fellow Umayyads, who failed to acknowledge the Prophet until his conquest of Mecca, was suspect. It was one of convenience rather than conviction. Egypt too had an Alid party. But the Umayyad caliph was fully able to cope with the situation. Sensing that Hasan was more interested in the harem than in the throne, he offered him whatever subsidy and pension he chose to fix for himself. As Hasan was satisfied, Hasanids were left no ground to stand on. Meantime, Mu'awiyah let his friend Amr take care of the Egyptian dissidents. These measures exemplified the new caliph's style of diplomacy. He formulated it in these words: "I apply not my sword where my lash suffices, nor my lash where my tongue is enough. And if there be but a hair binding me to others, I let it not break: If they pull I loosen, and when they loosen I pull."

Mu'awiyah's caliphate (661-680) was a landmark in the annals of Islam. It ended the simple, patriarchal Orthodox caliphate of

Medina. The limelight shifted to Damascus, which was Byzantine-oriented. The Umayyad series inaugurated by Mu'awiyah lasted till 750. Hejaz, with its sacred associations, receded into the background. Byzantine Syria, with its Christian majority, became the caliph's main support. The founder of the dynasty built his state machinery within the local framework. The state treasury was put under St. John of Damascus' grandfather, who had figured in the city's surrender. Greek remained the language of the register. Archaic features inherited from Arabia were eliminated. The army's tribal basis was abolished; its fighting units were "modernized," following the Byzantine model. Mu'awiyah built the first navy in Islam, using the old shipyard in Acre (Akka) and Alexandria, and himself became the first admiral in Arab history. (Both "admiral" and "arsenal" are of Arabic etymology.)

Summer raids made into the "land of the Romans" (Asia Minor) kept the fighting forces physically fit. The objective was booty rather than conquest, though the spectacle of Constantinople must have beckoned from the distant horizon. Indeed, on two occasions the Umayyad army stood before the triple wall of the mighty capital. From 668 to 669 it wintered at its Asiatic suburb, Chalcedon. Meantime, the navy was not idle. It harassed the Byzantine ports and at times engaged the enemy fleet. In the prolonged war of 674 to 680 the Arabs secured a naval base in the Sea of Marmora. Thence they conducted raids which resulted in the occupation of Rhodes and Crete. It was a newly invented weapon, the Greek fire, which drove them out of Marmora. This highly combustible compound "would burn on water." Neither Mu'awiyah's nor his successors' attacks, however, gave the Arabs a permanent foothold in Asia Minor. As it was never Semitized before, it was never Arabicized later. Nor was it Islamized until the Turkish conquest in the fourteenth century. Nature had raised the Taurus and Anti-Taurus as the first line of defense. The relatively cold climate served as a second line. For the Arab invaders the line of least resistance pointed in other directions.

The westward drive from Egypt was more productive of results. Climate and terrain suited Arab warfare. Berbers were on about the same general level as Arabians. Only along the shore had Greco-Roman culture and Christianity struck roots. The Phoenician colonization of earlier days perhaps added to the facility of conquest. The Byzantine masters had no strong hold on the country. Their fleet had lost mastery over the eastern Mediterranean waters. In a few years, therefore, what is today Libya and Tunisia were reduced. In 670 Qayrawan (Kairwan), whose ruins can now be seen near Tunis, was founded as a stopping place for caravans. It soon developed into the Moslem capital of North Africa and remained for centuries an intellectual and religious center for the area.

Equally successful was the eastward drive. In 674 Bukhara in distant Turkestan was reached. Here Islam established its first contact with an entirely different people and a strange culture. The Turks were neither Semites, Hamites nor Indo-Europeans. Their relation was with the Mongols. These conquests in the east and the west made Mu'awiyah the second founder of the Arab empire.

As Mu'awiyah conquered, he consolidated. As he consolidated, he counted heavily on the loyalty of his Christian subjects, especially the Syrians. His favorite wife was a Christian; so were his court physician and his poet laureate al-Akhtal, one of the best known in Arabic literature. In 679, the year before his death, the caliph nominated Yazid, his son by the Christian wife, as his successor. The introduction of the hereditary principle was an innovation in Islamic succession, which thus far had followed the Arabian, based on seniority in the tribe. To the Arab historians, however, mostly writing in the hostile Abbasid atmosphere, Mu'awiyah was not a favorite. The theocratic caliphate he inherited from Medina he passed on to his successors as a secular state, a temporal monarchy. He himself was its first king (*malik*), an unsavory title to Arab historians. Following the Byzantine precedent, he surrounded his throne with a bodyguard and a retinue of officials, including non-Moslems. Under him Islam began to look less toward the desert and more toward the West. It lost its puritanical character. To his successors, the first caliph served as a model. Many tried to emulate him, but few succeeded.

The death of Mu'awiyah and the accession of Yazid (680-683), a dissolute drunkard, encouraged Shiite uprising. A small band of relatives, harem and believers rallied behind Husayn, Hasan's brother. Some must have thought that, as the God-chosen imam, Husayn was invincible. But to an Umayyad contingent he and his band were an easy prey. The encounter took place at Karbala, twenty-five miles southwest of Kufa. The head of the Prophet's grandson was sent to Damascus but was returned to Karbala for burial. The Karbala shrine joined that of Najaf as a revered object of pilgrimage, more meritorious than Medina's. The son shared with the father the greatest honor of martyrdom. The anniversary of his passion is still commemorated with mourning and self-inflicted suffering in many places of the Shiite world. "Vengeance for Husayn" became a new battle cry for a community of Islam. Their chance came as the Umayyad regime began to totter on its way to final downfall.

The dynasty initiated by Mu'awiyah reached its meridian of power, glory and affluence in the days of his sixth successor Abd-al-Malik (685-705) and his son al-Walid (705-715). Under these two caliphs the second wave of Umayyad conquest rolled on eastward and westward. Transoxiana and western India were completely subdued. Balkh (Bactra of the Greeks), capital of Tukharistan and Samarkand, metropolis of Sogdiana, leading centers of Buddhist culture, became in due course leading centers of Islamic learning and civilization. Among other major cities added to the list of conquered were Kabul, now capital of Afghanistan, and Marv, capital of Khurasan. Therewith Islamic expansion reached its farthest eastern limit. The drive southward through what is today Baluchistan netted Sind and southern Punjab, the area in which Pakistan in 1947 was cradled. All this Turkish and Hindu territory was Islamized, and so it remained.

While these military operations were in progress, the eternal enemy in the west was not entirely forgotten. The drive against Constantinople, however, yielded no more results than earlier ones. The year after al-Walid's death an Umayyad army subjected the

Byzantine capital to a year-siege (716-717), ending in failure. Scarcity of provisions and the rigors of an unusually cold winter accounted for it. This was the third and last time in which Umayyad warriors cast covetous eyes on the city of Constantine.

The campaign against Constantinople's possessions in North Africa, however, fared well. Here the hero was Musa ibn-Nusayr, Umayyad viceroy, whose base and capital was Qayrawan. Musa was the son of a Christian Iraqi captive seized with other boys by Khalid ibn-al-Walid as they were in a church studying the Gospels. Musa's horse "was the first Arabian to drink from the Atlantic waters."

In a few generations the new conquerors accomplished what neither Byzantines nor Romans were able to accomplish. They Arabicized and Islamized not only the littoral but a large portion of the adjoining hinterland. The dominant language in the area is still Arabic, and the dominant religion Islam.

The westward thrust, having reached the Atlantic, took a new course, northward. Beyond the narrow straits, priceless treasures in palaces and rich vessels in cathedrals offered an irresistible invitation. In 711 a Berber freedman of Musa utilized boats from the Byzantine governor of Ceuta to cross the thirteen miles of water and landed at the southwestern tip of Spain. His name, Tariq, gave us Gibraltar (Jabal—mount of—Tariq). As in other cases the raid was a prelude to full-scale conquest. Dissension in the royal Visigothic family, discontent and disloyalty among the natives—particularly the Jews—facilitated the invaders' task. Musa followed his lieutenant. Like a row of pins, one city after another, including the capital, Toledo, fell. In six short years the country was overrun. The first European land was annexed to Islam. There it remained for centuries. One of the most sensational campaigns in Arab military annals was concluded.

From Spain the temptation to make incursions into Gaul was too strong to resist—the Pyrenees notwithstanding. But no firm foothold was established. In 718 the mountain was crossed, and the victorious march was not halted till it reached Tours in north-

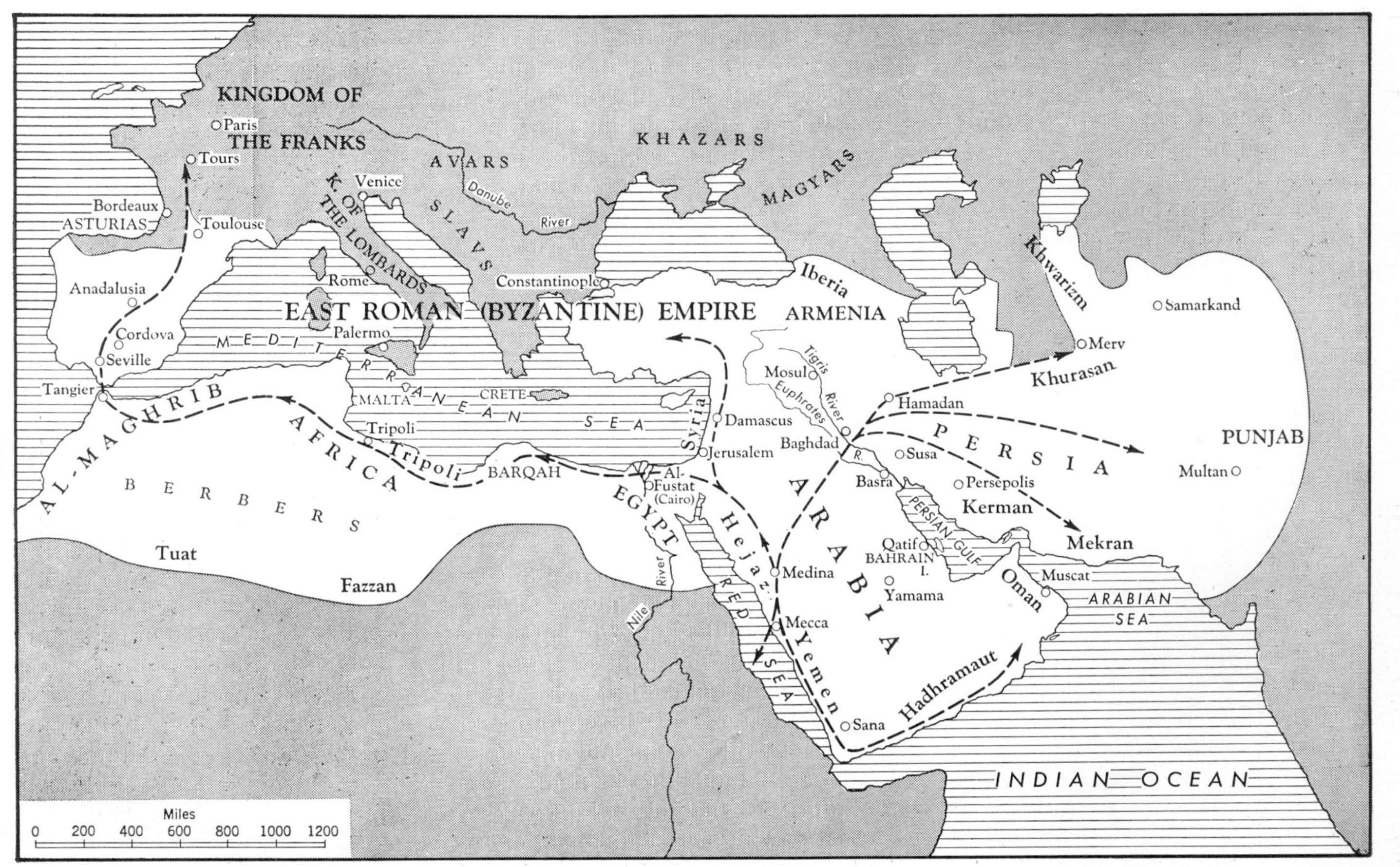

ARAB CONQUESTS IN THE FIRST CENTURY OF ISLAM, MARKING THE GREATEST EXTENT OF THE CALIPHATE

western France. There it was checked by a Frankish army under Charles, later named Martel (the hammer). The year was 732, marking the hundredth anniversary of the death of the Prophet. The place and date offer an opportunity to pause and look back. A hundred years after the death of the Arabian Prophet, his followers had mastered an empire extending from the Atlantic to central Asia—greater than that of Rome—and his name, joined with that of God, was being proclaimed five times a day all over the area. The word of his successor in Damascus was law throughout this vast domain.

Damascus, the oldest inhabited large city, took its place among the imperial capitals of the world. It rose to the occasion. An early Umayyad prince had supplied it with running water from the Barada (bibilical Abana), which supplied its surrounding orchards (Ghutah). Arab writers numbered the Ghutah among the four or five earthly paradises. Legend went further: As a young man Muhammad hesitated to enter the city because he did not want to enter Paradise but once.

In the center of the capital rose the caliphal palace, of which no traces are left. Next to it stood the Umayyad Mosque, built by al-Walid on the site of a Christian church and still ranking as the fourth sanctuary in Islam after those of Mecca, Medina and Jerusalem. One of its minarets is the earliest surviving structure of its kind and has served as a model for minarets in the area. In Jerusalem, the Dome of the Rock (misnamed Mosque of Umar) was built by al-Walid's father Abd-al-Malik on the rock whence Muhammad, so goes a tradition, ascended to heaven. The site commemorates the holiest place in the world, having been marked successively by a heathen, Jewish (temple of Solomon) and Christian (Crusading) place of worship. Close by stands al-Aqsa Mosque, also a product of Abd-al-Malik's architects. These architects, as well as those of Damascus, must have been native Christians trained in the Byzantine school. The dome of the mosque that bears its name copies the domes of a Syrian cathedral. The mosaics rank among the decorative masterpieces of the age.

It was at this time that the Arabicization of the state was completed. It took time to develop Moslem personnel, but at last Arabic replaced Greek as the language of the register. Coinage was also Arabicized. At first koranic phrases were superimposed upon Byzantine coins current in Syria and Egypt. Then Arab coins were struck in imitation of Byzantine and Persian ones. Finally, in 695, Abd-al-Malik coined the first Arab silver piece (*dirham*) and the first gold one (*dinar*). This caliph is also credited with the development of a postal service started by his great predecessor Mu'awiyah. Its primary purpose was, of course, to meet government needs. The system employed relays of horses shuttling between the imperial and the provincial capitals. Local postmasters acted also as intelligence agents for the central government.

The three major government functions of political administration, tax collection and religious leadership were now more clearly differentiated, defined and entrusted to separate personnel. The caliph remained the supreme head. He appointed the governors general, who were responsible for political and military administrations in their respective provinces. He often appointed the tax collectors, too. The army, which in early days was manned largely by Bedouins under Meccan and Medinese leadership, was now made up of Neo-Moslems and Christians. The judicial system evolved slowly, with the governors normally appointing judges in the provinces. Judges were theologians. Not only did they decide cases brought before them, but they administered pious foundations (wakfs), soldiers' stipends and state annuities to Arabian Moslems. Additionally they acted as guardians for orphans and the insane.

Dhimmis remained under their spiritual heads' jurisdictions. Islamic law was only for Moslems. Christian priests and Jewish rabbis handled not only personal status cases, but civil and criminal ones as well. But when a Moslem was involved, Islamic law was applicable. Adherents of other faiths, not originally included in the dhimmi category, were now treated as if they were.

Social classification began to take definite form under the Umayyads of the early eighth century. Moslem Arabians, headed by the caliphal household, stood at the top of the ladder. This aristocracy embraced government officials, warriors, veterans and a few town settlers. It specialized in government and warfare. It was an exclusive body to which admission was by birth certificate. Just below, Neo-Moslems were grouped. Theoretically they were equal to every other believer within the fraternity, but practically they were not. The state discriminated against them in government positions and could not afford to forego their land tax on conversion. Those who attached themselves to Arabian tribes became clients, a socially inferior rank. What made these second-class citizens especially resentful was that they represented the higher culture and were the ones skilled in crafts and learned professions. We shall hear more about them as their resentment predisposed them to espouse all kinds of doctrines heretical to religion and inimical to the state. We shall also find that as Persians, Aramaeans, Copts, Berbers swelled the numbers of new converts, they intermarried with Arabian Moslems and in due course contested the social and political leadership. The line of demarcation between Arabian and non-Arabian Moslems ultimately was thinned beyond recognition. As the original nationality of the individual Moslem receded into the background, any follower of Muhammad began to pass for an Arab. Today Arabian blood is indeed rare among those between Morocco and Iraq who go by the name of Arabs.

Dhimmis constituted the third social class. As professors of revealed religions they were placed under state protection but required to pay poll and land tax. Originally a majority, their ranks were being constantly depleted by conversion to the dominant religion. But at the time we are studying they must have still been so influential politically and economically as to arouse general Moslem jealousy. In response a caliph, Umar II (717-720), decreed the first discriminatory enactments against them. Umar holds the distinction of being the only pious caliph among the Umayyads. The new legislation excluded Christians and Jews from public offices. It required them to wear distinctive clothes, ride without saddles and, more damagingly, erect no new places of worship. But the fact that such enactments had to be renewed on at least two later occasions bespeaks looseness in enforcement.

At the bottom of the social ladder stood the slaves. Recruited mainly from war prisoners, slaves at this time must have reached unprecedented numbers. Viceroy Musa reportedly captured, in the course of his African campaigns, 300,000 of them, of whom he presented 60,000 to al-Walid. His triumphal entry into Damascus, the same sources boast, was graced by 30,000 Visigothic virgins. The Damascus slave market must have swarmed with white, black and yellow recruits from conquered lands. For an Umayyad prince, general or governor to have included hundreds of slaves in his household belongings did not seem extraordinary.

Canon law forbad enslavement of a Moslem by a Moslem, but guaranteed no franchise to one who embraced Islam after enslavement. Freeing slaves was considered a meritorious act. Female slaves could be used as concubines; any children from them were not free. The degrading effect of the institution on womanhood and labor can be readily surmised. Ironically many of the enslaved were more cultured than their masters and substantially enriched Arabic literature and Islamic civilization. Liberated slaves attached themselves as clients to their former masters, who then became their patrons. In many cases slaves and clients replaced their former masters. For two and a half centuries, as we shall learn later, a dynasty of slaves (Mamluks) ruled Egypt and Syria.

The Umayyad was a period of military expansion, political consolidation and social integration, but not of intellectual efflorescence. The Arabians brought with them from the peninsula no science, no art, no philosophy. Their two assets were religion and language. But in the lands they acquired they had sense enough to sit as pupils at the feet of the conquered. In Syria John of Damascus (d. 749) mediated Greek Christian thought. John started life as a successor of his father and grandfather in the Umayyad court, at which time he was a boon companion of Yazid and engaged with him in drinking bouts. After thirty-one years of service he renounced worldly life and retired to a life of asceticism and study in a monastery south of Jerusalem. Aramaic was his mother tongue, but he wrote in Greek and spoke Arabic. His eloquence as an orator won him the title of Chrysorrhoas (golden tongued). The hymns he composed mark the highest attainment of beauty by Christian Church poets and are still in use. His works include a standard textbook of dogmatic theology and a dialogue with a Saracen (Moslem) treating the divinity of Christ and the freedom of human will. John was the last great theologian of the Eastern Church and has been canonized by both Greek and Latin Churches.

This early confrontation of Greek and Islamic thought on Syrian soil laid the seeds of religio-philosophic movements which agitated Arab minds for centuries to come. Rudiments of the doctrine of free will, for instance, which conflicted with the Islamic concept of God's almightiness and man's predestination, can here be first detected. The doctrine became a cardinal point in the teaching of the Mutazilite (seceder, schismatic) school, which flourished in the early Abbasid period. Stimulated further by Greek rational and critical thought, this school boldly questioned the dogma of the uncreated and eternal character of the Koran on the ground of its inconsistency with the unity of God.

In Iraq intellectual activity took another form. Here on the borderline between the Persian- and the Aramaic-speaking territories, the need for Arabic study was keenly felt by Neo-Moslems desiring to understand the Koran or qualify for government offices. Islam the religion was not enough. Arabic was a prerequisite for joining the aristocratic élite. Basra and Kufa became renowned centers for linguistic studies. A Persian Basrite, Sibawayh (d. 793), composed the first Arabic grammar that lies at the basis of this science.

In Hejaz, Mecca and Medina concentrated on the study of religion, theology and law. At the basis of the three disciplines lay the Koran and the hadith (literally narrative), a collection of acts and sayings attributed to the Prophet or to one of his companions. Particularly to Medina flocked students to devote themselves to research on the mementos of the sacred past and to compile legal enactments, ritual practices and Prophetic traditions.

First among foreign sciences for which Moslems felt urgent need was medicine. Respect for the science and art of healing was crystallized in a saying attributed to the Prophet, "Science is twofold: that relating to religion [theology] and that relating to the body." Throughout the conquered territory the scientific tradition was Greek in Syrian or Persian hands. Greek medicine, it should be recalled, was indebted to an earlier Egyptian tradition. The Umayyad court physicians were Syrians. The earliest scientific book in Arabic was a treatise on medicine translated from Syriac by a Jew in Basra. Closely associated with medicine was alchemy, an Arabic word of Greek (ultimately Egyptian) origin. Arab legend cradles the alchemical "science" in the Umayyad age.

Arab or Moslem art was basically a combination of Syro-Byzantine and Persian elements and motifs, developed under the auspices of Islam and adapted to its needs and the proclivities of its society. We have just learned that the architects and artists who built and decorated the earliest monumental structures, those of Damascus and Jerusalem, were Byzantine-trained Syrians. The pulpit in these mosques was a copy of the Christian one, as was the dome. The muezzin took the place of the gong in calling the faithful to prayer—quite an improvement because of the superior effectiveness of the human voice. The niche (*mihrab*), indicating the direction in which prayers should be recited, appears for the first time in the Umayyad Mosque of Damascus. It was in all likelihood inspired by the apse of the Christian church. The ensemble of structure, dome, pulpit, niche and decoration, as represented in the Dome of the Rock, is of such noble beauty that it has scarcely been surpassed anywhere.

All this, clearly, was a far cry from the primitive mosque of the Prophet in Medina, which began as an open courtyard enclosed by sun-baked clay. To protect the congregation against the sun, the Prophet had the flat roof of the adjacent building extended to cover the open area. The main features of the Damascus and Jerusalem mosques traveled through Egypt into North Africa and eastward into Iraq. They were copied and perpetuated, serving notice on the world that the places of worship for followers of the new faith were in nowise inferior to the grand cathedrals of Christendom.

Not only in its architectural but also in its plastic and pictorial forms Moslem art was a non-Arabian product. Born and nurtured in subjugated lands, it was first executed by non-Moslems and then by Neo-Moslems. Islam with its uncompromising monotheism and strict prohibition of idolatry discouraged sculpture and painting. Such activities are forms of creation; creation is a privilege of God and God only. According to a hadith ascribed to the Prophet: "Those to be punished most severely on the judgment day are the painters."

The Moslem artist got around the difficulty by deriving his decorative motifs primarily from the vegetable and animal kingdoms and so stylizing and conventionalizing them as to preclude the possibility of their identification with any existing plants or animals. He developed a kind of ornamentation, called arabesque, with patterns of flowers, foliage or fruits fantastically interlaced. Geometric figures could, of course, be worked out into decorative forms with impunity. Then there were the Arabic letters which lent themselves admirably to such purposes. They were extensively used in the names of God, Muhammad and the Orthodox caliphs as mural mosque decorations. They still take the place of icons or pictures in churches.

But finding a way for justifying the representation of the human or animal form was more difficult. The Umayyad caliphs, not famed for their piety, felt no scruples in including among the mural decorations of their pleasure houses along the fringe of the Syrian Desert pictures of dancers, musicians and other entertainers. One such house, recently excavated near Jericho, has walls decorated with plump dancing girls with lipstick and scarlet-painted fingernails and toenails. We know also of Umayyad caliphs of Spain who had their concubines represented in sculptural form. We shall see later how Persian artists, with a highly developed esthetic feeling and a long artistic tradition, developed miniature representation, including human and animal forms, to a distinct art.

Music, as an art, was frowned upon by Moslem theologians. Muhammad may have looked with disfavor upon this activity because of its association with pagan religious rites. He is said to have declared that musical instruments were the devil's muezzins calling men to his worship. But to the new converts "wine continued to be the body, music the soul and joy their offspring." It did not take the old converts, beginning with aristocrats and caliphs—remember Yazid—to adopt the view.

Drinking and other vices of civilization, against which Arabians had developed no immunity in their homeland, began early to sap the vitality of the Umayyad regime and divert its members from their state duties. The successors of al-Walid (d. 715) surrounded themselves with a galaxy of singers, musicians, fun dealers and pleasure peddlers, some drawn from as far as Persia. To unlimited concubinage and superabundance of slaves was added the eunuch system, borrowed from the Sasanid court, which made the harem institution flourish. One of the son-successors of al-Walid was the first offspring of a slave to ascend the caliphal throne. Clearly the regime was engaged in self-destruction before it was engaged in battle with an enemy intent upon its destruction.

14

Baghdad: Political and Intellectual World Center

Weaknesses in the central government encouraged uprisings in the provinces. Among the provinces Iraq was seething with Shiite discontent and Persia with dissatisfied clients, freedmen and Neo-Moslems. Even certain Sunnite pietists sympathized with the Alid cause; they considered the Umayyad worldly and ungodly. A new claimant to the high office appeared in the person of abu-al-Abbas, a descendant of a paternal uncle of the Prophet. He provided the necessary adhesive force and leadership. An agent of his, abu-Muslim al-Khurasani, was the first to unfurl, in eastern Persia, the black Abbasid banner. Black was supposedly the color of the Prophet's banner and was adopted by the Shiites in mourning for Ali. Abu-Muslim had no difficulty in capturing Marv, capital of the province. Everywhere the white banner of the Umayyads was in retreat before the black banner of the insurgents. In October 749 public homage was paid in the Kufa mosque to abu-al-Abbas as a caliph.

Caliph Marwan II (744-750) resolved on a desperate attempt to stem the tide. At the head of 12,000 loyal Syrian troops, he headed eastward, reaching the Great Zab, a tributary of the Tigris, in January 750. Here he was decisively defeated. The proud capital, Damascus, yielded after a brief siege. Its fugitive caliph was caught hiding in a church in Egypt. He was decapitated; such was the fate of the fourteenth and last incumbent of the Umayyad throne.

The Abbasids now embarked upon a policy of extermination against the fallen house. Eighty princes who accepted an invitation to a banquet near Jaffa were treacherously cut down while eating. Their dead and dying bodies were covered with leather while their

Abbasid hosts resumed their meal. Not even the old dead were spared. Caliphal tombs in Damascus were desecrated and their contents exhumed. One of the two tombs unviolated was that of the pious Umar II.

A fortunate nineteen-year-old Umayyad prince, Abd-al-Rahman, escaped the massacre. Disguised, he wearily tramped through Africa from east to west, landing in Spain five years later. There he inaugurated the brilliant Umayyad dynasty of Cordova, which made of Spain the most cultured state of Europe. The secession of Spain ended forever the period in which Islam the state and Islam the religion were coterminous.

The fall of the Umayyads and rise of the Abbasids meant much more than the succession of one caliphate by another. It had geographic, economic, social and political implications. Syria lost its hegemony in favor of Iraq. The center of gravity moved eastward. Islam was now oriented toward Persia. The pure Arabian aristocracy gave way to a new one, nationally mixed and featured by Neo-Moslems, now called Arabs, more interested in trade and business than in warfare. Arabianism fell, but Arabism rose on its ruins and, hand in hand with Islamism, continued its triumphal march.

Abu-al-Abbas (750-754) took his seat in Iraq. The line he introduced was the most celebrated and longest lived (750-1258). The new caliphate claimed to be a reversion from the secular to the theocratic state, in which theologians and legists resumed their rightful role. The execution of its policy was indeed the reverse of that finesse in policy initiated by Mu'awiyah. The executioner now took his place by the caliphal throne. The founder took pride in his title al-Saffah, blood shedder, and his successors followed in his footsteps. His brother al-Mansur (754-775), of whom all thirty-five successors were lineal descendants, lost no time in liquidating old friends and supporters now dangerous rivals. Abu-Muslim, to whose sword the Abbasid cause owed its initial success, headed the list. He was unceremoniously disposed of in the course of an audience with the caliph. His rule of Khurasan was too independent. The turn of the Shiites came next. They had naïvely thought the Abbasids were fighting their battle. Their two idols, grandsons of

Hasan and leaders of uprisings in Medina and Kufa, were slaughtered. The realm from Khurasan to the Atlantic was pacified. Only Spain lay beyond the reach of the mailed caliphal arm.

For his capital al-Mansur chose the site of a Persian village, Baghdad, on the west bank of the Tigris. Lying in the valley which had seen the bloom and decay of many mighty capitals, the city of al-Mansur grew in a few decades into an emporium of trade and industry and into a political and cultural center of international significance. Its estimated population in a century was a million. The new capital was surrounded by a triple wall and a double moat. The city was circular in form and centered on the caliphal palace with its golden dome and golden gate. Nearby stood the mosque. Here the caliphal court was set up, surrounded by a Khurasanian bodyguard and conducted like a Chosroes' court. Persian titles, Persian wines and wives, Persian food and garments became fashionable. But Islam and Arabic remained the official religion and language.

Next to the caliphate in rank and authority was a newly developed office, the vizirate. Its first incumbent was a Shiite Persian, Khalid al-Barmaki. Khalid was head counselor, chief executive and treasurer of the state. He bequeathed this triple office to his descendants. The Barmakis used state revenues for canals, mosques and other public works, but amassed personal fortunes of fabulous size. They lavished bounties on friends and entertained admirers at banquets that won them a popularity eclipsing the caliphs'. A strong-willed grandson-successor of al-Mansur, Harun al-Rashid, could not tolerate two suns in his political firmament. In 803 he had the severed head of his Barmaki vizir impaled on one of the bridges of Baghdad and the two halves of his corpse on two other bridges. Other members of the family were imprisoned. All their property was confiscated. The vizirial family became extinct, but the institution continued, and Arabic was enriched by a new word, *barmaki,* still used as a synonym of munificent.

Under Harun (786-809) and his son al-Mamun (813-833) the Abbasid caliphate reached its prime of life. Before Harun became al-Rashid he headed (782) for his father a campaign through the "land of the Romans" as far as the Bosporus. Regent Irene, mother of nine-year-old King Constantine VI, signed a singularly humiliating treaty involving the payment of a substantial semiannual tribute. The victory won Harun the honorific title of al-Rashid (follower of the right path). But it was a temporary victory. For the fourth and last time the Byzantine capital was threatened by an Arab army.

It was not, however, military prowess that made Harun's court the most glamorous in Islamic annals. It was the extravaganzas enacted on festivals, weddings and ceremonial occasions, against a background of harem and eunuchs and amidst an elaborate setting of courtiers and functionaries. Harun's royal munificence made him the *beau idéal* of Islamic kingship. Like a magnet his court attracted musicians, singers, jesters, wits, poets from all over the realm. To a master musician-singer from Mosul, considered "the first in Islam to beat the rhythm with a wand and to be able to detect the ill-tuned instrument of a flute-player among thirty ones," the caliph assigned a monthly salary of "10,000 silver pieces." These were the men and women who furnished fiction and history with the theme for some of the fantastic anecdotes crystallized in the *Arabian Nights* and other Arabic literary works.

Al-Mamun's court drew and patronized intellectuals from Syria, Persia and other lands. Their scholarly activity was institutionalized in the famed House of Wisdom, established by the caliph in 830. This was a combination of academy, library and translation bureau. Of special significance was the translation work begun before this time and continued after it.

As early as the days of al-Mansur an Indian treatise on astronomy was done into Arabic at Baghdad, introducing this science into the Moslem world. The early celebrated scientist al-Khwarizmi (d. *ca.* 850), an Arabic-writing Persian of Baghdad, based on the translation his astronomical tables. These were in turn done into Latin (1126) in Toledo, Spain. With the Indian astronomical treatise came a mathematical one which introduced the so-called Arabic numerals. Al-Khwarizmi used these numerals in his textbook on algebra (*al-Jabr*), the first of its kind. This book by al-Khwarizmi, which was also translated into Latin, introduced this branch of mathematics and with it the Arabic numerals into Europe.

Persia and India collaborated in offering Arabic its first assortment of delightful tales intended to teach lessons through animals' experience. The fables were fathered on an Indian philosopher named Bidpai and done from Persian into Arabic by a Zoroastrian convert into Islam in the mid-eighth century. They became the earliest literary work in this language and were rendered into Spanish under King Alfonso the Wise (d. 1284), the great patron of Moslem learning in Christian Spain. Shortly after that they were translated into Latin. Since both the original Sanskrit and its Persian rendition have been lost, it was the Arabic version that has formed the basis of these fables in some forty European languages. The French fabulist La Fontaine acknowledges his indebtedness to the Bidpai tales.

Richer than Persian or Indian was the Greek source, which supplied the Arab world with its basic philosophic and scientific lore. The dean of translators in this field was a Nestorian Christian, Hunayn ibn-Ishaq (809-873). Hunayn headed the House of Wisdom and was himself a practicing physician. He knew Greek, from which he translated into his mother tongue Syriac, whence his son and nephew made Arabic renditions. The Hunayn school was responsible for making accessible to the Arabic readers the medical works of Galen and Hippocrates, the botany of Dioscorides and the philosophical masterpieces of Aristotle and Plato.

More than a scholar, Hunayn was a flower of Christian culture in the caliphal garden. When al-Mamun's son-successor al-Mutawakkil (847-871) ordered him, as his private physician, to concoct a poison for destroying an enemy, Hunayn categorically refused and was imprisoned for a year. He was then threatened with death if he persisted in his refusal. But he uncompromisingly explained that he could not comply because of his religion, which decreed that one should do good even to his enemies, and because of his profession, instituted for the benefit of humanity and limited to bringing relief and cure. Embarrassed, al-Mutawakkil explained that he was simply testing his physician's integrity.

Another Syrian shaykh of translators was Thabit ibn-Qurrah (836-901). Thabit, a star-worshiper of Harran, headed a school of relatives and disciples interested in astronomy and mathematics. His school is credited with putting into Arabic the works of Euclid and Archimedes. Earlier Harranians had produced the first Arabic versions of Euclid's *Elements* and Ptolemy's *Almagest*. This celebrated work of Ptolemy (fl. *ca.* A.D. 140), the astronomer-geographer of Alexandria, has survived in its Arabic translation, as indicated by the name.

This period of translation (roughly from 750 to 850) inaugurated the most momentous intellectual movement in early Islam and—considering its later impact on the Latin West—one of the most momentous in the history of thought. It put at the disposal of the Arabic-reading public some of the most precious treasures of the Indo-Iranian, Semitic and Hellenic heritages. Thereby Islam lost much of its primitive character and its Arabian nationalism, but took its place in the cultural unit that linked western Asia with eastern Europe. The movement had no parallel until the nineteenth century, when a stagnant Near Eastern culture was vitalized by translations from English and French. Properly viewed, transmission of thought by translation is of no less importance than origination. But for translation, the Decalogue, the Sermon on the Mount, the philosophy of Aristotle, the Code of Justinian would have been of limited value in time and place.

The early period of translation and imitation was followed by one of origination. This was again centered in Baghdad. It made of the city a world scientific capital, next to Jerusalem as a religious capital and Athens as a philosophic one. In theology and jurisprudence, philology and linguistics, Arab scholars had an early start in creative work. And now as they assimilated and adapted the translated works, they began to make their own contribution. This was particularly true in medicine, mathematics and geography.

Arab scientific medicine grew out of the Syro-Persian, based on the Greek tradition which, as noted before, owed much to Near Eastern—particularly Egyptian—lore. The first family in Arab history to distinguish itself in this field was founded by ibn-Bakhtishu, a Nestorian Syrian, dean of the Jundi-Shapur academy (central Persia). Stricken with a stomach ailment that baffled physicians, al-Mansur summoned ibn-Bakhtishu. He settled in Baghdad as court physician, maintained his Christian affiliation and passed on his profession and office to sons and grandsons. Resisting advances to conversion, he assured his caliph patron that his preference was for the company of his ancestors, be they in heaven or in hell. A grandson of ibn-Bakhtishu cured a slave of Harun al-Rashid from hysterical paralysis by pretending to disrobe her in public. At this time Baghdad saw its first hospital, modeled after Jundi-Shapur's and serving as a model for thirty others in the provinces.

The prevalence of eye diseases provided Arab doctors with their opportunity for research. A textbook on ophthalmology, ascribed to Hunayn ibn-Ishaq and lately published in English, is the earliest extant book of its kind. At the other end of the spectrum stood surgery. Islam's discouragement of dissection resulted in deficient knowledge of the anatomy of the body.

In the tenth century Islam began to produce its brilliant physicians whose independent productions enriched the Eastern as well as the Western heritage. They were mostly of Persian nationality but writing in Arabic. One of them, al-Razi (865-925), reportedly hung up shreds of meat in different quarters of Baghdad and chose, for site of a new hospital, the spot where they showed the least signs of putrefaction. From al-Razi's pen we have the earliest treatise with a clinical distinction between measles and smallpox. No such information has reached us from Greek or other sources. More comprehensive was this physician's book entitled *al-Hawi* (the comprehensive) which, translated into Latin in Sicily (1279) as

Continens, was repeatedly reprinted and used as a text in the early European schools of medicine. Al-Razi's contributions place him among the keenest and most original medical thinkers of medieval times.

No less original in his productivity was Ali Abbas al-Majusi (Latin: Haly Abbas, d. 994). His last name betrays Magian (Zoroastrian) origin. Al-Majusi's masterpiece was *al-Kitab al-Malaki* (the royal book), dedicated to his royal patron, a Buwayhid sultan in Baghdad. Among other points the book presents a rudimentary conception of the capillary system. It argues that in delivery the child does not come out by itself but is pushed by the womb's muscular contraction. Al-Majusi's was the only major scientific work done into Latin by Crusaders. It served as a textbook in both East and West until superseded by ibn-Sina's encyclopedic work.

In ibn-Sina (Avicenna, 980-1037), physician, philosopher, astronomer and philologist, Arab science reached its highest point. Born to an ultra-Shiite (Ismaili) family near Bukhara, young ibn-Sina was accorded the privilege of studying in the library of its Samanid ruler. Such was the appetite of this self-educated man that he is said to have devoured the library's contents and started on his professional career when still in his early twenties. His authorship recognized no disciplinary boundaries. Of the ninety-nine works ascribed to him certain ones deal with theology, art and poetry. His masterpiece was *al-Qanun,* a codification of Greco-Arab medical knowledge of the day. The book contributes among other points a clinical distinction between mediastinitis and pleurisy, a recognition of the contagious nature of tuberculosis and a discussion of the spreading of disease by soil and water. Translated into Latin in twelfth century Toledo by Gerard of Cremona, the *Canon* displaced earlier texts in medical education and was in vogue for centuries. In the East it remained a medical Bible till the introduction of English and French works in the nineteenth century.

With medicine went alchemy and botany, in both of which Arabs excelled. Alchemy, we learned earlier, was an Arab "science." Its most distinguished exponent was a Kufan, Jabir ibn-Hayyan (Geber, fl. *ca.* 775) who, more than any other worker in this field, recognized the importance of experimentation. Jabir scientifically described calcination and reduction, two principal operations of chemistry. He improved the methods of melting and crystallization. But like other alchemists before and after him, Jabir wasted time and energy in search of that mysterious something called the philosophers' stone. By this stone basic metal, such as tin, could be transmuted into precious metal like gold. Another will-o'-the-wisp sought by other alchemists was the elixir (Ar. *al-iksir*) of life, which could make young of the old and prolong life indefinitely. For generations Jabir dominated alchemical thought in the East and the West.

In botany, as an auxiliary to medicine, Moslem physicians had to depend upon the researches of a Spanish coreligionist, ibn-al-Baytar (d. 1248). Not satisfied with Dioscorides and other Greek sources, ibn-al-Baytar made firsthand study of plants in Spain, North Africa, Egypt, Syria and Asia Minor. His two books on *materia medica* and simple remedies comprise drugs from animals, minerals and 1400 plants, of which 200 were novelties.

Astronomy and mathematics were two sciences in which Arabs produced creatively. In al-Mamun's observatory at Baghdad, the first in Islam, Moslem scholars verified the length of the solar year, the precession of the equinoxes and other basic elements first discussed in Ptolemy's *Almagest*. Assuming the roundness of the earth, they measured accurately the length of a terrestrial degree at the meridian—a most delicate geodetic operation. Remarkably, these operations, headed by al-Khwarizmi, were conducted in an observatory equipped mainly with a primitive quadrant, astrolabe and dial globe. The Baghdad observatory was soon followed by thirty others. Next to al-Khwarizmi in this galaxy of Baghdad scientists stood al-Farghani (Alfraganus) who, as revealed by the name, was born in Transoxiana of possible Turkish origin. In 861 Caliph al-Mutawakkil commissioned al-Farghani to supervise the construction of a Nilometer at al-Fustat. His condensed, authoritative and readable book on astronomy, done into Latin in Spain (1135), attained unparalleled popularity.

If astronomy attracted some of the most brilliant minds of Islam, its handmaid, astrology, drew lesser and more numerous ones. This pseudo-science formed a sizeable part of the heritage from the ancient Near East. Its basic assumption was that human affairs were influenced by the stars and that terrestrial events could be foretold by the astral positions. At least one Moslem astrologer, abu-Mashar (Albumasar, d. 886), rendered a distinct scientific contribution. He explained tides on the basis of their relation to the moon's rising and setting. The twelfth century translation of four of his books into Latin established his reputation as the leading astrologer of the Middle Ages. Strangely, he figured as a prophet in Christian iconography, and many spurious works were attributed to him.

Arab astronomers have left on the skies enduring traces discernible to any student of the stars. Consider by way of illustration such names as Acrab (from Ar. for scorpion), Algedi (for kid), Altair (for flyer). Arab mathematicians have also left in European languages indelible marks of their scholarship. Take such words as algebra (Ar. *al-jabr*), algorism (from al-Khwarizmi), cipher, zero (both from Ar. *sifr*). Then add such medical and chemical terms as alcohol, alembic, alkali, antimony, julep, rob, soda, syrup, and you get a glimpse of the magnitude of the cultural debt the West owes the Moslem East.

Less conspicuous was Arab original production in philosophy. Here Moslem thought was conditioned by religion, and for a time there were no philosophers other than theologians. The intrusion of Greek thought, however, gave birth to a new variety of philosophical thinker, termed *faylasuf*. Al-Kindi, who flourished in Baghdad in the late ninth century, was styled *faylasuf al-Arab*. He had the distinction of being the earliest Arab scientist and philosopher of Arabian descent. Al-Kindi contributed a work on geometrical and physical optics, which influenced Roger Bacon, and another on the theory of music, the earliest extant in Arabic. As a philosopher, he was a Neo-Platonic who endeavored to combine the views of Aristotle and Plato and reconcile them with Islam. In his pioneering work this Arab philosopher was followed by one of Turkish nationality, al-Farabi (Pharabius, d. 950). Al-Farabi aimed at a syncretism of Platonism, Aristotelianism and Islamic mysticism (Sufism). His major production, undoubtedly inspired by Plato's *Republic* and Aristotle's *Politics*, presents his concept of a model city. Like the human body, it is a hierarchical organism. In it the sovereign, perfect morally and intellectually, corresponds to the heart, and is served by functionaries who in turn are served by others still lower. The citizen's happiness is the ultimate object of the association in this ideal city.

But the greatest Aristotelian philosopher Islam produced was not in its eastern but its western half. He was ibn-Rushd (Averroës, 1126-1198) of Cordova and Seville. In fact ibn-Rushd was more of a commentator than a philosopher. Commentators then differed from now. What ibn-Rushd did was to take the Arabic translation of Aristotle done in Baghdad, keep chapters and titles more or less intact, but paraphrase the contents so as to make them intelligible to his readers. First done into Hebrew and thence in twelfth century Toledo into Latin, ibn-Rushd's commentaries were more influential in the West than in the East. Averroism became a dominant school of philosophic thought despite conservative Christian opposition. It struck an intellectual spark that spread its flame far and wide. Thus did the Latin translation of a Hebrew rendition of an Arabic version of a Syriac translation of a Greek original find its way back into Europe and contribute to its intellectual renaissance.

Like other philosophers of his time ibn-Rushd was also a physician and an astronomer. In his medical work he recognizes the principle of immunity in cases of smallpox and correctly explains the function of the retina. Rightly he is considered the most eminent representative of intellectual Islam in its western half.

As philosophers, Moslem theologians had early competitors, but as lawyers they had no competitors until the twentieth century. The system of jurisprudence they evolved (*fiqh*) did attain the status of a science, but it was based on the Koran and the hadith (tradition). In the Koran about 200 of the 6000 verses are strictly legislative, but in hadith the sayings and deeds fathered on the Prophet and his immediate companions were numberless. The majority of hadiths were spurious, manufactured to meet the demands of new and changing conditions. The first task confronting scholars in this field was to compile, criticize, sift and choose what they considered genuine or plausible hadiths, and then to solve the problem of adequate coverage for the diversified civil, criminal, financial and international cases confronting an expanding society.

In time, four Sunnite schools of jurisprudence emerged. That of Medina, known as Malikite after its founder, Malik ibn-Anas (715-795), leaned to the conservative side. It soon dominated in Hejaz and spread into Egypt and North Africa, where it still holds its own. Concurrently a liberal school appeared in Iraq led by abu-Hanifah (d. 767), son of a Persian slave. The Hanafite school insisted on the right of juridical speculation, including analogical deduction. It prevailed throughout the Ottoman Empire and still claims about a half of Sunnite Islam. In between arose a rite, al-Shafiite, which accepted speculation but with reservations. Al-Shafii was born in Gaza, studied under Malik in Medina, worked in Baghdad and died at Cairo, where his tomb is still an object of pilgrimage. The Shafiite school still dominates east Africa, Palestine, South Arabia and the East Indies.

The fourth and last orthodox rite was founded by ibn-Hanbal of Baghdad (d. 855), a staunch supporter of conservative orthodoxy and an uncompromising adherent to the letter of the hadith. This made him a natural enemy of the Mutazilites patronized by al-Mamun. The caliph had set up an inquisition, the only one in Islam's history, which jailed and scourged the reactionary theologian. Ibn-Hanbal's compendium of 28,000 hadiths, which he assembled and commented upon, enjoyed a wide reputation but currently is a favorite of the Wahhabis. Among other devices intended to mitigate the rigidity of koranic and traditional Islam but rejected by Hanbalites was the authoritative character of consensus of opinion in the Moslem community, accepted in varied forms by the other schools. To give validity to this principle the following words were put into the Prophet's mouth: "My community shall not agree on an error." Thanks to this doctrine the pre-Islamic practice of circumcision, to which there is no koranic reference, was perpetuated, Muhammad's miracles in folklore were validated, sainthood of holy men and pilgrimage to shrines were accepted. To the Hanbalites and Wahhabis any compromise with the oneness of God smacks of polytheism, the unforgivable sin.

The Shiites had their own school of jurisprudence. It opposed to the community agreement the absolute authority of the imams, Ali and his successors. To this extent Shiites were a more conservative and authoritarian body than the Sunnite majority. But unlike the Sunnites they kept the "door of interpretation" open to their theologian-lawyers. Through this door all kinds of philosophic and non-Islamic elements were admitted to crystallize into numerous schools of thought and sects. The bulk of the congregation remained steadfast in its allegiance to the twelve imams, beginning with Ali, and became known as Twelvers. The twelfth imam, Muhammad al-Muntazar (the expected) disappeared (878) in a Samarra mosque (Iraq) under obscure circumstances. He thereupon became the "hidden" or "expected imam," who at the opportune moment will appear again as the Mahdi (the [divinely] guided one), to unify the believers, establish Islam as the universal world religion and usher in a short, happy millennium before the final end. This Messianic idea embodies the psychological reaction of a suppressed, frustrated minority and the personification of its hope in a leader. A startling Shiite doctrine that concurrently evolved made dissimulation not only permissible but mandatory on the believer in time of danger.

The seventh imam, Ismail (d. 760), was addicted to drinking, which sparked a controversy that split the Shiite body and gave rise to an offshoot styled Seveners or Ismailites. The Twelvers rejected the drunkard imam in favor of his younger brother, but the new group argued that he, as imam, was above the law. To his followers Ismail became the hidden, expected imam. Ismailism proved to be a fertile soil for Neo-Platonic and gnostic ideas leading to an esoteric interpretation of the Koran. It maintained that in addition to the exterior or literal meaning known to the commonalty, there is an esoteric, inner meaning known only to the initiated few. The Fatimids of Egypt (to be treated later) and the Assassins belonged to this group.

In the last decade of the eleventh century a Neo-Ismailite movement emerged giving rise to the Assassin order. Its founder was a Persian, Hasan al-Sabbah (d. 1124). Hasan started his dramatic career by gaining possession of Alamut, a strategically located mighty fortress in the Elburz 10,200 feet above the Caspian Sea. From this "eagle's nest" Hasan conducted his campaign of "new teaching," as he termed it, which brought together multitudes of economically and religiously dissatisfied Moslems and united them in a secret organization in quest of a better life. Headed by the grand master, the order was set up as a hierarchy with priors in charge of districts and "self-sacrificers" at the bottom. The self-sacrificers dared all, risked all and made assassination an art. They spread terror throughout the realm. According to a graphic but late secondhand account by the Italian traveler Marco Polo, the grand master would administer hashish (Ar. *hashish,* whence assassin) to his youthful disciples, let them loose in his beautiful garden with damsels and houris and then ordered them to go and destroy some enemy, promising similar visits to Paradise. Assassin fortresses in the Syrian mountains, still standing, provided the personnel which struck terror into Crusaders' hearts. Nor were Moslem leaders spared. An illustrious Persian vizir in Baghdad, Nizam-al-Mulk, was an early victim (1092). A later attempt on the life of Salah-al-Din (Saladin) was unsuccessful.

Other less obnoxious and more enduring orders, such as the Sufis, arose in Islam. Sufism, a form of mysticism, represented a reaction against cold intellectualism and fossilized traditionalism in religion. It stressed emotion (love), the "inner light" (intuition) and asceticism as a means of knowing God and establishing personal contact ending in union with him. The doctrine found ready devotees among Shiites as well as Sunnites, who tended to be conformists. As it developed, Sufism absorbed Christian practices, gnostic beliefs and even Buddhist ideas such as union with the deity to the extent of self-annihilation in him. The name comes from Arabic *suf* (wool), indicating that the favored dress copied that of Christian monks. The practice of solitary meditation and prolonged vigils also reflect Christian monastic life. In the twelfth century Sufis began to group themselves into fraternities housed each in a "monastery" (*takiyah, zawiyah*) of its own and headed by a shaykh. The shaykh instructed and initiated seekers of admission into his order. An order could have a number of branches, all ruled by a master shaykh. Orders developed their own ritualistic services, including songs and music abhorrent to puritanical Islam.

The earliest fraternal order was planted in Baghdad by Abd-al-Qadir al-Jilani (d. 1166). Known as Qadirite, it is presently one of the most widely spread, claiming adherents from Algeria to Java. Another Iraqi order, al-Rifai, bearing the name of Ahmad al-Rifai (d. 1175), is known for the strange feats of its members, such as swallowing glowing embers and passing knives through the body. Another popular order is the Mawlawi, or whirling dervishes, founded by a Persian, Jalal-al-Din al-Rumi, who flourished in Anatolia and died there in 1173. This order features music and songs composed by its founder and considered among the tenderest and most exquisite of their kind. A modern order is the Sanusi of Libya, to which the royal family belongs. It bears the name of an Algerian shaykh who founded it in 1837 and is distinguished by being a congregation state with military and political as well as religious aims. The war it waged against Italians in Libya contributed to the freeing of the country.

Sufis are credited, among other innovations, with the introduction, from Eastern Christianity, of the rosary, originally a Hindu instrument of devotion. Through the Crusades the rosary made its way into Europe and still figures in Roman Catholic worship. The cult of saints is another Islamic innovation fathered by Sufism. The cult spread far beyond Sufi circles. It supplied the need of bridging the gap between the finite worshiper and the infinite, transcendent worshiped. Founders of orders, shaykhs and other holy men who performed "miracles" were sanctified by popular acclaim. Even women were not denied the rank of "friends of Allah." An early example was Rabiah al-Adawiyah of Basra (717-801). When young, Rabiah was sold as a slave but was freed by her master on noticing a radiance around her as she prayed. She thereupon entered upon a life of celibacy, asceticism and otherworldliness, devoting herself to the instruction of a circle of disciples in

Garrett, Mysticism and Magic in Turkey (*Isaac Pitman, London, 1912*)

A MAWLAWI NEOPHYTE LEARNING THE WHIRL DANCE

the "mystic way" of self-denial and utter dependence upon God. In reply to a question as to whether she hated Satan, Rabiah said that her love of God so filled her heart that no room was left for hatred to anyone.

The man responsible in a large measure for reconciling Sufism with orthodoxy was al-Ghazzali of Tus (Khurasan, 1058-1111). Al-Ghazzali was perhaps the noblest and most interesting theologian of Islam and one of the most fascinating in religion's history. He started his career as an intellectual, a professor in the Nizamiyah college of Baghdad, which was founded by the above-named Nizam-al-Mulk to teach Sunnite Islam and which served as a model for later institutions throughout the Near East. Intellectualism failed the professor and he turned to Sufism, then skepticism. Finally, after physical and spiritual collapse, he became a mendicant dervish roaming for twelve years in search of peace of mind. The struggle ended in victory expressed in a pragmatic synthetic approach worked out in his masterpiece *Ihya Ulum al-Din* (revivification of the sciences of religion). In it he employed Greek dialectics to strengthen the structure of Islamic scholasticism and so treated mysticism as to make it palatable to the canon law. The scholastic structure he built has lasted to the present day.

As Persian thinkers dominated Islamic thought under the Abbasids, Persian artists dominated the esthetic field. In Damascus the Syro-Byzantine pattern of architecture and decoration prevailed, in Baghdad the Sasanid. But unfortunately civil wars, Mongol invasions and floods left us hardly a trace of congregational mosques or caliphal and vizirial palaces in the capital. All the Sasanid architectural features, including ovoid domes, semicircular arches, spiral towers, glazed wall tiles were continued in Abbasid art. Manuscript illustration and miniature decoration display Greek and Eastern Christian influences. Early among Arabic works to be illustrated were the Bidpai fables (*ca.* 1120). Heirs of a long artistic tradition, Moslem Persians excelled in color and ornamental designs, especially as related to industrial arts. Their delicate geometric and floral patterns became dominant in and typical of Moslem art in general. Human, animal and plant forms, as well as geometric and epigraphic figures, on tiles, plates and vases attained a beauty of style unsurpassed. Kashani (from Kashan, south of Tehran) tiles were imitated in Baghdad, Damascus, Cairo and Cordova. They later became popular in Turkey and India. Oriental rooms in the Metropolitan Museum, the Louvre, the British Museum exhibit with pride among their treasures specimens of illustrated manuscripts, vases and lamps from early Moslem centers. Syrians and Egyptians excelled in decorated silk fabrics, the Egyptians carrying on the ageless Coptic tradition. Crusaders and European merchants and travelers introduced such pieces into the West, where they were imitated.

The Abbasid society in which science and art flourished was radically different in structure and economy from its Umayyad antecedent. The change in structure was due to the process of fusion between Arabian and non-Arabian Moslems. Polygamy, concubinage and slavery contributed to the result. So thorough was the diffusion that even among the early caliphs only three—abu-al-Abbas, al-Mahdi and al-Amin—could boast free mothers; and of the three only al-Amin had both parents of the Quraysh. The rest were sons of Persian and later Turkish mothers. Among the bulk of the population the primitive tribal system at the basis of Arabian social organization was virtually obliterated. Meantime a new group of merchants, craftsmen, scholars and other members of the learned professions had replaced the old aristocracy based on Arabian blood and priority in Islam. The Arabian warrior caste was overthrown. Below them stood the mass of the Moslem community. A lower layer of farmers, herdsmen, manual laborers and simple country folk comprised the native stock, persisting in its old faiths.

This social change reflected a shift from an economy of war to one of trade and business. The wide extent of the empire entailed trade on an international scale. Baghdad, Basra, Siraf (on the Persian Gulf), Cairo and Alexandria became world centers of commerce. There is evidence that Moslem traders of the ninth and following centuries ventured east as far as China, west through North Africa into Spain and north into what is today Finland. An idea of the fortunes amassed by the industrial magnates and merchant princes of the day may be gained by citing the case of a Baghdad jeweler who—as the tale goes—remained wealthy after a caliph (*ca.* 930) confiscated 10,000,000 dinars of his wealth.

But it was agriculture that sustained the bulk of the population and provided the main item of state revenue. Agriculture remained for long in dhimmi hands even after landowners embraced Islam. The governments saw that irrigation canals in the river valleys of Iraq and Egypt were opened or reopened. Staple crops included dates, rice, cotton, flax and in certain areas oranges, sugar cane, nuts, lupines and eggplants. Perfume, including preparations from rose and violet petals, flourished as an industry in Damascus, Shiraz and other Persian towns. Our word attar is Arabic of Persian origin.

As dhimmis prospered in industry and agriculture they aroused their neighbors' jealousy. As they clung to their traditional culture patterns and persisted in their native tongues—Aramaic (Syriac) in Syria and Iraq, Iranian in Persia, Coptic in Egypt and Turkish in central Asia—they aroused hostility. This was reflected in legislation under two Abbasid caliphs, Harun and his grandson al-Mutawakkil. It reactivated the legislation of Umar II and decreed the demolition of churches erected after the Moslem conquest, and the affixing of wooden images of devils to Christian and Jewish houses. The jurists added a new disability, the unacceptability of a dhimmi's testimony against a believer. Egypt was subjected to further discriminatory enactments under a Fatimid caliph of the early eleventh century. The result was massive movements to Islam. By the eleventh century the conquest of Islam the religion was near complete except in such mountainous areas as Lebanon. This religious conquest entailed the linguistic, establishing the supremacy of Arabic.

As the body of Islam was bulging with new recruits, and while Neo-Moslem Syrians, Persians and Turks were playing the central role in the caliphate's intellectual life, Neo-Moslem governors and generals were busy amputating limbs of the political body, leading to its final destruction.

15

Dismemberment and Succession

The dismemberment of the Abbasid caliphate began early but moved slowly, and its completion was long delayed. Spain, we learned, was the first province lost. There in 755 the fugitive Umayyad prince, Abd-al-Rahman I, inaugurated an independent regime, centered in Cordova, that started a rival Sunnite caliphate. In 800 a governor sent by Harun to what is today Tunisia assumed the title of amir, ruling independently but acknowledging the spiritual authority of the Baghdad caliph. The amir seldom inscribed the caliph's name on the coinage. He passed on the amirate to his progeny. His successors extended Arab sway to Sicily (902), which they held until the Norman conquest in 1060.

On the ruins of the Tunisian state arose (909) a more powerful and enduring one, the Fatimid, which in 973 moved to its newly built capital, Cairo. The dynasty's founder, Ubaydullah al-Mahdi, claimed descent from the Prophet's daughter. As Shiites, the Fatimids considered the Sunnite Baghdad caliphate a downright usurper. They were the rightful imam-caliphs. A contemporary of Ubaydullah, Abd-al-Rahman III of Cordova, proclaimed himself in 929 a caliph, thus giving Islam its first experience of having three heads at the same time.

Under the fifth Fatimid, al-Aziz (975-996), the empire reached its zenith, extending from the Red Sea to the Atlantic. Even Mecca, Damascus and cities in Yemen and Sicily cited al-Aziz' name in the Friday prayers. But al-Aziz had no worthy successors. Al-Hakim (996-1021) persecuted Christians and Jews and declared himself, in accordance with ultra-Shiite doctrine, incarnation of the deity; he was accepted as such by the Druzes. These sectarians bear the name of his missionary Darazi and survive in Lebanon and Syria. Al-Hakim's court, however, was illuminated by the great Egyptian scientist ibn-al-Haytham (Lat. Alhazen, d. 1039), whose work on optics corrected the Euclid-Ptolemy view that eyes emanate rays which reach the object of vision.

To Western historians Fatimids are known for the part they played in the struggle against the Crusaders. In Eastern history they are distinguished for being the first and last Shiite dynasty that posed a real threat to Sunnite Islam. Its destruction was achieved by Salah-al-Din (1171), who added it to his Syrian domain and offered lip allegiance to the Baghdad caliph.

As the western extremity of the Arab eagle's wing was being clipped, the eastern wing was experiencing the same operation. There a governor, originally a Persian slave appointed over Khurasan by al-Mamun (820), moved the capital from Marv to Naysabur and ruled as a sovereign. He gradually extended his authority to the Indian frontier and even ignored mention of the caliph's name in the Friday prayers. By 874 the entire area from India to Baghdad and from Transoxiana to the Persian Gulf had slipped from Arab to Persian hands, represented by the Samanids.

In the Samanid regime, which endured until 999, the old Persian aristocracy was restored to power. It was a most enlightened regime, with its capital, Bukhara, almost eclipsing the caliphal capital in political and intellectual brilliance. The Samanids patronized Arabic- as well as Persian-writing authors. To one of them, al-Razi dedicated (914) his great medical work which was later done into Latin. Another member of this dynasty accorded young ibn-Sina the privilege of using the rich treasures of his private library. It was in this period that Persian literature enjoyed its early renaissance and its poetry attained full manhood. Suffice it to mention the *Shah-Namah* (book of kings), the world-renowned epic by Firdawsi (940-1020). Firdawsi was born in Tus, birthplace of al-Ghazzali and other luminaries of Islam. In his poem of 60,000 couplets, Firdawsi recounted with pride and glamor glorious deeds of Iranian kings and heroes, historic and legendary, from Adam to the Arab conquest. His *Shah-Namah* served as a source of perennial inspiration to later Persian poets and has been done in part or in whole into most living languages.

By the time Firdawsi finished his great work, the reins of power had passed into the hands of another racial group, the Turks. These Turks were originally slaves with whom Samanids had staffed their court. Their rise marked the first victory of this element over the Iranian for mastery of Islam. To one of the new rulers, Mahmud of Ghaznah, Firdawsi dedicated his *Shah-Namah*, but received no worthy reward. Turks had not yet reached the stage at which they could appreciate learning and poetry. Chagrined, Firdawsi penned a bitter attack on Mahmud and had to seek shelter beyond his reach.

As the Ghaznawids inherited the eastern part of the Samanid monarchy and expanded their authority from Afghanistan to western India, another dynasty, the Shiite Buwayhids, fell heir to the western part of Iran. Buwayh claimed Samanid lineage. So low had the caliphate's prestige fallen that a son of Buwayh advanced against Baghdad (945) and was received by the helpless incumbent and honored with the title Muizz-al-Dawlah (the strengthener of the state). For 110 years the Buwayhids exercised supreme authority, keeping the caliph as a figurehead. This ushered in an era of humiliation from which the caliphs never recovered.

The caliphal eclipse continued under the Buwayhids' successors, the Sunnite Turkish Saljuqs. On a cold day in December 1055 a band of Turkomans led by Tughril, a grandson of Saljuq, stood knocking at the guarded gates of Baghdad. Instead of resistance the caliph offered hospitality, accepted Tughril as a deliverer, bestowed on him the title of sultan (he with authority) and with it the authority. This was the title continued by the Ottomans, cousins and inheritors of the Saljuqs. Saljuq sultans renewed the traditional feud with the Byzantines. The decisive battle of Manzikart (Armenia, 1071), in which the Byzantine emperor was captured, opened the way wide to the western thrust. Tribes poured in and settled. The destruction of Hellenism and the Turkification of Asia

Courtesy of the Metropolitan Museum of Art,
Bequest of William Milne Grinnel, 1920

MINIATURE OF RUSTAM, HERO OF A *SHAH NAMAH* TALE, CAPTURING THE HORSE, RAKHSH

Courtesy of the Metropolitan Museum of Art, Gift of Alexander Smith Cochran, 1913

PAGE OF A MANUSCRIPT OF NIZAMI, *KHAMSAH*, DATED 1525

Minor began, an aspect maintained until the present. Nicaea (Niqiyah, Izniq) was reached in seven years. There, not far from Constantinople, the autonomous Saljuq Sultanate of Rum (Romans) was established. Shortly afterwards the seat of government shifted to Iconium (Konieh), the richest and most beautiful city in Asia Minor. This was the first Moslem state on the Crusaders' route to the Holy Land. The Saljuq realm now reached its zenith. It extended from Kashgar, the farthest eastern point ever reached by Moslems, to the proximity of Constantinople. The Saljuqs had sense enough to appoint and rely on Persian vizirs. The star among these was Nizam-al-Mulk, mentioned before as founder of the model Nizamiyah college and victim of the Assassins (1092). Nizam prompted the astonomers' conference (1074) that so reformed the Persian calendar as to be declared by a modern scholar as more accurate than the Gregorian calendar we use. One of the participants was Umar al-Khayyam (tentmaker, d. 1123), known to the West as a poet of wine. This cultured vizir is also credited with building mosques, canals, roads and caravanserais. So well guarded were the roads that, according to a biographer, one or two travelers could go safely alone between Transoxiana and Syria. A contemporary of al-Khayyam was the master of romantic poetry, Nizami, whose *Khamsah* (*Five Poems*) has been styled the five treasures of Persian literature.

Nizam's assassination marks the beginning of the weakening of the central Saljuq power, leading to the breakup of the house. The Saljuqs of Persia maintained a form of authority till 1117. Those of Rum gave way to the Ottomans about 1300. When the Crusaders arrived in north Syria they found it under Saljuq kinglets.

Thus far we have been dealing with Moslem states rising and falling within the caliphal state, each leaving the state weaker than before. This made it vulnerable to attacks from outside. First came the Crusaders from the west and then the Mongols from the east.

Viewed in its proper setting the adventures called Crusades were but a medieval chapter in the long story of action and reaction between Europe and Asia, a struggle which began with Darius and Alexander and ended with the second World War. This particular reaction was prompted by Saljuq Moslems knocking at the door of Christian Constantinople, preceded by Arab Moslems from Sicily raiding as far as Rome and Spanish Moslems threatening France. The warriors' wearing of the cross as a badge and the setting of the wresting of the Holy Land from Moslem hands as the goal gave the movement a religious overtone. As a matter of fact the motivation was mutlicomplex, including urge for commercial expansion on the part of Italian merchants, hunger for territorial acquisition by French and Norman princes, search for an outlet by restless adventurers, as well as penance for the devout through the holy pilgrimage. The immediate spark, however, was set by a fiery speech delivered by the French-born Pope Urban II on November 26, 1095, in southern France. Note the place and time. The speech urged the faithful to "enter upon the road to the Holy Sepulcher and deliver it from the wicked race." Judging by results, no more effective speech was delivered in medieval times. Like wild fire a strange psychological wave spread from France through Europe, engulfing high and low, rich and poor, old and young.

Constantinople was designated as the rendezvous. Thence the march started through Saljuq Asia Minor. Nicaea was captured in June 1097. On reaching Syria, Baldwin, leader of the Lorrainers and future king of Jerusalem, swung eastward and early in 1098 captured Edessa (al-Ruha, Urfa), an Armenian Christian principality. Edessa was the first Latin state. Tancred, leader of the Italian and Sicilian Normans, turned westward and occupied Tarsus, also under Armenian control. His kinsman Bohemond, shrewdest of all leaders, headed toward Antioch, cradle of the Christian Church (Acts 11:26) and key to all Syria. After an arduous nine-month siege, the city surrendered (June 1098), thanks to the treachery of an Armenian general under its Saljuq amir. Bohemond established himself as head of the principality. Raymond of Toulouse, devout leader of the Provençals, pushed southward through Tripoli to Jerusalem, the ultimate goal, and was followed by Godfrey of Bouillon, brother of Baldwin. Jerusalem was then under the Fatimids and was guarded by a thousand-man garrison. After a month's siege the holy city was stormed (July 1099) and its population given to the sword. The largest and most important of the Latin states came into being. Godfrey served as its head for one year and was followed by his brother Baldwin I (1100-1110), who assumed the title of king of the Latin Kingdom of Jerusalem. In the meantime Raymond returned to Tripoli, captured it from its Arab amir in 1109 and built in it a castle, the first of its kind and still a grand sight of that ancient town. Herewith the last major acquisitions by the Crusaders were accomplished. The three states of Edessa, Antioch and Tripoli owed feudal allegiance to that of Jerusalem. Under Baldwin I and his cousin Baldwin II (1110-1118) the kingdom attained its height.

It was time for Moslems to react. It all started with a Turk, Zangi, lord of Mosul and Aleppo, who in 1144 attacked Edessa and seized it. His were the first of the blows which were not to cease until all four intruding states crumbled to the ground. With Zangi the spirit of the holy war began its migration from the Christian to the Moslem camp. His son Nur-al-Din (light of the faith) captured Damascus from another Turk and made it his seat, thereby removing the only remaining barrier between Zangid and Latin territories. Nur's ambition to acquire Egypt and crush Latin Jerusalem between the upper and lower jaws of the military nutcracker was realized by his more energetic and aggressive successor Salah-al-Din (Saladin, rectitude of the faith).

Salah was born of Kurdish parents in Iraq. When a year old he moved with the family to Baalbak, where his father served as commander under Zangi. His first brilliant achievement was the destruction of the schismatic Fatimid caliphate of Egypt, noted above. With Egypt went Cyrenaica and Hejaz. His second was the decisive victory over the Crusaders at Hittin (July 1187), crater of an extinct volcano 1700 feet above the Sea of Galilee and traditional scene of the Sermon on the Mount. Here his fresh troops subjected the weary, thirsty Frankish army to a shower of arrows the like of which they had never experienced. Of the 20,000 knights and footmen only a few survived to tell the story. King

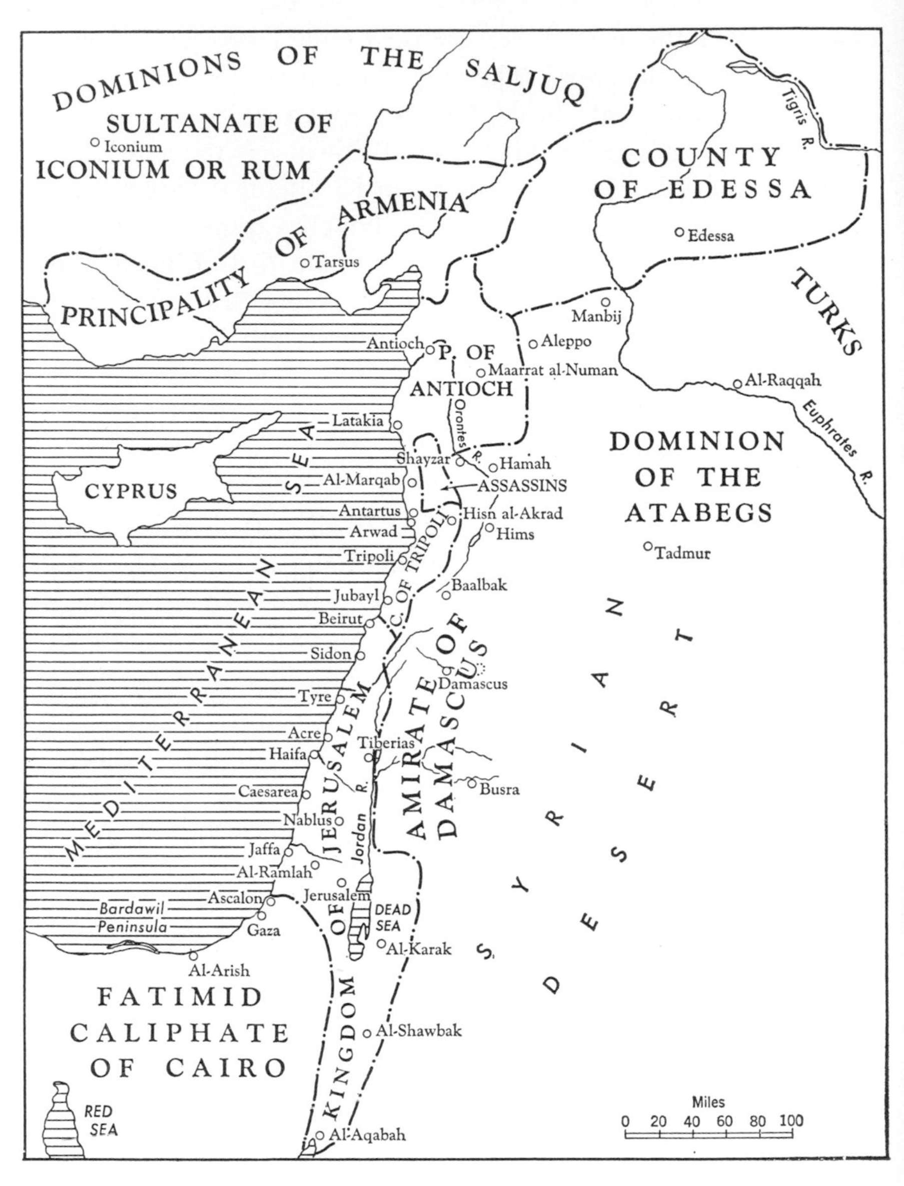

CRUSADING STATES OF SYRIA *ca.* 1140

Guy de Lusignan, who headed the list of captives, was treated by his chivalrous captor with consideration worthy of his high office. He was freed upon pledging never again to take up arms against Moslems. But his fellow captive, Reginald of Châtillon, lord of al-Karak Castle by the Dead Sea, who had laid audacious plans to attack Medina and carry away Muhammad's body for exhibition, deserved a different treatment. And he got it. In fulfillment of an oath he had taken, Salah killed his prisoner with his own hand.

Hittin sealed the fate of Jerusalem. In contrast to the treatment accorded its Moslem population in 1099, its Christian inhabitants were now offered an opportunity to ransom themselves or be sold as slaves. The fall of the Latin capital encouraged and facilitated the conquest of other cities in Palestine, but in Europe it aroused a new pitch of Crusading fervor. Three crowned heads—Philip Augustus of France, Frederick Barbarossa of Germany and Richard the Lion-Hearted of England—led a new massive campaign. Akka (Acre), considered the key to Palestine, was chosen as the main battleground. It was immediately subjected to a tight siege by Richard. Saladin rushed to its relief. The besiegers found themselves between two fires. The contest was long (1189-1191) and strenuous, with spectacular feats of valor on both sides. It involved the two heroes of the opposing camps, matching their military wits. Richard emerged as the victor. Of the prisoners, 2700, who could not pay ransom, were slaughtered. Haifa followed Akka. The coast from Tyre south reverted to Christian hands, but its hinterland remained a Moslem possession.

The death of Salah-al-Din (1193) removed from the scene the champion of Moslem orthodoxy and paragon of Arab chivalry, but left a shining legacy that the passage of centuries has not dimmed. Throngs still flock to his tomb adjoining the Umayyad Mosque in Damascus, and contemporary agitators invoke his name in the struggle against Western powers. Other relics of the past keep his memory alive. Seminaries, mosques and hospitals he started served as models for later institutions.

As often happens, Salah's successors, called Ayyubids after his father, parcelled out the domain. Cairo, Damascus, Hamah and other cities in Syria and Iraq developed into seats of autonomous Ayyubid dynasties. Anti-Crusading Islam lost its unified command as it lost its unified domain. The Crusaders were in no position to take advantage of the new situation. In 1238 a fresh Crusade directed against Egypt by the French King Louis IX ended in utter failure. The leader was taken prisoner but released on the payment of a ransom. He proceeded to Syria, where he fortified several coast towns. His castle in Sidon is a feature of that town. In nobility of character Louis stood unique among his Christian contemporaries and well deserved the canonization he received.

The Ayyubids were succeeded by the Mamluks (1250-1517) as rulers of the Syro-Egyptian kingdom and as champions of Islam in its anti-Crusading struggle. "Mamluk" means possessed, slave, and a dynasty of slaves it was. This unique series of rulers was started by Aybak (1250-1257), an ex-slave of the last Ayyubid's bodyguard. Aybak married his predecessor's widow and established a military oligarchy in which succession in most cases went to a slave of his predecessor or to a member of his bodyguard. Though generally uncultured, untutored, ruthless novices in Islam, the Mamluks rendered three distinct services: They cleaned their realm of the remnant of the Franks, checked the advance of the redoubtable Mongol hordes of Hulagu and Timur and on the cultural side adorned their capital with mosques and other structures that are still treasured among the most precious relics of its past.

The Mamluk line culminated in Baybars (1260-1277), who rolled back the Mongol wave that had destroyed Baghdad (1258) and swept over Syria-Palestine. Baybars consolidated his realm and resumed the deadly blows begun with Zangi and continued by Nur and Salah. One after the other of the Frankish-held towns and the formidable castles garrisoned by Templars and Hospitalers yielded under his onslaughts. In 1268 Antioch surrendered. The entire city with its ancient citadel and venerable churches was set to flames. Some 16,000 of its garrison and people were slaughtered and about 100,000 were taken prisoners. So glutted did the slave market become that a boy could fetch only twelve silver pieces and a girl five. From this blow the once glorious capital of Seleucids and Romans never recovered.

HISN AL-AKRAD

Three years later the tenacious Hisn al-Akrad (Kurds' castle, Crac des Chevaliers), garrisoned by Hospitalers, yielded. The Hisn could house as many as a thousand Hospitalers, and for years it had stood as a sentinel on the route linking Tripoli and the coast to Hims and the hinterland. Abandoned thereafter as a castle, it housed a poor community of farmers until cleared under the French mandate. The Hisn headed the mountain type of citadel, dominating the east-west passes through the mountain from the coast to the interior, while its equally formidable and impressive sister al-Marqab (watchtower, Castrum Mergathum) watched over the north-south passes of the maritime plain. After a thirty-eight-day siege al-Marqab was reduced (1285) by Baybars' successor, Qalawun (1279-1290). Like his predecessor, Qalawun was a

Turkish slave for whom his master had paid the unusually high price of a thousand (*alf*) dinars. Hence his surname al-Alfi, in which he took pride. After al-Marqab came the turn of Tripoli, south of it. In 1289 the city fell and was left in ruins. Akka, the only place of military importance left, was stormed in May 1291 by Qalawun's son-successor. Its Templar defenders were promised a safe-conduct, but nevertheless put to the sword. Therewith the curtain fell on the last act of the East-West medieval drama.

The periods of truce in the two Crusading centuries, strange as it may seem, were longer than the periods of war. From the harvest of benefits the West reaped the larger share. From that of detriments the East was the greater recipient.

The Crusading movement gave Europe a needed chance to expand politically and brought it culturally into contact with a more advanced society. On the military side Crusaders acquired new techniques including the use of fire for signaling at night and courier pigeons for conveying intelligence. Economically the movement opened new markets for European merchants. It popularized such Near Eastern products as rice (Ar. *arizz*), lemons (*laymun*), attar (*itr*), ginger (*zanjabil*) and sugar (*sukkar*). Warriors, merchants, sailors and pilgrims returned with rugs and other fabrics which were later imitated. In European languages are embedded words that stand witness to this fact: damask (from Damascus), muslin (from Mosul), taffeta (*tafta,* originally Persian), satin (*zaytun,* originally Chinese).

On the intellectual level the stream of infiltration was disappointingly meager. On one side was an Arab society starting on its downward cultural path; and on the other a European community lacking in cultural appreciation and responsiveness, prejudiced by religion and a hostile climate and handicapped by linguistic differences. Only one major scientific work, the medical masterpiece of al-Majusi (*al-Kitab al-Malaki*), is known to have been translated at this time into Latin. Short stories, in which Arabic literature abounded, proved especially fascinating and were transmitted, mostly orally. They began to appear in Latin literature. Chaucer's *Squire's Tale* had an *Arabian Night* antecedent.

An especially interesting by-product of the Crusades was the initiation of Christian missionary work among Moslems. The military failure prompted a more peaceful approach. Converting the Moslem seemed easier than conquering him. A mid-twelfth century Crusader founded the Carmelite order, bearing a Palestinian mount's name and still active in the area. In Europe a Catalan ecclesiastic, Raymond Lull (d. 1315), was the earliest European to sense the value of Oriental studies and stress their use for mission work in North Africa and western Asia. Once begun the missionary activity, first Catholic, then Protestant, persisted.

The ejection of the last Franks before the end of the thirteenth century turned towns held by them into a shambles. The Mamluks then came in to add havoc and devastation especially to the coastal areas. Fearing the enemy's return they dismantled towers and castles, blocked harbors and discouraged habitation in seaports. A scorched-earth policy was launched. Remembering that Druzes, Nusayris and Shiites were not fully cooperative and loyal, Mamluk sultans tried to enforce conformity on these dissidents and drive them back to the Sunnite fold. As for the Christians, headed by Maronites in Lebanon, Jacobites and Armenians in Syria, their day of reckoning was at hand. Military campaigns were conducted into their territories and a heavy price was exacted in terms of life and property. The Christians, it should be remembered, were the ones who mediated Greek and other European thought into the world of Islam. Rapport with the West then became more difficult. To man-made misery, nature added its quota. Drought, famine and pestilence became more frequent and, naturally, more destructive. No less than four plagues of considerable severity are chronicled in the fourteenth century. One, the Black Death, raged with fury for several years in the middle of that century, reportedly carrying away 300,000 Cairenes. It worked its deadly way to western Europe. Interpreting the blight as a sign of God's wrath, a Mamluk sultan sought atonement by fresh exactions from his Christian and Jewish subjects.

Under Mamluks the population of Syria and Egypt was reduced by about a third. With that went cultural decline, which had begun in the Crusading period, as well as the economic decline—all of which continued under the Ottomans, successors of the Mamluks.

Before it closed, the fifteenth century gave rise to two international developments of major impact that adversely affected the trade and general economy of the area under study. The discovery of America in 1492 opened new vistas resulting in shifting world-trade routes and turning European eyes westward toward new markets. No more could the Atlantic be called the "sea of darkness," nor the Mediterranean the "middle of the earth" sea. Six years after America's discovery, a Portuguese navigator (Vasco da Gama) rounded the southern tip of Africa, known to us as the Cape of Good Hope, and unfolded a new page in the map of the world. He continued his voyage to India, blazing a new and considerably shorter trail not only to southern Africa but to southern Asia, with its greatly desired and highly priced spices, and to the Far East. The Near East was by-passed and its Moslem area outflanked. The area had to wait until the opening of the Suez Canal in 1869 before it could partially recover from the blow to its trade.

Other world-shaking developments were brewing on the political horizon. A new star was rising in the north, that of the Ottoman Turks. These upstarts were now posing a challenge to the supremacy of both Persian shahs and Mamluk sultans. Though Sunnites, like the Ottomans, the Mamluks now cast their lot with the Shiite Persians, considering them the lesser of the two evils. In 1515 an army from Constantinople under an energetic sultan-warrior, Salim I (1512-1520), cut down the Persian cavalry and routed the entire force behind it. Armenia, where the encounter took place, was added to the rapidly rising Ottoman Empire. Tabriz, capital of Shah Ismail (1502-1524), was occupied. The Mamuks' turn came.

At Marj Dabiq north of Aleppo the Egyptians, wedded to antiquated methods of warfare involving reliance on personal valor, fared no better than the Persians against the Ottomans with their superior artillery and other long-range powder machines. Stricken with apoplexy, the aged Mamluk sultan, Qansawh al-Ghawri (1500-1516), fell dead from his horse on the battlefield. His governor of Aleppo deserted with his troops. The battle proved decisive. Salim entered Aleppo. All Syria lay at his feet. Early in the following year (1517) his guns, stationed on the Nile banks, were turned against Cairo. Its fortifications crumbled. Qansawh's successor and ex-slave Tuman-bay (1516-1517) fled to a Bedouin camp nearby but was caught and hanged on one of his capital's gates. Thus ended the Mamluk sultanate after an existence of 267 years. With it the entire Arab era may be said to have definitely ended. The center of gravity, once in Medina, Damascus, Baghdad and Cairo respectively, now moved to Constantinople. There the ruling race was different, the language was different, the culture was different, but one element remained the same—Islam. Under its aegis these relatively new converts marched on to fresh heights of victory.

16

Under the Ottoman Crescent

The Flag of the Ottoman Empire

The fathers of the Turkish nation originated as nomadic tribesmen in central Asia, drifted first to Persia, where they were Islamized, and thence to Anatolia, which became their homeland. In Anatolia they absorbed their Saljuq kinsmen—both were ethnically affiliated with the Mongols—and inherited their state. Their semihistorical first great leader was Uthman (Osman, *ca.* 1299-1326), who gave them the national designation by which they became known. All thirty-six Ottoman sultans, ending with Muhammad VI Wahid-al-Din (1918-1922), were his lineal descendants.

The principality founded by Uthman in Anatolia around 1300 grew into an empire under his seventh successor Muhammad II the Conqueror, was expanded and consolidated under Muhammad's grandson Salim I and reached its zenith under Salim's son, Sulayman the Magnificent. Muhammad (1451-1481) achieved what no Arab caliph of Damascus or Baghdad was able to: He captured Constantinople in 1453 and destroyed the Byzantine Empire, then more than a thousand years old. Installed astride the Bosporus with one foot in Europe and the other in Asia, the new giant dominated the Near East and the Balkans. In its Near Eastern dominance only one power, Moslem Persia, partially shared.

If the hero of conquest on the eastern front was Salim I, that on the western was Sulayman the Magnificent (1520-1568). Sulayman codified, on the basis of the sacred law and tradition, a system that remained intact and supreme until the nineteenth century reforms. Hence the honorific title by which he is known to his people, al-

Qanuni (the lawgiver). The public works undertaken by his architect Sinan, a Christian ex-slave from Anatolia, have survived, more intact than his code of laws. These include a masterpiece of a mosque (Sulaymaniyah) in the early capital Adrianople. Designed to eclipse Saint Sophia (Tur. Aya Sofya), the Sulaymaniyah is an exquisite structure, topped with a dome eighty-eight feet in diameter. Its tiles in the Saljuq style and its mosaic and faïence following Persian models exemplify the height of artistry in decoration and color. Sinan is credited with over three hundred mosques, palaces, schools, hospitals and public baths in different cities, including Constantinople, Jerusalem and Mecca.

Under Sulayman Turkey became a mighty naval power. An Ottoman corsair of Greek birth, Khayr-al-Din Barbarossa, had under the sultan's father added Algeria (1518) to the realm. He now built up the fleet, manned it largely with Greek and Italian renegades and made it an effective instrument of imperial aggression. In 1534 Khayr-al-Din invaded Tunisia which, however, did not become a Turkish province till 1574. The reduction of Tripoli (1551) completed the acquisition of the Barbary states. Only Morocco remained outside the Ottoman fold.

Meanwhile the land forces were neither neglected nor idle. Their core was an infantry corps styled Janissaries (Tur. new troops) recruited first from slaves, conscripts and subject Christians received as tribute. The new troops were trained, disciplined, screened, brain-washed, Islamized and Turkefied. They were able to carry Ottoman striking force eastward to Persia and westward to the heart of Europe. The Balkans as far as Hungary were included in Sulayman's empire. Vienna was besieged in 1529 and later in 1683. As the Turks retreated from this second siege they presumably left bags of coffee (from Ar. *gahwah*) which introduced this delectable drink into central and thence the rest of Europe.

Under Sulayman the Ottoman flag acquired a new meaning. One horn of the crescent stretched from beyond Budapest to the head of the Persian Gulf, and the other from the western border of Algeria to the Red Sea coast of Arabia. The master of such a realm could well address the king of France in such bombastic style as:

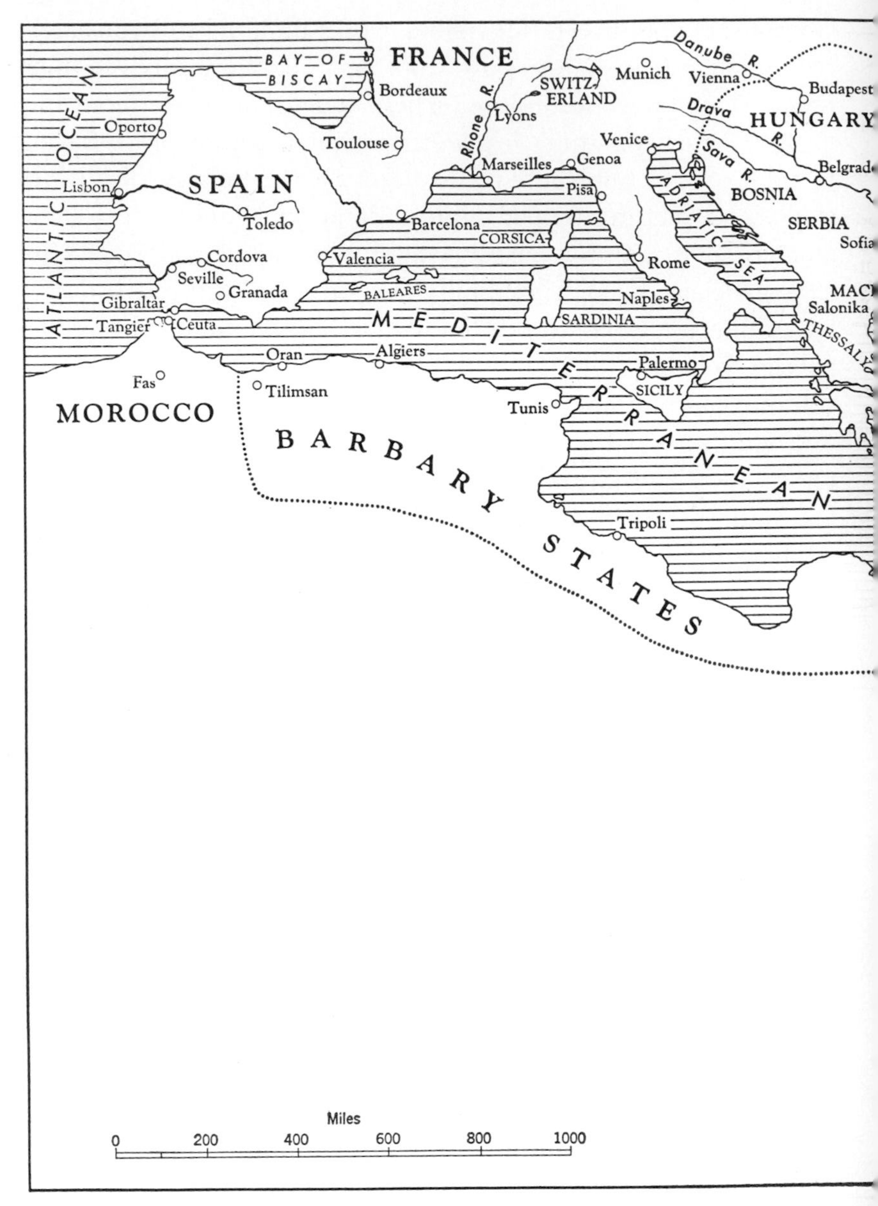

THE OTTOMAN EMPIRE AT ITS HEIGHT *ca.* 1550

ARAL SEA
Oxus R.
Volga R.
Don R.
Rostov
COSSACKS
CASPIAN SEA
MOLDAVIA
Odessa
ALLACHIA
CRIMEA
ucharest
Danube R.
BLACK SEA
GEORGIA
Baku
Batum
Tiflis
ULGARIA
Constantinople
Trebizond
ARMENIA
drianople
ONIA
Erzerum
Ankara
Sivas
Tabriz
Brusa
ANATOLIA
Diyar Bakr
PERSIA
Smyrna
Koniah (Konya)
Mosul
thens
Tarsus
Alexandretta
Aleppo
Tigris R.
Isfahan
Antioch
Latakia
RHODES
Hims
Tadmur
Baghdad
CYPRUS
Tripoli
Euphrates R.
CRETE
Beirut
Damascus
Basra
Shiraz
Sidon
SEA
Acre
Jerusalem
Gaza
PERSIAN GULF
Alexandria
ARABIA
Cairo
EGYPT
HEJAZ
Medina
1st Cataract
RED SEA
Mecca
Jidda
Nile R.
YEMEN
HADRAMAUT
SUDAN
Aden
GULF OF ADEN
ETHIOPIA

"I, who am the sultan of sultans, the sovereign of sovereigns, the dispenser of crowns to the monarchs on the face of the earth . . . , to thee, who art Francis, king of the land of France."

The framework in which the imperial setup developed was now largely drawn. The institution was essentially a military dynasty headed by a descendant of Uthman who came to be regarded as a sultan-caliph. Under him the state power resided in a military group ("people of the sword") consisting of ministers, governors of provinces, generals and other military officers. No matter how high a government official rose, he remained a slave over whom the master could—and at times did—exercise the power of life and death, to say nothing about property confiscation. Under ministers and governors lay a bureaucracy of clerks, accountants and secretaries ("people of the pen"). This category was recruited mainly from native Turkish stock. Then came the religious group ("people of learning," ulema) comprising theologians, canon lawyers, judges (sing. *qadi,* cadi) and muftis—interpreters of law—headed by shaykh al-Islam. This shaykh's office recalls that of the Greek Orthodox patriarch of the defunct regime. In contrast to the military and governmental hierarchy, the theological was recruited almost to a man from persons of Moslem origin.

The commonalty was a heterogeneous complex of religious, linguistic and ethnic groups—Slavs, Greeks, Kurds, Armenians, Arabs, Moslems, Christians and Jews—artificially held together by the sword of the sons of Uthman. Throughout, the Turks remained a minority, but an expanding minority, incorporating only those who professed Sunnite Islam, spoke Ottoman Turkish and conformed to the general pattern considered by that minority as correct. Anatolia was the only land east of the Bosporus where the Turks grew into a majority. In it alone a solid base for a Turkish state was developed. All subjugated peoples, Christian or Moslem, were designated rayah (flock), a pastoral term denoting a reciprocal relationship between a shepherd, who guards his cattle, and the cattle, which supply the shepherd with his sustenance. The subjects themselves used the term with no feeling of opprobrium, as they would use "citizen" today.

The religious grouping was termed *millet* (Ar. for religion, nationality). The identification of religious with nationalistic grouping was deep rooted in Near Eastern tradition. Moslem and Rum (Romans, Greek Orthodox) formed the two major millets. Jews, Armenians and other Christian denominations were also so termed. The religious head of each millet was officially recognized as responsible for administering the laws relating to the personal status of his community. Moslem laws of marriage, divorce, inheritance and adoption were not applicable to non-Moslems. Ecclesiastical and rabbinical courts handled them. This made Ottoman society into a cluster of partially self-governing groups and widened the gap between governed and governor. The millet status was extended to European residents of the empire. First among these were the Venetians, with whom Sulayman in 1520 signed a treaty in thirty chapters (Lat. *capitula,* whence capitulations). This practice had antecedents in Byzantine days. Fifteen years later the French obtained their first capitulations; the British followed in 1580. Ironically these privileges bestowed by a strong monarch on foreigners in his domain became traditional rights opening the way for foreign powers to interfere in Turkey's internal affairs. They could not be entirely shaken off until the first World War.

The government of the provinces followed its Byzantine and Arab precedents. For each province (Tur. *vilayet,* from Ar. *walayah*) a governor general was sent from Constantinople charged primarily with collecting taxes, providing conscripts, maintaining law and order and executing justice. External security was the responsibility of the central government. The practice of farming out tax collection, with all its evils, was of course continued. Mountainous Lebanon, distinguished by its liberty-loving Maronites and Druzes, deserved a different treatment. It was left under its feudal lords, the Mans and after them the Shihabs. These native rulers transmitted their fiefs to their sons, offered no military service to the imperial army and exercised autonomous control. One of them, Fakhr-al-Din II al-Mani (d. 1635), went so far as to conclude a treaty with the Medicis of Florence including a military article directed against his suzerain. In other than Lebanon the typical provincial governor (wali) would buy his office in Constantinople and concern himself with recovering his investment, aware that his tenure of office at best was of short duration. Admittedly, relative internal security and general stability were maintained. For long centuries the entire population was held tightly in the Ottoman grip. But no sustained effort was made to exploit the resources of the lands or improve their manpower. Agriculture and industry languished in the rut into which they had fallen.

The period of imperial glory under Sulayman did not survive him for long. During the reign of his son Salim II (1566-1574), for whom wine and women had more attraction than state affairs, dissipation and corruption became rife. Under Salim's successors wars were carried out fitfully with Persians on one front, Hungarians, Austrians and Poles on the other. The unsuccessful attack on Vienna in 1683 marked the beginning of the decline of imperial power. Attempts by grand vizirs to stamp out corruption, reform the recalcitrant Janissary corps and improve the bureaucracy could neither reverse nor halt the current.

The seeds of weakness embedded in Ottoman state and society began to yield their bitter fruits in the late sixteenth century. A state primarily organized for warfare rather than peace and welfare lacked the capacity to adapt to changing conditions. The concentration of its supreme authority in one man, the sultan-caliph, meant remote and ineffective control of the unwieldy, far-flung provinces. It further meant that when that authority fell, as it often did, into incompetent hands, the results could be disastrous. The situation was further complicated by ambiguity in the line of succession to the throne. This led to endless intrigues and civil strife in which the main actors were brothers or sons of the throne incumbent. Sulayman had his eldest son strangled to clear the way for the dissolute Salim, son of his favorite concubine. Salim's son-successor Murad III (1574-1595), who sired more than a hundred children, inaugurated his reign by murdering five of his brothers. A more humane practice was introduced around 1603, when the ruling sultan simply immured his oldest male relative in a special pavilion (*qafas*, cage), surrounded by a high wall and kept under strict surveillance. One such "caged" sultan was Muhammad V Rashad (1909-1918), who showed the expected signs of arrested mental growth.

As for the conglomeration of peoples constituting the bulk of the population, they felt no strong bonds among themselves and no developed loyalty to the ruling class. Only the Moslems among them could find in religion a common ground for meeting. As these peoples persisted in their ancestral methods of agriculture and traditional techniques of home industry, their economy deteriorated more and more. The Syrian area between Aleppo and the Euphrates, anciently yielding enough to support kingdoms, had assumed by the mid-eighteenth century the desert aspect it maintained to the present. Between the Iraq of that century and the flourishing Tigris-Euphrates valley of Nebuchadnezzar and Harun al-Rashid the difference was so vast as to make the one almost unidentifiable with the other. The population of Syria-Lebanon-Palestine, which in Roman days reached about six million, had by the end of the eighteenth century dwindled to about half that number. Meantime Egypt, where epidemics were more deadly and more frequent, had been reduced in population from some eight million to about two and a half million.

Internal troubles synchronized with external ones. As imperial Turkey waned, imperial Europe waxed. Political ambitions sought new territories and expanding industrial productivity searched for new markets. The challenge to an Asiatic state anchored in Europe was on all fronts: political, military, economic and cultural.

In the seventeenth century the problem was aggravated by the emergence of two formidable neighbors, first Austria-Hungary and then Russia. Austria and Hungary had an old score to settle and a new urge for territorial annexation to satisfy. Russia, hitherto an Asiatic country, was under Peter the Great (1689-1725) beginning to open its doors to European civilization and strive for a place among European powers. Trading rights in the Black Sea constituted the first bone of Russo-Turkish contention. Russia, with its ice-locked northern ports, coveted access through the Black Sea to warmer Mediterranean waters. The struggle against Turkey was carried on by Catherine the Great. In 1774 Catherine forced on defeated Turkey the treaty of Kuchuk Kainarji, imposing a heavy indemnity and exacting the right of free navigation in Turkish waters. Other terms laid the basis for the right of interference to protect the Greek Orthodox subjects of the sultan. No more humiliating treaty had been signed by a Turkish ruler before. Hostilities in the nineteenth century culminated in the Crimean War (1854-1856), provoked by Russia's claim of protective rights over Palestine's holy places and by Czar Nicholas I's designs on Constantinople. Nicholas had called Turkey the "sick man of Europe" and invited Britain to participate in the burial and share in the legacy. But the Crimean War found both England and France fighting on Turkey's side, ostensibly to preserve the integrity of its empire but in reality to contain Russia. The two West European powers had commercial interests in the area, both in itself and as a segment of their imperial "life lines" to east Asia and Africa. It was this rivalry between European powers that gave decadent Turkey a new lease on life. The so-called Eastern question of the nineteenth and early twentieth century was in reality a Western question involving European powers, each jealous of the other and desirous of promoting its own interests in a temptingly weak state.

In the meantime the urge for reform on the part of Ottoman statesmen was not entirely lacking. The point of departure was military considerations. After the Kuchuk Kainarji experience, Ottomans were rudely awakened to the fact that in the science and art of warfare they had been far outstripped by their European adversaries. A bold attempt was made by Salim III (1789-1807) to enforce discipline on the unruly Janissaries and to establish a new militia modeled after the French. But he was opposed by the old corps, forced to abdicate and finally put to death with other advocates of reform. More radical remedial measures were taken by Salim's nephew and disciple, Mahmud II (1808-1839). On a secretly kept day he had his new corps' artillery turned on the barracks of the old one, burying underneath the rubble some eight thousand Janissaries. Those in the provinces were in turn pursued and exterminated. A huge roadblock was thus removed from the path of progress. Mahmud was now free to proceed with his program, featuring the promotion and more extensive study of French. Originally introduced to implement military reforms only, this language thereafter served as a key for unlocking a treasury of knowledge—political, social, economic, scientific, philosophic. The break in the linguistic barrier opened the way for long-needed intellectual cross-fertilization. The reign of this greatest of reforming sultans would probably have been more productive of good had it not been signalized by the Balkan wars which ended in the independence of Greece (1828) and by the Egypto-Syrian war waged by his provincial governor Muhammad Ali.

Mahmud's son Abd-al-Majid (1839-1861) followed in the father's footsteps. Until the advent of these two sultans there was hardly a legal innovation. Canon law (shariah) had ruled supreme. In 1839 a judicial body emerged and began to encroach upon the jurisdiction of the shariah in commercial cases involving non-Moslems. This body developed (1851) into commercial courts based on French models. Seven years later a criminal code was promulgated, again after a French model. All cases relating to personal status, however, remained within the jurisdiction of religious courts until the Young Turks' regime.

Two decrees issued by Abd-al-Majid under the titles of the "noble script" and the "imperial rescript" proved too ambitious. They guaranteed the lives, property and honor of all Ottoman subjects regardless of creed and nationality. All were declared equal before the law. The new regulations aimed at abolishing the farming out of taxes, the annulment of the civil powers of the Christian Churches and the allowance of full liberty of conscience. Largely premature and lacking in adequate implementations, the new laws remained to a large extent ink on paper.

By this time the liberal cause had gained a number of adherents and advocates from among journalists, poets and other writers and thinkers. The inspiration came understandably from French sources. Had the two progressive streams—the political and the intellectual—effected junction, they might have broken the dam of conservatism and swept away the old regime together with its institutions. But the appearance on the scene of a shrewd, dedicated dictator, Abd-al-Hamid II, stood in the way.

Abd-al-Hamid (1876-1909) started well. For prime minister he had Midhat Pasha, one of the most enlightened and liberal-minded statesmen Turkey ever produced. Midhat was a member of a secret society of young Turks working for constitutional reform and had served with distinction as wali of Baghdad province. On his recommendation the newly installed sultan solemnly proclaimed a constitution (*dustur*) which, while recognizing Islam as the state religion, enjoined freedom of thought and conscience, within the limits of the law, and guaranteed protection to all religions in the empire. The proclamation further created a representative parliament modeled after French and Belgian originals. Elected members from all provinces held their sessions in the capital. In February 1878, however, the crafty ruler abruptly dismissed the parliament and sent Midhat into exile in Arabia, where he died.

The sultan now retired to a life of isolation behind heavily guarded palace walls fearful of losing his life and throne to rebellious Bulgarians and Armenians with nationalistic aspirations, or to disloyal liberal-minded fellow Moslems. For information he relied on reports from spies, secret police and press censors, and for self-preservation on force. Repressive measures were taken against suspicious individuals or societies, Christian or Moslem. The Armenian massacres of 1894 and 1895 shocked the civilized world and earned him the title of red sultan. Posing as champion of Islam and rightful head of Moslems everywhere, he stressed his caliphal office, conjuring the Pan-Islamic bogy against European powers with imperial interest and designs in India, Egypt and North

Africa. Simultaneously he tried to pit one European power against another. In Germany he thought he found an ally. Its Kaiser Wilhelm was then launching his "drive-to-the-East" policy and in 1898 paid an official visit to Constantinople, Beirut, Damascus and Jerusalem. He was received everywhere with acclaim. The visit paid dividends in terms of concessions, chief of which were the building of the Baghdad railway and the sending of military missions to modernize the Turkish army. The new railway was meant to link Constantinople to its provinces. This Berlin-Baghdad railway, as it was called, became a focal point in the Eastern question, with the British and French viewing it as a threat to their interests and an index of growing German influence at the Sublime Porte.

At long last the internal pent-up discontent exploded. A military coup, engineered by the Committee of Union and Progress of the secret society of Young Turks, caught the sultan-caliph unaware. The aim, as indicated by the two names, was to rejuvenate Turkey, unite its people and set it on the highway of modernism. Abd-al-Hamid professed readiness to cooperate. He immediately announced the restoration of the constitution and the abolition of espionage and censorship. All political prisoners were pardoned. A wave of jubilation spread throughout the realm. Christians and Moslems embraced in the streets. "Liberty, equality, fraternity" reverberated in orations, poetry and song. Utopia was around the corner. But somewhere en route lurked the crafty sultan. Caught intriguing with his palace officials, he was unhesitatingly deposed (April 1909). His doddering brother Muhammad V Rashad was installed in his place. A new era did dawn, but it was that of the Young Turks tackling, with more courage and zeal than knowledge and experience, a colossal task. Ottomanism was the key to the new policy. The presumption was that the sundry communities of the empire could and should be fused into a monolithic body, using one language, owing loyalty to one ruler and protected by a constitution. Little did they realize that before room could be found for such innovations the entire structure of the state with its political and legal institutions, as well as the fabric of society with its loyalties, traditions and cultural elements, had to be demolished.

17

Cultural Institutions

The Turkish bands, we learned before, which became known as Ottomans in western Asia, started with no more than a primitive nomadic culture. The Islam they picked up en route from Persia was but a thin veneer. The Arabic alphabet they borrowed was ill fitted for their Altaic language. With Islam and the alphabet went countless technical terms—religious, literary, political, legal, scientific, philosophic—for which Turks had no concepts. As they assimilated their Saljug relatives and replaced the Byzantines, they acquired new sources of knowledge. From them they received the general military and governmental patterns, which they followed mainly in Anatolia and European Turkey. When Muhammad the Conqueror seized Constantinople (1453), he encouraged Greek-speaking scholars to remain and even coerced native architects, artisans and textile weavers who were tempted to flee. Byzantine artistic motifs are manifest in Ottoman palace and mosque decorations, and Byzantine patterns are equally apparent in Ottoman silk and cotton cloth. Genoese and Venetian merchants who hitherto had carried Byzantine textiles into Italy and thence Western Europe kept busy with the new products from Constantinople and Brusa.

Persian influence is also clear in Turkish woven textiles, which in the sixteenth century achieved distinction in fabric, coloring and design. Equally clear is Persian influence in Turkish architectural and artistic development, as evidenced by miniatures, mosaics and other structural decoration. Especially conspicuous was Persian impact on Turkish literature, particularly in its poetic form. The

Islam which the early Turks embraced was tinged with Persian mysticism.

More copious than the Byzantine or Persian source of influence was the Arab, with its two channels of religion and language. With religion went law, hadith, linguistics and related sciences. From Arabic, the language of religion throughout Moslem lands, numberless words were first borrowed, then domesticated. Mustafa Kemal's attempt to purge Turkish from such borrowings was only partially successful, but his substitution of Latin for Arabic characters was fully so. Arabic historical, literary, scientific and philosophic works served as models for early Ottoman authors, some of whom even found it preferable to compose their works in Arabic. Hajji Khalifah (d. 1657), to cite an example, wrote his most valuable bibliographical and encyclopedic work in Arabic. With borrowing and imitating went translation. Translation from Persian and Arabic featured Turkish literary activity in the fifteenth and sixteenth centuries.

Until then Turkish writers were largely dependent on foreign patterns. In the mid-sixteenth century the classical period began. A Turkish poet of love, Muhammad Fuzuli (d. *ca.* 1562), was one of the first to write with originality and distinction. The love he sang displays the mystic tinge that characterized later Turkish poetry, especially in its folk form. Fuzuli was of Kurdish origin and wrote in a different idiom from the Ottoman. In the prose literature of the period the work of Evliya Chelebi (d. 1679) stands out. For forty years Chelebi journeyed in the empire, amassing a storehouse of information on its history, geography and folklore to which he added his experiences and observations. Though rich in legend and misstatements, Chelebi's work has not yet entirely outgrown its usefulness. The classical period lasted till the impact of the West in the nineteenth century.

In Sufi literature members of the Bektashi order excelled. This was the most popular order in the country. It practiced its ritual in secrecy and favored the native idiom, whereas the two other widely spread orders, the Mawlawi (whirling dervishes) and the Rifai (howling dervishes), drew upon Persian ritualistic and linguistic sources. In common with other Sufi orders the Bektashis emphasize love as the chief means of achieving union with the deity. Love is pictured as the nostalgic longing of man to return to God, whence he derives his being. The order distinguished itself further by practices betraying Christian borrowings. These include a variety of the confession of sins and a form of communion in which bread, wine and cheese are shared. Celibacy is practiced to a certain extent. Allah, Muhammad and Ali constitute a trinity, with Ali corresponding to Christ.

Legend brings Hajji Bektash, who gave his name to the order, in the mid-fourteenth century from Khurasan in Persia, endows him with miracle working and bestows a special blessing from him on the Janissaries. But no Janissaries were then in existence, and there is no clear reference to this order by name till the sixteenth century. The order established early intimacy with the Janissary corps and provided it with chaplains who lived in the barracks. Bektashis were often involved in the Janissary revolts. The fatal blow Mahmud gave the corps (1826) came near being fatal to the order. But it revived and survived for a century. The reforms of Mustafa Kemal did away with all Sufi fraternities.

Prior to the nineteenth century, borrowings from the West were largely material and technical, conditioned by military considerations. Gunpowder was introduced as early as the fourteenth century; shipbuilding, navigation and military engineering followed. A Hungarian renegade, Ibrahim, introduced (1728) the printing press. Its first product was the translation of an Arabic lexicon. Traces of the traditional Persianizing and Arabicizing school continued till the reign of Mahmud II (1808-1839). It was not until then that a European language, French, began to be diligently cultivated. Religious instruction, based on the Koran, continued to monopolize elementary and secondary education. In 1861 Constantinople opened its first school for girls. Eight years later the University of Constantinople was founded. By then Turkish students educated in the West had become available for teaching and writing.

An early student in France, Ibrahim Shinasi, specialized in linguistics and published in 1859 a small volume of translations from French poets. In 1860 he was appointed editor of the first government newspaper on whose pages Turkish flowed from his pen with less artificiality and more comprehensibility. Shinasi's disciples continued in the new style. Other translations from Molière, Victor Hugo, Rousseau, Lamartine appeared. The Turkish writer then discovered that, after all, his native tongue could be adapted to modern literary and scientific expression, and that his reader could relish a menu of foreign philosophy and thought.

An increasing number of leaders of thought and action became convinced that their whole society was lagging behind in all walks of life and needed repairs, if not reformation. The blind belief in the excellence of the traditional way of life and the efficacy of its institutions, engendered and fostered by past phenomenal success and resultant national pride, was shaken to its very foundations. It was more generally realized that Europeans had become organized into new states, nationalistic, dynamic, based on unprecedented industrial growth and rapidly expanding trade and imbued with militant political aggression.

In any cultural change, education is deeply involved. The Ottoman educational system followed the prevailing pattern throughout Moslem lands. Elementary education was carried out in mosques and, as already noted, was restricted to language, the Koran in Arabic and other religious subjects. In its advanced form education was generally conducted in private homes under learned shaykhs. It comprised, besides religious subjects, linguistics and mathematics. The system was topped by the *madrasah,* basically a theological seminary featuring theology, law and hadith. Early Ottoman scholars, not content with their madrasahs, patronized such renowned centers of learning as Mecca, Damascus and Cairo.

From the outset the trend among Ottoman theologians was toward conservatism. In the second half of the sixteenth century three of them, charged with freethinking, were executed. The purge left the extreme right in control. Under its direction madrasahs declined into stagnant reservoirs of theology, shut off from the invigorating streams of physical sciences and foreign languages. The study of Persian was discouraged; it was tainted with unorthodox mysticism. The curriculum had no place even for Persian-modeled Turkish poetry. The import of European books was banned, and remained so until the second quarter of the eighteenth century. So influential was the theological hierarchy that a grand vizir of Ahmad III (d. 1730) who dared encourage the study of Persian and mathematics in a school he founded faced a revolt that cost him his life and the sultan his throne. Printing by Moslems was forbidden until about that time. By then non-Moslem subjects including Greeks, Armenians, Arabs and Jews had introduced their own presses. When the new convert, Ibrahim, was permitted to adapt an Arabic machine for Turkish use, he was forbidden to publish religious works. When he died in 1745, his press had produced seventeen books, one of which was a cosmology of Hajji Khalifah.

Sufi and military orders conducted their own education in their own ways. The Bektashis gave training in music, and the Mawlawis emphasized Persian precisely because of its mystic elements. The military schools opened their doors to the French language long before the madrasahs did. The first outstanding military institute was founded by Muhammad the Conqueror and lasted until Mahmud II's reign. The course was stiff, covering twelve to fourteen years. It was a fairly well-balanced course, combining liberal arts, arts of war and government. Those who distinguished themselves in intellectual attainment were given further training. The others were drafted into the navy on the Janissary corps. An idea of the effectiveness of such education may be gained from the fact that the majority of the grand vizirs and statesmen who gave the empire its stability, and of the officers who defended and expanded it, were its product.

The reign of Abd-al-Aziz (1861-1876) bored new holes in the wall isolating his country from the West. He was the first sultan to visit Europe. The immediate attraction was the Paris exposition, but the sultan also visited Vienna and London (1867). Shortly after his return, Constantinople saw its French *lycée*. An American institution had preceded it. This was Robert College, founded (1863) through the efforts of an American missionary and the generosity of a New York merchant, whose name it bears. This was the earliest American college overseas. Though aimed at Christian minorities—Greeks, Armenians and Bulgarians—the institution has in recent years undergone radical transformation in character and personnel. It now follows the national system of education and serves primarily Turks. It is distinguished by a flourishing school of engineering. In 1871 a sister American college for girls was added on a picturesque site commanding a view of the Bosporus and the shore of Asia.

Dynamic ideas, introduced in the nineteenth century by Ottoman students educated in the West and by French and American institutions in Turkey, were disseminated by the printing press and supported by a growing urge for a better life and by fear of European imperialism. They took full effect in the first decade of the twentieth century. The tangible result was the emergence of the Young Turks, whose stormy career we shall sketch in the next chapter.

18

From Absolutism to Republicanism

The task facing the young rulers who seized power in 1908 to 1909 could be expressed in simple terms but—as they were soon to discover—could not be solved by easy methods. In essence it involved the transformation of a decrepit, outmoded state into a nationalistic one viable in the world of the twentieth century. But the Christian constituent communities—Slavs, Bulgarians, Greeks, Armenians—and even Moslem Kurds and Arabs had already developed their own nationalistic feeling and were in no hurry to change. Worse than that, they considered the moment opportune to assert their separate identities. In 1909 Armenian demonstrations provoked a massacre in Adana. Moslem Kurds attacked their Turkish neighbors and were attacked by them. Disturbances in Yemen forced the Porte to guarantee its autonomy (1912). In the following year an Arab congress, the first of its kind, met in Paris and demanded decentralization of the Arab provinces.

Nor were Turkey's powerful neighbors eager to cooperate. To the contrary, they were ready to take advantage of the new situation. Before 1908 was over, Austria-Hungary formally annexed Bosnia and Herzegovina. Bulgaria declared its full independence. In 1911 and 1912 Italy initiated its colonial career by sending its troops across the waters to occupy Ottoman Tripolitania and Benghazi (now Libya). Greece seized Salonika. In 1912 to 1913 two Balkan wars were waged in the course of which Serbia, Bulgaria, Montenegro and Greece—all once under Ottoman rule—battled against their former sovereign. The net loss to Turkey in the first four years of the new regime covered most of its European possessions, including Moslem Albania.

In this boisterous sea the Young Turkish ship of state floundered.

Its first policy of an Ottomanized modern nationalism under Turkish leadership yielded opposite results. It stimulated separatism under local leadership. Resort was made to Pan-Islamism. But when on the entry of Turkey into the World War in 1914, the nominal sultan Muhammad V evoked the ghost of the holy war (*jihad*), Pan-Islam was found to be dead as under Abd-al-Hamid. Neither the Moslems of India nor those of North Africa rose in arms against the British or French. In their desperation the theoreticians of the regime went still farther back and concocted a new pan-, Pan-Turanianism, Turan being the legendary ancestor of Turkish-speaking peoples everywhere. But the new formula, instead of rallying speakers of Turkish in Russia, Persia and central Asia to the support of their Ottoman cousins, served to alienate the non-Turkish elements of the empire still further. Nothing was left but force, and the new regime used it to suppress opposition more ruthlessly than the old one. Martial law, censorship and espionage were tightened, and terrorism found new means of expressing itself. These measures were ready made when on November 14, 1914, the Young Turks cast their lot on the side of the Central Powers.

Turkey then went under a triumvirate headed by Enver as minister of war, Talaat as prime minister and Javid as minister of finance. All three were now pashas. Enver was an officer in the war against Italy in Libya. Talaat began his career as a telegraph operator. Javid belonged to a secret Jewish community that professed Islam. This community had financed the Committee of Union and Progress.

Turkey's plunge into the conflict vastly extended the area of operations to the disadvantage of the Allied Powers. On its frontiers the country tied up over a million of their troops, while outside of its territory its troops fought on three fronts: Persia, the Balkans and Galicia (now in Poland). Though unprepared and enfeebled, it lost no time in taking the offensive against Russia in the Caucasus region, and in initiating operations from Palestine against the Suez Canal held by the British, who had declared Egypt a protectorate. Egypt, occupied by the British since 1882, was still under

Turkish suzerainty. The operations were lengthy but ineffectual. More successful and spectacular was the stubborn and long-drawn-out defense of the Dardanelles, through which the Allies sought to reach Constantinople and establish easy communication with their landlocked ally, Russia. The defense, centered in Gallipoli Peninsula, was conducted by a German general assisted by Colonel Mustafa Kemal. After months of futile fighting and heavy loss the Allied attempt was abandoned. No supplies could reach Russia that way.

Another German general conducted the defense of Iraq against Anglo-Indian troops operating from India. The attack began in November 1914 and was designed to occupy the territory at the head of the Persian Gulf, protect the oil pipeline from Persia and impress the Arabs of the region. After a humiliating reverse at Kut al-Amarah, where a British general was forced to surrender, the invading troops occupied Baghdad and reached Mosul (1917). Mesopotamia went the way of Hejaz.

All the while the internal situation was deteriorating. In 1915 the Armenians, accused of aiding the Russians, were subjected to deportation and massacre, and after their revolt in Van their entire community in the country was virtually wiped out of existence. After months of wandering and deprivation some sixty thousand found refuge in Lebanon. In its capital Beirut, they have since built up a flourishing community. In the following year (1916) Sharif (descendant of the Prophet) Husayn of Mecca raised the banner of revolt, declared the independence of Hejaz and proclaimed himself "king of the Arabs." In this he was encouraged by the British. He sent a contingent under his son Faysal, later king of Iraq, to cooperate with the Anglo-French forces working their way northward through Palestine. Those were the operations in which T. E. Lawrence figured dramatically. In 1917 to 1918 Palestine, Lebanon and Syria were all amputated from the Ottoman Empire.

Throughout this area the Allied troops were well received by the inhabitants. Their four years of indescribable misery under a Young Turk governor and army general, Jamal Pasha, at last came to an end. Jamal had ruled with an iron hand. Syrians in general were considered pro-Arab, Lebanese pro-French and both anti-Ottoman. Their leaders were jailed, banished or hanged in the public squares of Damascus and Beirut. Jamal lost no time in abrogating Lebanon's autonomy, which had been internationally recognized since 1861. For his attempt at the Suez Canal he drained the young manhood of these countries, requisitioned their beasts of burden and gave priority of provisions to his troops. With the Allied blockade of ports, the imports of drugs, cloth and other necessities of life vanished. Epidemics spread. Before the war was half over Lebanon faced starvation. Out of its 450,000 population some 100,000 were reportedly lost.

The autumn of 1918 marked the dawn of relief for the occupied Arab provinces and also the collapse of Turkey. The armistice that followed, signed October 30, ended Turkey's four-year war but started other wars which lasted as long. The Allies stretched the truce terms to the point of violation. Their troops occupied Constantinople and its straits. It was then disclosed that they had bound themselves by secret treaties giving Constantinople and its straits to Russia, Smyrna and other cities with a Greek population to Greece, and the southeastern coast of Anatolia to Italy. What was left of the empire was to be partitioned between the "big two," Britain and France. Russia, under the Bolshevik forerunners of the Communists, renounced the czarist treaty, but Greece landed troops in Smyrna and Italy in Adalia (Antalya). In August 1920 the peace treaty of Sèvres (France) was signed by Sultan Wahid-al-Din. In it Turkey renounced all claims to its non-Turkish territories and ceded its islands to Italy and Greece. Syria and Lebanon were to be mandated to France, Iraq and Palestine to Britain. Hejaz was recognized as independent. This dismemberment reduced the empire to Constantinople and its environs in Europe and the bulk of Anatolia.

The peace treaty brought no more peace than the truce treaty had brought truce. A new leader was in the making. His name was Mustafa Kemal. It was he who galvanized a seemingly dead nation.

THE VICTORY MONUMENT AT ANKARA WITH MUSTAFA KEMAL ON HORSEBACK

A national assembly, inspired by him, met at Ankara and set up a new government. The new government repudiated the treaty of Sèvres and laid the claim to being the true representative of the nation rather than the sultan. Mustafa Kemal was proclaimed (1920) head of the provisional government by the national assembly. Two years later the sultanate was abolished, then the caliphate (1924). Constantinople became Istanbul and ceased to be the capital. Smyrna, from which Mustafa Kemal had thrown out the Greek invaders, became Izmir. The Italian intruders were with greater facility driven back whence they came. The ground was cleared for a new treaty, that of Lausanne (July 1923). In this treaty the new Turkey renounced all claims to non-Turkish territories, recovered a slice of its European territory, paid no reparations, abolished the capitulations and won recognition as a fully independent state within its ethnic frontiers. On October 29, 1923, the Turkish Republic was proclaimed with Mustafa Kemal (later accorded the family title of Atatürk, 'father" or "preceptor of the Turks") as its first president and his comrade at arms, Ismet Inönü as prime minister.

Once such a radical break with the past as the destruction of both sultanate and caliphate and the separation of the state and Islam was achieved, further steps toward secularization, modernization and the adoption of Western institutions and ideas could be taken. And they were, with breath-taking celerity. All religious orders were prohibited. Polygamy was legally abolished; the veil was ordered removed. A new judiciary system based on the Swiss code replaced the old religious code. The hat was substituted for the fez. Arabic script was abandoned in favor of Latin. A constitution was proclaimed in Ankara (1934) guaranteeing individual rights and civic liberties for all citizens, men and women. It placed all legislative power in the national assembly. Sporadic outbursts of opposition to the new measures were dealt with ruthlessly.

The displacement of Arabic by Latin script strengthened the trend toward simplification of the Turkish idiom, its purification from Arabic and Persian influences and its Westward orientation. Moreover, it tended to utilize the unexplored riches of native folklore and indigenous themes. A new group of poets, story-tellers and fiction-writers appeared on the scene. The break with the past on the literary level was as near-complete as it was on the political level.

Elected first as president of the Turkish Republic in 1923, Mustafa Kemal was re-elected three times, throughout which he ruled

REPUBLIC OF TURKEY

as a dictator. He, however, regarded his dictatorship as a temporary necessity. On his death in 1938 Ismet Inönü was chosen as his successor.

The second president of the republic continued the domestic and foreign policies of his predecessor, but proceeded with more caution and deliberation. In internal affairs state socialism was the cardinal point. It differed from European theoretical socialism in trying to maintain private initiative while putting the nation's economy in state hands. But a new development, the outbreak of the second World War in September 1939, subjected both internal and external affairs to extraordinary strains.

Throughout this international holocaust and despite wooing from one of the opposing sides and threat from the other, Turkey managed to maintain its posture as it straddled the fence. In anticipation of the conflict France, mandatory power over Syria, had conceded to Turkey the right to incorporate the frontier district of Alexandretta (now Hatay), which was partly Turkish populated. Britain concurred. Additionally the three powers signed a pact of mutual assistance in case of war in the "Mediterranean area." On the other hand the entry of Italy (1940) into the conflict on the side of Germany, the collapse of France (1941) and the occupation of Greece and the Balkans by German troops posed a threat which Turkey could not ignore. A few days before Japan's sneak attack on Pearl Harbor (December 1941) President Franklin D. Roosevelt had declared the defense of Turkey vital to the security of the United States and offered it lend-lease aid. But not until American military successes against the Axis Powers had dispelled all doubt about the final outcome of the struggle did Turkey's neutrality become positively beneficial to the Western Allies. Its declaration of war on Germany and Japan in February 1945 was a token one intended to insure it a seat in the contemplated United Nations charter meeting held two months later in San Francisco.

The great war left Turkey in a sad condition. Its armed neutrality had strained its economy to the breaking point. Essential imports had practically ceased; prices soared, currency depreciated and rationing was extended to most staples of life. The resultant social and political unrest necessitated a stricter enforcement of martial law. In the meantime the polarization of world power into two main centers, capitalist America and communist Russia, and the ensuing cold war enhanced Turkey's geopolitical importance in Western eyes. The so-called Truman doctrine, involving the expenditure of millions of dollars, was initiated by the president of the United States to help Turkey and Greece against the spread of communism. To Turkey were also generously extended the benefits of the Marshall Plan, originated by the American general and statesman to offer economic assistance to war-stricken Europe. Other United States agencies accorded the country credit and sent experts and technicians for promoting its industry and commerce and for improving its systems of communication.

The republic, hitherto under the domination of one party, the Republican People's party, was now subjected to democratic pressure from the West and to demands of liberal opinion inside. It began to yield. President Inönü ended martial law and proclaimed a new law guaranteeing free elections. The first such election (1950) was a landslide in favor of the opposition, the Young Democratic Party, headed by Jelal Bayar. President Bayar's regime moved cautiously against the salient features of state socialism. It eased press censorship, encouraged private enterprise and welcomed investment of foreign capital. In 1955 the country joined the North Atlantic Treaty Organization (NATO) and took the initiative in concluding with Iraq a defensive treaty which was joined by Britain, Pakistan and Iran. Signed in Baghdad, the treaty became known as the Baghdad Pact. It was designed to build a northern Near Eastern tier against possible Soviet aggression. The United States remained outside but offered moral and financial support. Russia vehemently denounced the pact, viewing it as a link forged by the West between NATO and the Southeast Asia Treaty Organization (SEATO).

It was not long, however, before the new liberal course was reversed. Prime Minister Adnan Menderes undertook a program of extensive construction projects, on borrowed money, that took the country to the brink of bankruptcy. Prices soared. Inflation spiraled. Discontent spread. The regime resolved to crush opposition. It committed hundreds, including journalists, writers and influential leaders, to jails. Public opinion turned to the army. In May 1960 the army struck. The Democratic government, turned dictatorial, was overthrown. General Gürsel, a fellow-warrior with Mustafa Kemal at the Dardanelles, was installed as president. Both President Bayar and his prime minister were sentenced to death for "crimes against the state." Menderes was executed, but Bayar's sentence was commuted to life imprisonment. Four years later he was freed.

This military coup came as a surprise in a country that had enjoyed stable government under Kemalist principles. The new government introduced a new constitution (1961) including a reference to "social justice" as one of the aims of the state. There was no departure from the Kemalist policy of confining Turkey to Anatolia and the narrow European strip and abandoning all thought of territorial expansion or empire building.

19

Imperial Persia

Other than Ottoman Turkey, Persia was the only state to play an imperial role in the modern Near East. This was particularly true under the Safawid dynasty (1501-1736). This dynasty bears the name of a Moslem Sufi saint, Safi-al-Din, who claimed descent from Ali. But it was founded by his descendant Ismail I (1501-1524), who, following the careers of his father and grandfather, added the role of warrior to the profession of sanctity. This was the first nationalist dynasty in centuries.

In one battle after another Ismail subdued the petty states that had mushroomed under the descendants of the Mongol conqueror Timur (d. 1405), and before them under the descendants of another Mongol empire-builder, Hulagu (d. 1265). Ismail consolidated his realm, extending it from the Oxus to the Persian Gulf and from Afghanistan to the Euphrates. He proclaimed himself shah, an old Persian title for king, and recognized Shiism as the state religion. Clearly this was turning a new page in Persian history. But just as the Sasanids and Parthians had found themselves contesting Byzantine and Roman supremacy in the Near East, the Safawids now find themselves doing so vis-à-vis Ottoman Turks. In the first round the Turks came out on top. Reference already has been made to Salim I's victory in Armenia (1514) and his triumphal entry into Ismail's capital, Tabriz. Salim's son Sulayman repeated his father's performance on Persian soil, but these episodes merely served to rally the Persian people with intensified loyalty around the nationalist throne.

The empire founded by Ismail had to be refounded by his fifth successor, Abbas I (1587-1629), worthily entitled the Great. Abbas

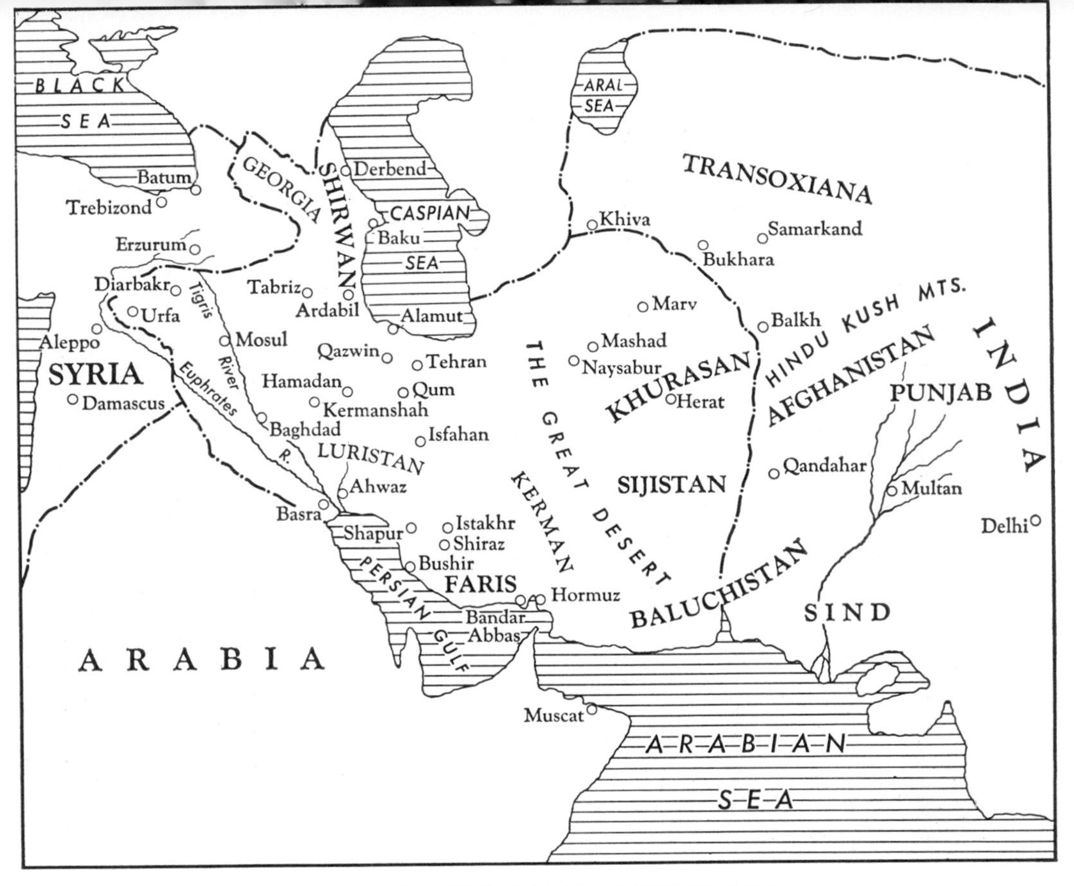

THE SAFAWID EMPIRE AT ITS HEIGHT *ca.* 1515

was not only the ablest shah modern Persia produced but one of the most enlightened and respected. Under him Safawid power attained its meridian. His starting point was the army, hitherto made up—like the early Moslem Arabian army—of tribal units under tribal leadership. The Ottoman forces then in occupation of the western sector of his country served as a model for a new military organization consisting of infantry and artillery, manned mostly by Armenian and Georgian converts, all on a paid basis. His first campaigns were naturally directed against the occupying Turks, from whom he first recovered Tabriz. He then drove them out of the land, pursued them into Mesopotamia and occupied Baghdad, Mosul and other key towns in Mesopotamia, which as of old was the bone of contention.

Abbas was great not only in the arts of war but in those of peace. The palaces, mosques, gardens, public squares and baths he built made his new capital Isfahan a "wonder of the world." Persian writers never tire of singing its beauty. Statisticians claim it enclosed within its mud-brick walls 600,000 inhabitants, 162 mosques, 48 seminaries, 1802 caravanseries, 273 public baths. What remains of these structures still attracts and delights more tourists than any other place in the land. Such lavish expenditure of money on public works presupposes an increase in domestic production and in international trade. Before Abbas' days Venetians and Portuguese had discovered and exploited the Persian market. Carpets, cotton, wool, fruits and gum were its chief exports. Hormuz on the Persian Gulf served as the main port. Then, there was the overland trade route to India. Through the English East India Company the British under Abbas established a firm commercial foothold in the land and gained influence in the shah's court. They began to monopolize Persian Gulf trade. Since then they have been the paramount power in the Gulf area. The French were not permitted to trade in Persia until later.

Abbas' successors were inept rulers. For this he was partly responsible. Unable to stand the popularity of his sons, he had murdered one of them and blinded two others. The rest of the royal princes were immured under eunuchs' guardianship. Patricide was practiced by one of his predecessors. Fratricide was exercised by more than one shah, though not on a high scale as in Ottoman Turkey. The dynasty started on its downward course. Internal weakness encouraged external aggression. The Turks, under a warrior sultan, Murad IV, renewed their attacks. They occupied Tabriz for a time, annexed (1638) Baghdad and with it Mesopotamia, which they held till the first World War. A new enemy, czarist Russia, threatened from the north. Under Peter the Great it entered upon an ambitious career of conquest. In 1724 Russia negotiated an agreement with Turkey to dismember the common enemy, giving Turkey the western provinces and keeping for itself the already occupied Caspian provinces. The death of Peter and the ensuing Russo-Turkish war saved the victim's skin.

Temporary external security was not paralleled by domestic security. Persian minorities, mainly Afghans and Turkomans, both Sunnites, were on the march. One province after another fell into their hands. The remaining tiny Safawid territory was shared by many members of the royal family. Anarchy spread. Out of it emerged a new figure, Nadir Quli, chief of a Turkoman tribe, who in 1736 seized the supreme power and was proclaimed shah.

Nadir (d. 1747) initiated a new line of four shahs termed Afsharid (1736-1796) after the tribe to which he belonged. The new shah was born in a Bedouin tent in Khurasan. His diversified career included camel driving, robber-band leadership and military service in the Safawid army. As shah he not only restored the Persian kingdom to its fullest extent but added Afghanistan, pushed on to Lahore and sacked Delhi. Westward he moved against the Turks and annexed Iraq. Northward he forced Russia to yield the Caspian provinces. In a decade Nadir Shah became the acknowledged master from the Indus to the Caucasus and the Euphrates. Among the spoils from India were the fabulous Peacock Throne constructed by the Mogul emperor Shah Jahan (builder of Taj

Mahal) and the equally fabulous diamond Koh-i-noor ("mountain of light"). Both are now among the guarded treasures of the British crown in the Tower of London.

The war lord proved to be a poor statesman, lacking in administrative ability and civil experience. His military exploits had overtaxed the country's manpower and economy. Not enough was received in return. The imperial structure began to tumble down. Iranian, Afghan and Turkoman chieftains scrambled for slices. At last another tribal chief, Agha Muhammad Khan of the Turkoman Qajar tribe, seized power. A new leaf was turned in Persian annals. In the next chapter we shall read what was written there.

The Safawids, it will be recalled, raised their empire on the ruins of Mongol and Timurid states. The legacy was not only political but also cultural and artistic. In architecture Safawid artisans featured, as their predecessors had done, glazed tiles, polychronic mosaics and faïence. Examples are extant particularly in palaces, mosques and shrines built by Abbas in his new Isfahan. Abbas went further; he invited from China three hundred potters with their families whose refined designs and delicate coloring distinguished sixteenth-century Persian porcelain. Textiles and carpets of the period manifest the same influence. Carpet weaving served as an outstanding medium of the period's decorative arts. Hitherto a small home industry, it now rose to high cooperative levels, and has so remained. The material was wool or silk; the design was usually centralized on a medallion. Other designs featured trees, flowers and animals, real or fictitious. Human beings were rarely depicted. Tabriz, Kashmir, Isfahan and Kerman were and still are among the leading weaving centers. Their products during the Safawid age have never been excelled.

Painting was another artistic activity bearing the Chinese impact. Its miniature variety was born in the Mongol period and combined Persian and Mesopotamian elements. First used to illustrate epic or romantic poetry, miniature illustration developed into a popular art. Miniatures were not executed separately and then inserted in a book, as in the modern practice of book illustration;

they were rather interpenetrated with the text to blend with its calligraphy. The favorite themes were foliage or gardens, animals—again fictitious or real—and at times men. Calligraphy itself developed into a respected art primarily because of its association with the Koran. Arabic letters in which Persian was written, lent themselves to decorative use. Among Moslems Persian calligraphers ranked highest. Last came the leather worker to produce a cover embossed, tooled and harmonized with the painting and with the writing inside, giving the ensemble a pleasing look. More than an external protection, the cover was an artistic part of a prized possession cherished for generations. Books were treated as treasures.

The master in miniature artistry was Bihzad. Bihzad, born in Herat about 1455 under a Timurid monarch, labored and died in Tabriz (1537), early Safawid capital. His products were distinguished for their refinement, minute details and lifelike representation. He excelled in battle scenes. So great was his reputation that Shah Abbas is said to have declared him as worth half his kingdom. For centuries his signature was faked on miniatures by his imitators. Among his authenticated paintings are those illustrating Sadi's *Bustan* in the Egyptian national library (Cairo) and Nizami's *Khamsah* (*quinte*). The *Khamsah* is a collection of five long poems styled the treasures of Nizami (d. 1202), considered one of the greatest romantic poets of his country.

Sadi (*ca.* 1189-1292) was one of the brightest jewels in Persia's literary crown. He was born in Shiraz, traveled in Syria, where he was taken prisoner by Crusaders and put to dig ditches in Tripoli. Ransomed by an Aleppo merchant and freed on marrying his benefactor's daughter, he returned home. Besides his *Bustan* (fruit garden), Sadi composed another masterpiece, *Gulistan* (rose garden), which became a classical model for later Persian prose and poetry. Beautiful Shiraz, counted by Persian geographers one of four terrestrial paradises, numbered among its sons another great classical poet, Hafiz. Hafiz was singer of the pleasures of love, wine and women and of the beauty of nature particularly when awakened from its winter slumber. In his countrymen's esteem Sadi stands above all other poets of wine and women, Umar al-Khayyam included. His *Diwan* (collection of odes) has been done into several languages, European and Asiatic. Hafiz died in 1389, two years after Timur's invasion of his native town.

Poetry no less than painting was in those days a court art. Without leisure and patronage the talent for art could not develop. Mongols and Timurids, feeling strange in the lands they ruled, may have encouraged poets and artists as a means of *rapprochement* with their subjects. The Safawids, on the other hand, patronized theologians of the Shiite brand and fostered the praise of Ali's descendants. Under them a new intellectual hierarchy arose which attracted and diverted ambitious young men from possible belletrist pursuits. Shiite abuse of power and its intolerance toward Sunnites was partly responsible for the Safawid dynasty's fall. The following period of instability under Afghans and Turkomans was not conducive to the development of art or literature. Only one Turkoman dynasty, the Qajars, merits special consideration in our study.

20

Qajar Persia and European Involvement

The Turkoman dynasty of Qajars lived long (1779-1925) but achieved little. It had a bad start under its founder Agha Muhammad Khan, a mutilated eunuch and pathological personality dominated by vindictiveness, avarice and sadistic lust for power. Agha seized power in 1779, captured Tehran, which became and remained state capital, suppressed revolts in Georgia and Khurasan and militarily consolidated the kingdom. But when it came to administering it, he was found wanting. He lacked capacity, training and experience. His assassination in 1797, by two servants whom he had sentenced to death for trivial reasons, was met by a sigh of relief on the part of his subjects.

Agha's nephew-successor, Fath Ali (1797-1834), set an example of ruling the country as though it were an enemy to be exploited for the benefit of the ruler. The shah indulged in a high life of pomp and splendor. He established a new precedent in favoritism. This was the time when the European urge for political and economic expansion assumed impelling proportions and acquired competitive aspects. First came Britain which, since Abbas the Great's reign, had shown special concern in Persia as a buffer for its Indian possessions. For a rival, England had now Russia, beginning its successful thrust into central Asia. For a time Napoleon Bonaparte played a third role in Persia's involvement in European power politics. In 1806 the French conqueror sent a mission offering to assist Persia in the reconquest of Georgia from Russia and in an attack on India. Once opened for foreign infiltration, the door could not very well be closed.

The Russo-British tug of war was marked first by an Anglo-Persian treaty (1814), which left Persia virtually dependent upon its ally in its foreign policy, and then by a Russo-Persian treaty (1828) which ceded to Persia much of the Caucasian territory, imposed Turkish-modeled capitulations and put the country's foreign trade in Russia's hands. The capitulations were soon extended to other European powers and were not abolished until 1928.

In 1834 the two contending powers, changing their tactics, reached a new agreement guaranteeing the "independence" of the helpless victim but keeping it a pawn in the game of world politics. Imperialism took a novel form: controlling the natural resources, trade and certain foreign relations of a country without changing its color on the map to conform to that of the ruling party.

Of Fath Ali's successors only one, Nasr-al-Din (1848-1896), showed any marked ability or concern for his people's welfare. But throughout this shah's long reign foreign control of the country's economy remained unchecked. Nasr ascended the throne at the age of sixteen but was fortunate in having an open-minded and energetic prime minister. But the two had neither the purse to introduce financial and military reforms nor the sword to deal with the rising disorders and tribal recalcitrance. With a desire to learn how to increase state revenues and reinforce his effectiveness as a ruler, Nasr undertook three trips to Europe (1873, 1878, 1889), visiting London, Paris, St. Petersburg, Munich and other important centers. This made him the first shah to step on foreign soil except as an invader or exile. But instead of good, evil accrued to the country. Such was the strain on its economy, due to travel expenses, that it was found necessary to give a European group of capitalists monopoly over the tobacco industry, including its cultivation and trade. Tobacco was one of the most popular pleasures, and its monopoly aroused a storm of national indignation. Prodded by religious leaders, the indignation took the form of an uprising and the monopoly had to be canceled. In itself the tobacco uprising may not have been of great significance, but, being the first time in which the Persian people defied their government, it established a precedent. Fifteen years later a second and more serious uprising was staged.

The country sank deeper and deeper into debt. Loans from England and Russia did not restore health to a sickly economy. Nor did concessions, mainly to the British. These included telegraph lines, navigation and banks. As they loaned and received concessions, England and Russia tightened their grip on the country's life. Opposition which began in 1890 against foreign interests and control flared up again in December 1905. It was now fed by dissatisfaction with the incompetent rule of Muzaffar-al-Din (1896-1907) and his corrupt prime minister. The revolution spread. The shah was forced to yield to popular demand. In the summer of 1906 he dismissed his minister and agreed to the convocation of a general assembly (*majlis*). The assembly met in Tehran and drew up a constitution of the liberal type. The British encouraged the revolutionary movement; their legation extended refuge to several thousands of them. But the Russians opposed it.

At this juncture a vigorous young European power, Germany, began knocking at the front door of the Near East. Its admission was considered by the two contending powers as inimical to their respective interests. The two thereupon compromised their differences and signed an entente (1907) recognizing the northern half of Persia as Russian sphere and the southern half as British sphere. A neutral belt was left in between. The agreement paid the usual lip service political hypocrisy pays sincerity by reaffirming the "independence and integrity" of the country. But none were fooled, least of all the people concerned.

Muzaffar's son Muhammad Ali (1907-1909) had no more desire to support the new order than his father had to promulgate it. In this the shah was seconded by his reactionary minister. Urge for more freedoom and opposition to absolute rule, hitherto centered in the merchant class, the theologians and a few intellectuals, were now agitating the masses. The teachings of Jamal-al-Din al-Afghani, for a time closely associated with Nasr-al-Din, and the success of the bold Young Turks' revolution were having their effect.

Muhammad Ali was forced to abdicate. His twelve-year-old son Sultan Ahmad (1909-1925) succeeded.

The national assembly turned its face in an entirely new direction, the United States. The Department of State sent (1911) a young banker, W. Morgan Shuster, who had no knowledge of the economic, social or political problems awaiting him. Shuster was made treasurer-general and given free hand. Russia objected. She rushed two ultimatums and backed them up with forces that moved against Tabriz and bombarded Mashhad, one of the holiest places to the Shiah. The American mission was withdrawn the following year.

By this time a new source of national income was developing, petroleum. In 1909, after eight years of planning, drilling and spending money, oil was found in commercial quantities. The site was 125 miles north of the Persian Gulf. The Anglo-Persian (later Iranian) Company was formed in London. This was the first time that "liquid gold" was found in an area later described as an island floating on a sea of oil. The company proceeded with the construction of roads and built a pipeline to Abadan. Abadan's refinery today is perhaps the largest in the world. But before much income could be realized the first World War was on the way.

At the outbreak of European hostilities in the summer of 1914 Persia proclaimed her neutrality, a state she lacked the power to maintain and the belligerents the desire to respect. The capital became a hotbed of international intrigue with Russians, British and Germans as the chief participants. Russia and Britain tightened their grips on their respective spheres, while Germany and Austria used Turkey as a spearhead against its eastern neighbor. Emboldened by their victory at the Dardanelles, the Turks crossed the frontier and attacked Persia more than once. The smashing defeat they administered in 1916 to the Anglo-Indian expeditionary force at Kut al-Amarah (Iraq) released more troops for that front. Even Tehran was occupied. But in 1917 the tide turned. Turkey's loss of Iraq and the collapse of czarist Russia gave Persia a breathing spell. At the Paris Peace Conference in 1919 its delegation demanded the restoration of the Caucasian and Caspian territories annexed over the years by Russia, the abrogation of the Anglo-Russian treaty of 1907, the cancellation of the capitulations and reparation for war damages. The British, on the other hand, proposed a bilateral treaty verbally respecting the independence and integrity of the country but practically reducing it to a protectorate. An incompetent, irresponsible shah, seconded by a weak and corrupt cabinet, signed the agreement. But the national assembly stood firm. In this it was encouraged by an American diplomatic statement. The assembly refused to convene for ratification. It won. Persia was recognized the following year as a fully independent member of the League of Nations.

The first World War sealed the fate of the Qajar dynasty. A military coup against Sultan Ahmad was staged in February 1921 by a brigade commander, Reza Khan. Fearful for his life the shah subsequently left for Europe, to which he had made frequent sojourns and had become a habitué of its night clubs. He was dethroned, unlamented, in 1925. With the ascension of Reza Khan more than a dynasty—an era—was ended.

The dynasty founded by Reza Khan was named Pahlawi ("Parthian," later "brave," "noble"), emphasizing its old Iranian origin, as against the Turkish dynasties in control for a century and a half. The new era was one of uneasy reform and strained modernization.

The seeds of dissatisfaction with traditionalism in religion and absolutism in rule—the two closely related—had been laid early in the Qajar period. The crop began to bear fruit in the mid-nineteenth century. In May 1844 a theologian from Shiraz, Ali Muhammad, proclaimed himself the Bab (door), the gateway to the esoteric knowledge of divine truth. Resort was made to the old technique of allegorical interpretation of the scriptures. The new prophet had his own sacred book. He taught the equality of sexes, abolished legal ablution and reduced the number of fasting days of Ramadan. Starting as a spiritualized mystical movement, Babism, as often happens in such cases, served as a rallying center not only for religious dissidents but also for political, economic and social malcontents. It generated a religio-political rebellion that the government had to suppress by stern military measures. The Bab himself was shot (1850) on orders from the government. An attempt on the life of Nasr-al-Din Shah resulted in banishing the leaders.

Officially dead, Babism gave birth to another movement, Bahaism. Baha-Allah (God's splendor) claimed to be the next manifestation of the divine will foretold by the Bab. In his place of exile, Akka (Acre, in Palestine), to which he moved in 1868, Baha formed a new system with mystic, Christian and modernistic elements grafted on a Shiite trunk. He condemned war, stressed love, preached universal brotherhood and advocated an international language. He was succeeded in 1892 by his son Abbas Effendi, who took the title of Abd-al-Baha (Baha's slave). The spread of Bahaism into America after the 1893 Chicago fair and into Germany encouraged its new leader in his aspiration to make his a universal religion. Its American activity centers in Wilmette, Illinois, and New York City.

More rational was the reform movement originated by Jamal-al-Din al-Afghani (1838-1896). Jamal was a rare combination of the

JAMAL-AL-DIN AL-AFGHANI, PAN-ISLAMIST AND REFORMER

Pan-Islamist and modernist. Two cardinal points in his teaching stood out: the adoption of Western science and technology and the union of Moslem states under one headship, the caliphate. These, to him, were the only means of reviving Islam and insuring resistance to European encroachment. Of all nineteenth century Islamic reformers Jamal was perhaps the most effective. Wherever he went —Afghanistan, India, Egypt, Turkey—his impressive personality, eloquent tongue and facile pen won him disciples. Eminent among them was Muhammad Abduh, mufti of Egypt. The impress this Persian thinker left on the liberal movement of the Near East in general is still a living force. In his native land it furnished elements leading to the awakening of public opinion against foreigners and the final adoption of the constitution.

In discussing forces paving the way for twentieth century reforms under the Pahlawis, European Catholic and Protestant missionary activity cannot be ignored.

As early as the days of Abbas the Great a papal Carmelite mission had started operation (1604) in the country. It was joined later by Capuchins and Jesuits. True, the work was patronized mostly by non-Moslems—Armenians and Syrians—but as in similar cases Christians mediated Western learning to their neighbors. Besides schools, missionaries built hospitals, orphanages and other humanitarian institutions in which Moslems could more freely participate. On the Christian side two Uniat communities were created in Persia and Iraq: the Armenian Catholic (split from the Gregorian) and the Chaldean (split from the East Syrian or Nestorian). These are still flourishing in the East.

The Protestants entered the field late. In 1811 Henry Martyn arrived in Shiraz from India, where he was chaplain of the East India Company. His chief work was the translation of the New Testament into the native tongue. The Church Missionary Society established its first station in Isfahan (1866) and stressed educational and medical work. One of its workers translated the Old Testament.

American missionaries did not find their way into the area until

1834, when the American Board of Foreign Missions (Congregational) sent its first representatives. Urmia in the Syrian Christian district was chosen for base. In it a high school and hospital were founded. Transferred later into the Presbyterian Church, the mission extended its activities into Tabiz, Tehran, Hamadan, Mashhad and other towns. Its educational work culminated in the College of Tehran (1925), which had humble beginnings going back to 1873. The institution is now known as Elburz (Alburz) College and belongs to the ministry of education.

The educational track blazed by Western teachers did not remain a one-way track. In 1810 the government sent its first students to study medicine in England. Others were sent or independently went abroad to prepare themselves for civil service or professional careers. The United States, Germany and other countries have them today by the thousands.

When Reza Khan Shah (1925-1941) launched his program of reform, the domestic climate was not, therefore, entirely unfavorable. Externally there was the striking model of Mustafa Kemal, whom the shah admired and visited at Ankara. Starting with the assumption that Western institutions could not very well be accommodated to medieval Oriental systems of politics, economics and society, Reza resorted to radical, dictatorial measures. In only one sphere, religion, he did not follow the Kemalist precedent. The constitution he kept, but the national assembly he reduced to a ratifying body. The laws he introduced aimed at the emancipation of women and equalizing their rights with those of men. Titles of nobility were abolished. An attempt was made to replace sons of aristocratic families with more meritorious officials. In 1935 he had the name of the country changed to Iran, the ancient one. In that year the University of Tehran was organized by joining the faculties of law, science, literature, theology and medicine. Engineering and agriculture were added later. By then the modern system of elementary and secondary education, introduced by the government, was yielding adequate supply for higher learning.

Military and economic measures included building up the army, developing roads and starting the construction of a railroad from the Caspian to the Persian Gulf, which took twelve years to complete. To meet the mounting expenses state monopolies were expanded to cover most fields of production. The United States financial mission, headed by Arthur C. Millspaugh, which had been in the country since 1922, remained until 1927, receiving the shah's full support.

Equally enlightened was the shah in his foreign relations. Early in his reign he abolished the century-old capitulations. He later extended the Anglo-Iranian Oil concession and revised its rate of royalty in favor of the state. With his neighbors, Turkey, Iraq and Afghanistan, he signed (1937) a non-aggression pact guaranteeing each other's borders and binding each country to refrain from interference in the others' internal affairs.

Reza's reforms were not as thoroughgoing or as effective as Kemal's. His subjects were less responsive than the Turks, who had been exposed for centuries to European influences. Persia was too close to Najaf and Karbala, the two fountainheads of conservative Shiism. The Persian religious hiearchy, after the destruction of Babism and Bahaism, stood triumphant. The non-urban population had no urge for change, and the government had neither the will nor the power to enforce its decrees. The outbreak of the second World War injected new factors and created more urgent international problems for which neither the government nor the people were prepared.

The shah tried to keep his country out of war, but he could not keep war out of it. By the summer of 1941 Russian troops had occupied its northern part, while British troops had occupied the southern. In the meantime the shah and his high officers, impressed by the initial display of might on the part of Hitler and Mussolini and by the collapse of France (1940), were showing a leaning toward the Axis Powers. Under pressure from the Allies and to save the throne for his son, the shah abdicated (September 1941) in favor of his twenty-two-year-old son and left the country. His more democratic successor, Muhammad Reza, leaned in the other direction. He entered into treaty relations with the two occupying powers guaranteeing the independence and territorial integrity of his country and pledging the withdrawal of their troops at hostilities' cessation. His government then declared war on Germany. The new orientation was dramatized in 1943 when Iran's capital played host to a summit conference of Churchill, Stalin and Roosevelt. In appreciation Iran was promised and received substantial material aid for the war period and after.

But such was the need that the aid, mainly American, could not cope with the worsening situation. Transport facilities had to yield priority to military requirements. Stoppage of the importation of certain essential commodities resulted in a drastic shortage of consumers' goods. A crop of profiteers mushroomed. Prices soared to ten times their prewar level. A Soviet-inspired leftist party made capital of the situation. So did a religious group eager to recapture their former prestige and stung by the Russo-British occupation. Disturbances followed in Tehran and other centers. Millspaugh was again invited and granted broad powers to reorganize finances. One tangible result of his two years' work (1943-1945) was a graduated income tax. Another American mission under Colonel Norman Schwartzkopf was sent (1943) to organize and direct the gendarmery.

With the hostilities' termination tension diminished and Iran began to reap certain war benefits. As the Allied troops withdrew they left an enlarged and improved system of communication, to say nothing about valuable electric and other installations. The shah in 1949 initiated a program of distributing or selling at reduced prices lands inherited from his father. In the same year he paid a state visit to Washington. The visit netted technical aid, military equipment and loans for purchase of supplies from the States, but not much by way of private American investment of capital. Restoration of self-sufficiency remained illusive.

Rather than improving the economic situation the nationalization of the oil industry in 1951 worsened it. The measure was prompted by Prime Minister Muhammad Mosaddiq. Mosaddiq had a substantial following among nationalists, anti-foreigners and others who complained that the British-owned company excluded natives from high technical and executive posts and that it yielded inadequate royalty. Oil was the main source of national revenue in a country that stood fourth among the world's oil-producing areas. All attempts by the British at compromise or the submission of the dispute to arbitration failed. The closing of the oil operations left some fifty thousand wage earners unemployed. As expected, unrest spread. Martial law was extended. The premier aimed at disposing of the shah and seizing authoritarian power. He succeeded to the extent of forcing the shah and the queen out of the country in August 1953. But a royalist revolutionary coup ended in jailing Mosaddiq and restoring the royal family.

The revolutionary spirit which expressed itself in the nineteenth century in religious innovations and in the early twentieth century in nationalism and constitutionalism manifested itself later in literary and artistic activities. Poetry, prose and art tended to free themselves from the classical tradition. No more was the bard to sing the praises of the shah and aristocracy, nor was the painter or sculptor to seek court patronage. The new poetry was exemplified in the works of abu-al-Qasim Arif Qazwini (d. 1934), a pioneer in folk ballads, a genre which became popular. Writers and journalists addressed themselves more to the common man and had to change their style accordingly. Following the Kemalist precedent Reza Shah charged the Iranian Academy with purging the language from Arabic loanwords, but the study revealed that that would affect about fifty per cent of its vocabulary. Prose writers discovered new themes to treat, such as the emancipation of women. Under Western stimulation a short-story writing was reborn in a land that co-originated the *Arabian Nights*. The first collection of such stories was published in 1922. Three years later the first historical novel, by Musa Hamadani, was written. Comedies after European models followed.

Again under Western stimulation modern sculpture and painting were introduced. New academies for the fine arts were established. If the present West provided the stimulus, the Persian past had the encouraging memory of some of the world's finest artists to offer. The academy of music had achieved some success in transposing native music into polyphony and making it most agreeable to modern generations.

Thus did Iran join the caravan of progress in which it was preceded by Turkey and followed by the Arab states.

21

Ottoman Background of Arab States: Egypt

Of the Arab world, extending from the western shore of Morocco to the eastern boundary of Iraq, only Egypt, Arabia and the Arab Crescent concern us in this study. Geographically in North Africa, Egypt belongs historically and culturally to the Near East.

Sultan Salim I's destruction of the Mamluk dynasty (1516-1517) incorporated Egypt into the Ottoman Empire but introduced no radical changes in its way of life. The country was put under a Turkish viceroy, titled pasha, who controlled a corps of Janissaries. The average pasha knew little about the language and manners of the people he governed, and cared less. His term of office was at best of short duration—by 1800 no fewer than a hundred such pashas had succeeded each other—and his chief concern was to reimburse himself the money he paid at Constantinople to win the high post. Under him were the Mamluk district governors, called beys, constituting a caste and replenished with fresh comers from the Caucasian slave market. Each bey had his own troops and slaves but acknowledged the new suzerainty by the payment of annual tax. The beys, though at times involved in intrigues and even wars against each other, had distinct advantages over the pashas. On more than one occasion the powerful among them would reduce the pasha to a passive spectator, and defy Constantinople by failing to pay what was due.

One such Mamluk was Ali Bey, for twenty years the chief figure in Egyptian history. Reportedly son of a Caucasian priest, young Ali fell into brigands' hands and was offered as a gift to a Mamluk who in the mid-eighteenth century virtually dominated Egypt. The slave succeeded the master and was recognized by his peers as their leader. In 1769 he went so far as to expel the viceroy, striking coinage in his own name and declaring his independence. The audacious Mamluk then launched a double attack on Arabia and Syria. Egyptian troops under his son-in-law, formerly his slave, occupied Mecca, captured Damascus and conquered almost all Syria. At the height of his power Ali Bey was betrayed by his victorious general and son-in-law, who sought to dethrone him. In 1773 Ali was mortally wounded on the field of battle. Ali Bey's ephemeral rise gives us an insight into the vulnerability of Ottoman rule in a remote Arab province. Other Mamluks were equally rapacious. Between pashas and beys the interests of the Egyptian people were lost. Their burden of misery grew heavier.

Napoleon Bonaparte must have sensed the situation well, when twenty-five years after Ali Bey's death he fell upon the country without warning. In his Arabic proclamation on landing at Alexandria, he stated he was coming to rid Egyptians of the Mamluks, who were not as good Moslems as he and his fellow Frenchmen were. His real purpose was to cut the lifeline between Britain and her Eastern possessions, or perhaps to fight his way back into France through Constantinople and the Balkans. In either case his bid was the old one for world domination through the Near East. After capturing Alexandria and winning the battle of the pyramids in Cairo he requested from the shaykh of the Azhar a religious declaration enjoining submission to his rule. The shaykh in turn requested submission to Islam, to which the invader offered two objections: lack of circumcision and addiction to wine. Feeling secure in his new conquest, Napoleon proceeded to Palestine but met his first Waterloo at Acre under a local governor, al-Jazzar. In the defense a British squadron assisted. The British at the same time were busy destroying the French fleet at Aboukir (Abuqir) in Egypt and cutting its line of supply. Napoleon was forced back to France, leaving a force which by 1801 was overwhelmed or withdrawn.

Thus ended the first attempt of its kind since Crusading days. Its significance as a military venture fades to the vanishing point when compared with the political and intellectual reaction chain it set. The year 1798 is generally considered as the one marking the beginning of rivalry among European powers for domination or influence in the Arab East and the breaking of the barrier in the way of Western cultural infiltration. The consequent impact has been the most pregnant fact in the last 165-year annals of the area.

In the Ottoman army that frustrated Napoleon's designs on the valley of the Nile was a native Albanian, Muhammad Ali, destined to dominate the Egyptian scene for almost half a century. Four years after the expulsion of the French the Sublime Porte appointed the young officer as governor. The new governor worked his way into the viceroyalty and from viceroyalty into virtual independence. Dependence upon Constantinople was expressed in the usual tax payment. In 1941 the office was made hereditary in the Alid family, the last representative of which was King Farouk (Faruq), deposed in 1952.

The innovations, some were no doubt reforms, introduced by Muhammad Ali Pasha during his long reign make him without a peer among his Moslem contemporaries. They justify entitling him father of modern Egypt. By 1811 the new pasha had come to the conclusion that he could not be supreme as long as there were Mamluks in the land. He then invited the leading ones among them to a banquet at the citadel built by Saladin overlooking Cairo and had them treacherously slaughtered one after the other. Only a few escaped and fled to Upper Egypt. The almost 600-year-old Mamluk problem was solved forever.

Muhammad Ali was now free to exercise unrestricted authority. By appropriating fiefs and confiscating land and properties with irregular titles, he gradually made himself virtually the proprietor of the country. By imposing monopoly over the export of grain, sugar and other products of the land, he became almost its sole producer. But he did not stop there. He improved methods of agriculture and industry; imported textile plants and a sugar refinery;

opened canals and built a huge barrage; and introduced new crops, such as rice, hemp and cotton. Cotton is still a main source of national income. Himself an illiterate Turkish-speaking man, the lord of Egypt established a ministry of education; he founded the first school of engineering in Arab lands, the first school of medicine and the earliest Arabic press by a Moslem. The press, founded in 1822, carries a name, Bulaq, known wherever Arabic is read. The medical school (Qasr al-Ayni), to which he invited first a French physician, is today the largest medical center in the Near East. The phenomenal military success of the French invader opened Egyptian eyes to the superiority of the West. European professors were invited to Egypt, and Egyptian students were sent to France, Italy and Austria. In the thirty-six years ending 1849 (the year of the viceroy's death) 311 such students were sent at state expense.

The military was, of course, not neglected. A substantial fleet was built, and the army was modernized by a French officer. The armed forces made their first venture (1811) into Wahhabi Arabia. The request came from the Sublime Porte. The seven-year war began with the occupation of Mecca and Medina and ended with the subjugation of Hejaz and Nejd to the Persian Gulf. All were held until 1840. The second military venture was into the Sudan (1820-1822), source of the Nile, and the supply of gold and slaves. Nubia and other parts were occupied and held in some form until the mid-twentieth century.

More serious were the naval and land campaigns against Greece (1825-1828), again at the behest of the viceroy's sovereign, Mahmud II. These were under the brilliant command of his son Ibrahim Pasha, conqueror of Arabia and future conqueror of Syria. Victory was snatched from the Turko-Egyptian forces in 1827, when the combined fleet was destroyed at Navarino by an Anglo-Russo-French fleet. The war ended with the liberation of Greece.

As a price for his participation Muhammad Ali demanded Syria, and when this was denied (1831) he ordered his son Ibrahim to move against it. Before the end of 1832 Ibrahim had overrun Syria, penetrated through Anatolia to Konya, whence he pushed on to

150 miles from Constantinople. He came near overthrowing the Ottoman house. Britain and France, however, preferred a decrepit Ottoman state, in which they could gain spheres of influence, to a youthful vigorous one. Once again Western European intervention deprived Egyptians of the fruit of their victory. Anatolia was immediately evacuated, but Syria, where Ibrahim had a powerful ally in Bashir al-Shihabi II of Lebanon, was held until 1840, the year north Arabia was evacuated. The day dream of an Arab empire, the first of its kind in modern times, was shattered. It had no basis in the masses' consciousness.

The dream was entirely that of a father and a son. The two were the new Egypt. The son died in 1847, two years before the father. A grandson of Muhammad Ali, Abbas I (1849-1858), succeeded. Rather than turning the hands of the clock forward the new viceroy turned them backward. He closed Western-style schools, plugged the inflow of new ideas, abolished trade monopolies and halved the army. In his efforts he was backed by theologians and reactionaries. Abbas' successor, Said (1854-1863), tried to push the pendulum back in the direction of progress. Said Pasha granted his subjects the right to own landed property and dispose of it freely. He gave concessions for a telegraph line. He encouraged foreign capital investment. But his crowning achievement was granting a French engineer, Ferdinand de Lesseps, a concession to build the Suez Canal. The concession was for ninety-nine years from the opening date. The royalty included preference shares yielding fifteen per cent of the net profit. Egypt was to provide four-fifths of the required labor, which was met by conscription. Said's name has been memorialized in Port Said at the north entrance of the canal.

The canal was opened in 1869 under Ismail Pasha (1863-1879), son of Ibrahim. The 300-mile cut represented the greatest and most influential change that had thus far been made on the face of the earth. It was meantime the greatest abbreviation of distance between the West and the Far East. The occasion under a viceroy given to ostentation in both private and public affairs was marked with pomp and magnificence that is said to have cost £1,000,000.

Emperor Francis Joseph of Austria, Empress Eugene of France and the crown prince of Prussia led the roster of honor guests. At the newly built Opera House at Cairo, the first of its kind in that part of the world, the renowned Italian composer Verdi performed. Two years later *Aïda* was presented.

The opening of the canal materialized a dream that had haunted Pharaohs, Achaemenids, Ptolemies and caliphs. It opened a new chapter in the economic history of the Near East. It brought the area back into the main stream of world trade and international affairs and made up in part for the loss sustained because of the Cape of Good Hope route.

Ismail, educated in France, was credited with the saying that Egypt was part and parcel of Europe. He opened the door wide to the flow of Western ideas, extended the railway and telegraph lines, increased the number of public schools and introduced the mixed courts. These courts established uniformity in legislation and served as a model for native courts. Under him Rifaat al-Tahtawi (d. 1873), one of the early scholars to go to France, pioneered in translating European codes and medical works.

Ismail's generosity knew no bounds. It encompassed Alid princes, pashas and officials—largely of non-Egyptian origins—who had taken the place of the Mamluks and were busy exploiting the country. It reached Constantinople. There it took the form of increase in the tax paid the sultan and was rewarded by the title khedive (from Pers., lord, ruler) and the right of primogeniture in his own line. This almost amounted to an acknowledgment of full sovereignty. The third successor of Ismail, Husayn Kamil (1914-1917), was elevated from khedive to sultan by the British.

The extravagance of the khedive and the cost of projects undertaken by him were beyond anything the state could stand. The total debt reached a staggering hundred million guineas. This gave the British and French loanholders a chance to establish a dual control over the country's finances. The British government itself, by purchasing Ismail's shares in the canal, had become its largest single shareholder.

MODERN EGYPT

As Christian European interference in Egyptian affairs became more apparent, resentment among theologians, government officials, armed forces and peasants increased. Burdened by taxation and suffering from the *corvée* system, by which the government could force any able-bodied male to work for nominal pay or none at all (as was done under the Pharaohs), the peasants had their own reasons for resentment. The discontented found a champion in a young colonel, Ahmad Arabi (Urabi, later pasha), son of an eight-acre-land cultivator and former student of al-Azhar. Anti-foreign riots spread. A major one broke out in polyglot Alexandria costing the lives of about 57 Europeans and 140 Egyptians. The British thereupon shelled the city (July 1882), landed troops in Port Said and seized the canal. France disassociated itself from the affair. Two months later the hastily assembled army of Arabi was routed in a village near Cairo and the leader was banished to Ceylon. Vague as it was in its ideology the Arabi movement, with its slogan "Egypt for the Egyptians," may be considered the earliest expression of nationalist feeling in modern Egypt.

The developments of 1882 led to an estrangement between England and France, leaving England in sole control of Egypt. Under the unpretentious title of British resident and consul general, Lord Cromer was the virtual ruler of the country for about quarter of a century. For force he depended upon the army of occupation. For political implementation he had "advisers" in all key posts who exercised ill-defined but effective control. No minister or provincial governor could long maintain his post if the adviser's advice and the resident's "recommendation" went unheeded. The authority of the khedive and the suzerainty of the sultan-caliph were maintained as a diplomatic fiction.

Under the strong rule of Lord Cromer the country's finances were ordered, exports and imports trebled, taxation revised in favor of the peasant, the *corvée* abolished, public security improved and the level of justice, which remained in native hands, raised. But little was done for public education or for the promotion of self-government. Some improvement was made in secondary education designed more for preparing candidates for civil service than for its intrinsic liberal values. Illiteracy, however, remained widespread. In international affairs the outstanding event was the insurrection against the hated Egyptian rule in the Sudan led by one who set himself as the long-awaited prophet (*mahdi*). Between 1881 and 1885 the Mahdi gained control of the country. A joint Anglo-Egyptian force under Lord Kitchener recovered the lost territory (1896-1898) and thereby re-insured for Egypt its water supply. The Anglo-Egyptian Sudan, as it was then called, was put under joint sovereignty headed by a governor general appointed by the khedive on the British government's recommendation. Its first governor was Lord Kitchener. Beginning in 1924 the Sudanese step by step Sudanized the government and ultimately gained control of their land. On the first day of January 1956 the British and Egyptian flags in Khartum were ceremoniously lowered and the Sudanese flag was hoisted. Sudan joined the caravan of newly freed African nations.

The reconquest of the Sudan by Kitchener was accomplished under Khedive Abbas II (1892-1914), a headstrong young man who resented British tutelage and tried to shake off Cromer's domination. In this he had French support. By this time Egyptians educated in Western style had increased in quality and quantity, and nationalist feeling was beginning to assert itself. One group, influenced by Jamal-al-Din al-Afghani's teachings, was attracted by the Hamidian Pan-Islamic ideal. Khedive Abbas leaned in this direction. Another nationalist group concentrated on Egyptian independence and constitutional government. This movement found an eloquent spokesman in a French-educated lawyer, Mustafa Kamil. In 1907 the first nationalist congress was held under his leadership and adopted a liberal, pacific program. On the death of the leader (1908) at the age of thirty-four, the successorship was assumed by a more articulate and experienced leader, Sad Zaghlul. Sad was an Azharite lawyer who was born to a peasant family. He had fought under Arabi Pasha and held several high posts, including two cabinet ones, and the vice presidency of the general assembly. A creation of Cromer, the assembly consisted of fourteen members nominated by the khedive and sixteen elected. It was more consultative than legislative. Under the new resident, Lord Kitchener of Khartum (as he was now called), a faint attempt was made to satisfy nationalist demands. The old assembly gave way to a new and expanded one, largely elective, with powers to initiate legislation, supervise the budget and in general represent the people. The assembly held its first session in January 1914, a year in which no such bodies could survive.

No sooner had Turkey taken a position of hostility against the Allies than a state of war was declared (November 1914) in Egypt. Martial law was immediately imposed and censorship applied. It is to the credit of the British that until then no such measures had been taken. In December Egypt was pronounced a British protectorate. Khedive Abbas II was deposed, and his brother Husayn Kamil (1914-1917) was installed as sultan. The country served as a military base. Its importance as a source of grain and beasts of burden and the land of the Suez Canal was now multiplied. The use of the canal was denied to enemy shipping. When commodities and services were not acquired by regular means, they were requisitioned against inadequate compensation. Especially exasperating were the drafting of men and the requisition of animals for defense, under General Allenby, against Turkish attacks from Palestine. The cost of necessities of life rose to prohibitive heights, and the hardship, of course, fell upon peasants and laborers.

As the war progressed British rule became more odious. Nationalist agitators could then count on far wider support. The crushing blows Turkey received in Palestine, Syria and Iraq weakened the Pan-Islamist wing of Egyptian nationalism. On the other hand, the Anglo-French declaration that in waging war on Turkey the Allies contemplated the enfranchisement of the peoples under its rule strengthened the more provincial school. So did the novel doctrine of self-determination enunciated by Woodrow Wilson.

The crisis came shortly after the armistice (November 1918), when a delegation (*wafd*) headed by Zaghlul was denied permission to go to the Peace Conference and plead the cause of their country's independence. Instead, the leaders were deported to Malta. Nothing could have more inflamed the patriotic zeal. The party now became known as that of the Wafd. In the meantime there was a new resident, General Allenby, fresh from his successful defense of the Suez and triumphal campaigns in Palestine, Lebanon and Syria. In February 1922 the British yielded. They unilaterally pronounced the protectorate terminated and declared Egypt an independent sovereign state of the hereditary monarchical type. But there were four reservations relating to British communication, national defense, protection of foreign interests and native minorities, and the status of the Sudan. Fuad (1922-1936), brother of the sultan, assumed the title of king. In the following year a Belgian-modeled constitution was promulgated. Egypt turned a new page in its long and checkered annals. That will be treated later.

We noted before that throughout the period of occupation, beginning in 1882, except in wartime, Egypt enjoyed freedom of expression and thought. This made of it an intellectual oasis in an Arab desertland. It attracted French- and Anglo-Saxon-educated young men, particularly from Lebanon and Syria. Presses, modern newspapers, learned magazines and societies flourished as nowhere else. Egypt's writers served as pioneers in the intellectual renaissance of the entire Arab world. Other emigrants sought employment in government service. Still others took advantage of the developing business opportunities.

On the religious side the awakening led by Muhammad Abduh took the form of reform, echoing earlier—but less intellectual—attempts in Arabia and Persia. The Egyptian reformer was born in 1849 to a peasant family and educated at al-Azhar at a time, luckily for him, when al-Afghani was lecturing there. The young scholar espoused the nationalist cause, but moderately, opposed excessive Europeanization of his country and participated in the Arabi revolt. This landed him as a deportee in Lebanon. There and later in Paris he was exposed to Western thought. On his return home he engaged in teaching and preaching, rising to the rectorship of al-Azhar and the muftiship of his country, the two highest intellectual and religious posts in the country. Like his predecessors ibn-Abd-al-Wahhab and al-Afghani, Muhammad Abduh started from the premise that the contemporary condition of Islam was unhealthy and that it required an over-all reform. But his prescription varied. He held that religious issues should be separated from political problems. He stressed the spiritual and intellectual rejuvenation of Islam by accepting the products of scientific research, and deprecated the use of force as an instrument of reform. His writings were singularly free from xenophobia. He was the first Arab Moslem intellectual to wrestle with the problem of rendering historically conditioned beliefs and practices plausible to his contemporaries. Certain koranic passages that seemed in conflict with modern thought and practice he interpreted somewhat freely and flexibly, thereby opening the way for rethinking the old in terms of the new. In this he was following Christian exegetes who for centuries had been reading into their Scriptures modern ideas which had never occurred to the writers.

The Egyptian reformer's immediate influence among his fellow countrymen was limited to a few intellectuals, such as Qasim Amin, who in 1898 wrote the first Arabic work on the emancipation of womanhood. His greatest disciple and commentator was born in a village in what is today Lebanon.

22

The Arabian Peninsula

The Ottoman background and heritage of the peninsula was not as extensive or significant as that of Egypt or the Arab Crescent. As heirs of the Mamluks, the Turks acquired Hejaz early in the sixteenth century and shortly after that conquered Yemen. In both cases, particularly that of Yemen, the control was remote and ineffective. In both areas, as in other parts of the vast and barren peninsula, the land was divided and subdivided among tribal chiefs and shaykhs often in struggle for existence or mastery. The urban settlements were under lords and amirs living in walled towns and exercising shadowy authority over neighboring tribes. The lords in Hejaz were the sharif descendants of the Prophet, centered in Mecca and drawing prestige from custodianship of the holy places. Those of Yemen were the imam descendants of a great-grandson of Ali, named Zayd, and quartered mainly in Sana. The sharifs were Sunnites, but the imams were Zaydi Shiites.

The Ottoman rulers naturally took more interest in Hejaz. So precarious was their hold on Yemen that in 1633 an imam expelled their wali from Sana. Not until 1849 did the Porte succeed in imposing its nominee as wali. The walis' chief concern became keeping insurgent tribesmen down.

The modern kingdom of Yemen was a child of the first World War. In it it freed itself from Ottoman rule. The Turkish garrison at Sana found itself isolated and ineffective, and in 1918 its remnant withdrew from the land. The imam of Sana, Yahya, became master of the country and on adding the title of king became the absolute spiritual and temporal ruler. Finding himself between two powerful rivals for influence in Yemen—Italy in Ethiopia and

Britain in Aden—Yahya naturally leaned toward Italy, for he considered occupied Aden a Yemeni territory. But the treaty of friendship and commerce he signed with Italy in 1926 did not leave the medieval country's door ajar to fresh breezes from outside. Italian physicians were invited to staff his newly built hospital in Sana and Italian engineers to irrigate largely his estate at Taiz, but the country as a whole remained isolated and insulated. Besides the frontier disputes with the British, Imam Yahya had those with the emerging ibn-Saud in the north which led to a losing war (1934).

In the second World War Yahya's preference was initially for the Axis Powers, but British military successes in Egypt and neighboring Arab lands changed it. In 1945 Yemen joined the League of Arab States and two years later the United Nations. In that same year it received the first diplomatic mission from the United States and signed a treaty of friendship and commerce. A military coup in 1948 ended in Yahya's murder and the succession of his son Ahmad.

Ahmad did allow American interests to build a road in his country, the first that could be so called, and to explore for oil and minerals, which did not turn out to be plentiful. But basically his policy remained old fashioned and his methods autocratic. A coup in 1955, engineered by Abdullah, his brother and representative at the United Nations, ended in disaster to the conspirators. It cost Abdullah his head. Headless bodies of the conspirators were exhibited in the public square of Taiz. Three years later Yemen federated itself with the new combination of Egypt-Syria called United Arab Republic, but before the end of 1961 the federation was dissolved.

On the death of Ahmad the following year his son Badr succeeded him as imam-king. A week later a revolt broke out headed by an army colonel, Abdullah al-Sallal, and supported by Egypt. Al-Sallal seized the capital and declared a republic modeled after the Egyptian. Saudi Arabia supported the royalists, and the country was plunged into a prolonged civil war.

For over a thousand years after the Orthodox caliphate, based in Medina, Hejaz played no noteworthy part in Arab or international affairs. Under Umayyads, Abbasids and Fatimids its status was that of a marginal province in the far-flung caliphate. Anesthetized by the aura of sanctity emanating from its holy cities, Hejaz lived on visitors and sank deeper and deeper into its medieval slumber. Unlike Yemen it had no cultivable potential; its population remained mostly nomad. Its first awakening shock was administered by the Nejdis, Muhammad ibn-Abd-al-Wahhab (d. 1793), a puritanical theologian-reformer, and Muhammad ibn-Saud (d. 1765), a tribal chief and son-in-law. This was the first ibn-Saud in history. The marriage of sword and religion, as often happens in Islam, gave birth to victory. Moslems practicing what ibn-Abd-al-Wahhab considered forbidden innovations were fought by ibn-Saud to the point of conversion or extermination. Innovations included the cult of saints, veneration of shrines, visitation to tombs, the use of the rosary and other practices savoring of idolatry. Tobacco smoking, silk clothing and other modern luxuries were frowned upon. The new sectarians called themselves Muwahhidun (unitarians); their enemies called them Wahhabis. The koranic law enjoining stoning the adulteress and amputating the thief's hand was enforced.

As converts mounted, political control widened. Every new convert of ibn-Abd-al-Wahhab was a recruit to the fighting machine of ibn-Saud. In 1773 Riyad, future capital of Wahhabism, was seized. From central Arabia the Wahhabi double-cause spread into eastern Arabia. Early in the following century it burst upon unsuspecting neighbors, Iraq and Hejaz. Karbala and Najaf, most revered Shiite shrines, were sacked and the population massacred. Mecca and Medina, holiest Sunnite cities, were not spared (1803-1806). Forthwith the two cities were purged of their venerated tombs, relics of paganism. Syria's turn came next. Damascus was reached (1808). Never since the Orthodox caliphate had such a vast area fallen under one man's scepter.

Constantinople was aroused. At the behest of Mahmud II, the Egyptians conducted a series of military campaigns. The first, in 1818, virtually razed the kingdom's headquarters and sent Abdullah ibn-Saud and other members of the royal family into exile. The first Wahhabi empire came to an end.

Restoration came in the early twentieth century. Its hero was young Abd-al-Aziz ibn-Saud, who had been a refugee at Kuwait. At

Courtesy of Arabian American Oil Company

KING IBN-SAUD, FATHER OF SAUDI ARABIA

the head of a band of two hundred followers, the twenty-one-year-old Abd-al-Aziz dashed through the intervening desert, entered Riyad by night, slaughtered the governor and his guard and established himself firmly in his ancestral capital. This was early in 1902. The governor was ibn-Rashid, supported by Constantinople. By way of unifying and consolidating his realm the new leader launched a policy of colonization aimed at settling his nomad followers in units, each under strict Wahhabi discipline and responsible for a contingent of armed force. The settlers (*ikhwan,* brethren) developed into a formidable warring machine. In 1913 ibn-Saud was ready to strike outside of Nejd. Al-Hasa on the Persian Gulf was wrested from the Turks. It brought him close to the British-dependent Arab states on the coast.

In the west ibn-Saud had a formidable rival in Husayn ibn-Ali al-Hashimi, sharif of Mecca and aspirant for general Arab leadership. The outbreak of the World War gave the descendant of the Prophet his golden chance. Arab nationalists in Damascus, Baghdad, Beirut, Cairo turned to him for leadership against the Turks. So did the British and French. In October 1914 the British gave him a conditional guarantee of independence. Two years later he proclaimed the full independence of Hejaz, attacked the Turkish garrison in Medina and assumed the title "king of the Arabs." His son Faysal, we learned before, was entrusted with organizing and leading guerrilla battalions against the Turks in Hejaz and Palestine. By 1917 all Turks had been dislodged from Hejaz. Reinforced by an Australian division Faysal took the inland route to Damascus, entering the city in November 1918.

At the Versailles conference (1919) it became clear that the Allies had no intention to honor their war promises to the Arabs or to recognize Husayn as king of the Arabs. Indeed, by then the Arabs had learned that as early as 1916 the British, French and Russians had reached a secret agreement parceling out not only Turkey but Syria, Iraq and Palestine among themselves. A Syrian national assembly enthroned Faysal (1920) in Damascus, whence he was immediately thrown out by the French who were then given the mandate over Syria and Lebanon. The British, however, installed him the following year as king over Iraq. His elder brother Abdullah was made by the British, who held the mandate over Palestine and Iraq, amir of Transjordan. The father, taking advantage of the abolition of the Ottoman caliphate, added to his title that of "caliph of the Moslems."

It was time for ibn-Saud to act. In five years ending 1924 the sultan of Nejd and its dependencies had utterly destroyed the Hashimite house of Hejaz. Two years later in the grand mosque of

Mecca he was proclaimed king of Hejaz. In 1932 the king of Hejaz and Nejd became the king of Saudi Arabia, covering almost all north and central Arabia.

Satisfied, the conqueror turned his attention, single-mindedly, to the stupendous economic and social problems. To a land where tribal warfare was endemic, Bedouin raids a sport and pillage a noble profession, the first Saudi king introduced a measure of unity, security and orderliness never known before. Where subsidies did not entice and alliances did not work, force suppressed. When theologians and obscurantists could not be convinced or reconciled, they were ordered silenced. Telephones, telegraphs and radios, strictly innovations in Wahhabi eyes, were introduced. Roads were built. Motor vehicles began to roll where only camels had trod. Pilgrims reached Mecca and Medina by buses rather than caravans.

The holy pilgrimage, for over a millennium the main source of revenue, had now a new competitor, oil. Oil was first discovered in Bahrain in 1932. It ushered in a new era in the economic life of the entire area. The following year a concession was given in Saudi Arabia to the Standard Oil Company of California, which became the nucleus of the Arabian American Oil Company (Aramco). From escalating royalties the king was able to finance his projects. Early in the 1940's, when war necessities and priorities curtailed oil operations and reduced pilgrim traffic, the United States through Britain offered generous aid. In 1953 the king died, bequeathing the throne to his eldest son Saud.

Saud's government followed a policy of cautious modernization. It inaugurated a new university at Riyad. A few students were sent to Cairo and Beirut and even to England and the United States. In 1964-1965, 490 Saudis were enrolled in American colleges. A small middle class of intellectuals, technicians, businessmen and professionals emerged, threatening the traditional social structure. The new spirit of Arab nationalism and its concomitant urge for Arab unity expressed itself through this class. Upheavals would probably have taken place but for Saud's displacement by his brother Faysal

ARABIAN PENINSULA

(1964). Faysal followed a more determined, though cautious course of economic and social progress, one more attuned to changing times.

Almost the entire southern and eastern territory of the peninsula, with its shaykhdoms and sultanates, is still British dominated. British interest stemmed from its concern for India's security and continued desire to control the area's trade routes.

The Muscat and Oman territory was the first to fall into European hands; the Portuguese held it for 180 years beginning in 1508. British treaty relations with Muscat began as early as 1798 through the East India Company. Other treaties followed, involving suppression of slave trade, customs agreement, navigation and commerce. Similar treaties were later signed with eastern Arabian states. The modern history of these states would have been uneventful but for the advent of the British and the discovery of oil. Prior to that the people lived on date growing, boat building and pearl fishing. The bulk of the population was nomadic. The richest and only independent (since 1961) state among them is oil-rich Kuwait. That the area is a desert floating on a sea of oil is especially true of this tiny state. Kuwait, Bahrain, Qatar and Saudi Arabia together with Iraq and Iran make the Near East the leading oil center in the world. Its fabulous income is revolutionizing not only the economic but other aspects of life.

23

The Arab Crescent

The incorporation of Syria (1516-1517) by Sultan Salim into the Ottoman Empire made no radical change in its Mamluk-inherited administrative system. Its three main provinces of Damascus, Aleppo and Tripoli became walayahs, each under a wali entitled pasha. The Mamluk governor of Damascus, who had betrayed his Egyptian suzerain, became the virtual viceroy. But the betrayer of his first master did not hesitate to betray the second. He declared his independence in Damascus and struck coins in his name. But Sulayman's Janissaries meted out such a punishment to the Syrian capital that its inhabitants ever after associated the word Janissary with terror.

Turkish walis followed one another in breathless sequence, averaging in the first century less than two years each. Their authority gradually shrank and was limited to towns and their environs. No systematic planning was undertaken to develop the natural resources of the land or its manpower. As economy decreased, insecurity increased. Villages in northeast Syria depopulated under Mamluks disappeared under Ottomans. Eventually the country's population was reduced to a third of its size under the Romans. Predictably, adventurous and unscrupulous local leaders emerged. Most conspicuous among them was Ahmad al-Jazzar. Originally a Christian Bosnian slave, young Ahmad landed in Cairo in the possession of the Mamluk Ali Bey. The distinction he won as executioner for his master won him his surname, meaning butcher. From Cairo he moved to Sidon and worked his way to the governorship of the city. Gradually he extended his authority to Acre, which in 1799 he successfully defended against Napoleon. Prior to that the sultan had added to his governorship Damascus, making him viceroy of

Syria. Throughout al-Jazzar lived up to his reputation of ruthless dealing with enemies, real or imaginary. On his death in 1804 a sigh of relief went throughout the land. His rise exemplifies the chaotic conditions in the provinces at this time.

Iraq was not secure in Ottoman hands until 1638 under Murad IV. Its distance from Constantinople, its proximity to Shiite Persia and the large Shiite element in its population created special problems. As late as 1733 Nadir Shah laid siege to Baghdad; ten years later he attacked Mosul. In 1801 and 802 Iraq's Karbala and Najaf shrines, we learned before, were sacked by puritanical Wahhabis from Nejd. Unwieldy Kurdish tribes in the north were and remain a thorn in its side. The Kurds are Sunnites but ethnically and linguistically closer to Persians.

In 1750 Iraq passed into the hands of Mamluks, who behaved no better than their opposite numbers in Egypt. The Mamluk historic theme revolved on personalities and intrigues in the capital. Their primary concern was themselves. Constantinople was satisfied with the annual tribute. Under them as under Ottoman pashas, before and after, it was the people who suffered the consequences of corruption and misrule. Not until 1831 was Constantinople able to reassert its authority. The Mamluks were exterminated. An Ottoman garrison was stationed in Baghdad. In the series of walis that followed, the record of only one, Midhat Pasha, shines with unusual brilliancy. Liberal-minded and progressive, Midhat was considered too dangerous by a grand vizir and therefore sent to distant Baghdad. Here he launched a program of public works, including clearing clogged-up canals, opening new roads and a savings bank, starting horse-tramways and founding a technical school, that stands unique in provincial annals. He even contemplated a railway. But official jealousy would not allow him time. He was recalled to Constantinople, where a change of regime favored him. As prime minister under Abd-al-Hamid II he inspired the short-lived constitution of 1876. His last days he spent as an exile in Taif, Hejaz, where he was strangled (1883), after varied attempts at his life, by agents of the Porte.

Lebanon, the least governed of the Ottoman Arab provinces, was the best governed and perhaps the happiest. In the decisive Turkish-Mamluk confrontation of 1516 the Lebanese feudal lords followed their time-honored tactics of wait-and-see. But no sooner had Sultan Salim victoriously entered Damascus than Fakhr-al-Din I al-Mani, of the Shuf district (southeast of Beirut), with other lords, presented himself to offer homage. Aware of more potentially dangerous enemies, Salim followed the easiest course. He confirmed those lords of the mountain in their fiefs, allowing them the same privileges as under the Egyptian Mamluks and imposing a relatively light tribute. For 181 years after that the Manis ruled a large part of the mountain. Of uncertain origin, they had entered Lebanon in the early twelfth century and settled in a village, Baaqlin, overlooking the Beirut-Sidon road, to harass Crusaders on the shore. They embraced Druzism, the religion of their subjects.

Under Fakhr-al-Din II (1590-1635) Manid hegemony reached its apex. So diminutive was Fakhr in stature that, according to his detactors, if an egg fell from his pocket it would not break. But his energy and ambition were great. Besides, he had unusual interest in developing his fief's resources and promoting the welfare of its people. To that end he encouraged the flax and silk industries, constructed bridges, built caravanserais (khans) and favored trade with such European cities as Venice, Florence and Marseille. To European traders and missionaries he extended capitulary privileges. Meantime he was busy extending his mountainous realm inland to include the fertile Biqa' plain and seaward to include the coast from the Dog River to Mount Carmel. The lord of Lebanon laid out plans for a greater Lebanon, and setting it on the path to independence and progress. He went so far as signing a treaty with the duke of Tuscany in Florence, comprising a secret military agreement against his suzerain.

At last the Porte moved against its vassal. Before long Fakhr found himself confronted with superior land and sea forces from Damascus and Constantinople. He fled to the court of his ally in Italy. There he spent two years. Taking advantage of a change of regime in Constantinople, he returned home, more intent than ever upon carrying out his plans for expansion and progress. After Fakhr routed Turkish forces sent against him from Damascus and captured its wali, the Porte acknowledged the *fait accompli* and designated him "lord of Arabistan," from Aleppo to Gaza. He then invited engineers, architects and agricultural experts from Tuscany and permitted European Catholic missions to settle in the land under his patronage. The rumor spread that he himself was baptized by his Capuchin physician. Once more the suspicious eye of the Porte turned toward him and its arm against him. The Lebanese prince put up a valiant fight against heavy odds. The expected aid from Tuscany did not come. In 1635 he was led captive to Constantinople and publicly strangled. His plans failed of realization but pointed out the way to the future.

Fakhr-al-Din's policy of breaking with the past, political and cultural, was not resumed until the rise of Bashir II al-Shihabi (1788-1840). Bashir's career almost duplicated that of his illustrious predecessor. The Shihabis were descended from the noble Quraysh tribe. They entered Lebanon half a century before the Manis, with whom they intermarried and allied themselves. First Moslems, they partly became Christians. For about a century and a half ending in 1843, from their capital Dayr al-Qamar, they ruled Lebanon through an intricate system of feudal hierarchy of princes and shaykhs. Like their predecessors they followed the principles of hereditary succession and home rule, exercising even the power of life and death on their subjects. Their feudal strength rested on universal military service involving no special training. As long as they sent Constantinople its annual dues they had little interference.

With the conversion of the fourth Shihabi governor, Mansur (1754-1770), to Maronitism, Lebanon's door was opened wider to Capuchins, Jesuits and European traders. French-Maronite relations go back to Crusading days and were tightened by Louis XIV's policy of promoting trade with the Levant and protecting its Catholic population. In 1584 Pope Gregory XIII founded a college in Rome for Maronite students. This college graduated scholars who remained in Europe to introduce or promote Oriental studies in Rome, Paris, Madrid and other cities; or who returned home to start Western-style schools or serve their church as priests, bishops or patriarchs. A Rome graduate introduced into Qazhayya monastry a press in which the first Arabic Psalter (in Syriac characters) was printed (1610). At a time when the thick Ottoman curtain had been lowered between Turkey and Europe, it was these graduates of Rome and their pupils who transmitted the torch of enlightenment and kept it aloft and aflame.

Courtesy of The Macmillan Co., Ltd.

BASHIR AL-SHIHABI II. FEUDAL LORD OF LEBANON

For fifty-two years beginning in 1788 Bashir ruled his realm with an iron hand. Tall of stature, with piercing eyes and impressive personality he struck awe in his subjects' hearts. Tales of his stern execution of justice and tracking down criminals have become part of the Lebanese saga. With security went a measure of prosperity. Bashir maintained the Mani-Shihabi tradition of religious tolerance. In the manificent palace he built at Bayt al-Din (near Dayr al-Qamar) he had a chapel and a mosque. The palace is still a show place in the country. In the early 1820's American missionary enterprise found a lodging in Lebanon and contributed to making it a center of intellectual radiation to nearby lands.

Bashir's first test of ability on a high level came when Napoleon in 1799 solicited his aid against al-Jazzar in Acre, promising more independence, additional territory and lighter taxes. The amir of Lebanon waited to see. He also made the right choice in 1810 when he responded to the Porte's solicitation for aid against the invading Wahhabis. The time to break with the Porte did not come until he had entered into secret understanding with the Egyptian viceroy Muhammad Ali. Bashir cooperated with the viceroy's son, Ibrahim Pasha, in the conquest (1831) of Syria. Nine years later, when a coalition of Turkish and European powers forced Ibrahim's withdrawal, the lord of Lebanon was taken to Malta and then to Constantinople, where he died. His reign added to the country a new dimension—the international.

Bashir's withdrawal from the scene left the country internally in a state bordering on anarchy. In five years civil disturbances between Christians—mainly Maronites—and Druzes began, culminating in the 1860 massacre. All told, some 12,000 Christian lives were lost, with the Porte's connivance. The tiny country was drawn into the orbit of power politics. Five European powers (France, Britain, Russia, Prussia and Austria) joined with Turkey to draw a new statute for its government. Lebanon was stripped of its seaports and the Biqa' plateau and put under a Christian governor general (*mutasarrif*) of Ottoman nationality. A new corner was turned in its modern history. Lebanon became an internationally recognized autonomous state contributing no troops to the imperial army and paying no tribute to its treasury. This Mutasarrifiyah of Mount Lebanon, as it was called, survived till the first World War. Despite its restriction to the mountainous area, it enjoyed a measure of prosperity and security that gave rise to the saying, "Happy is he who owns but a goat's enclosure in Mount Lebanon."

In this period Lebanon became an open arena for the interplay of Western economic and cultural forces. In 1895 a French company completed the Beirut-Damascus railroad—the first in the area

—which later connected these two cities with Turkey, Iraq and Egypt. Catholic and Protestant missionary schools began to dot the towns and villages. Overpopulation found a safety valve in emigration. Sons of Lebanon, in the tradition of their Phoenician ancestors, spread over a large part of the civilized world.

The World War of 1914 to 1918, besides interrupting the course of progress, brought the country untold misery. Its autonomy was abolished. Its Christians were suspected of pro-French sympathies, and its non-Christians of pro-Arab leanings. Both parties were regarded as anti-Turkish. Leaders were hanged or sent into exile. The country's main sources of national income dried up. Transit trade ceased. Tourism vanished. Disease and famine took their toll. It is estimated that a fourth of the population perished. After the war Lebanon with Syria was given by the League of Nations as a mandate to France, Palestine and Iraq to the British.

24

Modernization and Mandates

Before the mandates were instituted the Arab Crescent had been exposed to modernizing, Westernizing influences. The mandates intensified and accelerated the processes. The resultant transformation was one of the most thoroughgoing since the rise of Islam. It involved all aspects of life. In Turkey, we learned before, introduction to Western culture was prompted by politico-military considerations, in Egypt by politico-economic conditions; but in the Arab Crescent it was effected by cultural media. Lebanon provided an especially favored locale. Its tradition of tolerance and hospitality, together with its salubrious climate and Christian majority, made it so.

Catholic missionaries had been active in the area since Crusading days, but many chose Lebanon for headquarters. Capuchins had entered the country in 1627 under Fakhr-al-Din. By the nineteenth century this order had established eleven centers between Tyre and Aleppo. Under Fakhr-al-Din's Shihabi successors the Jesuits became particularly active. They served as the main medium for introducing French culture. In 1734 they founded in a village the first European-style school. Other schools for boys and girls followed. Jesuit educational work was crowned (1881) by the Université Saint-Joseph in Beirut, which now includes schools of medicine, dentistry, pharmacy, law, engineering and theology. It has supplied the Lebanese Republic with most of its presidents and ministers.

In 1819 the first Protestant American missionary landed in Beirut, which became headquarters of the mission for the Arab Crescent. Teachers, social workers, physicians and nurses followed. Primary and secondary schools for boys and girls were established not only in cities (Beirut, Tripoli, Sidon, Zahlah) but also in mountain villages. By 1848 a new sect, the Protestant, had been organized. Two years later Abd-al-Majid gave legal status to the new religious body.

The massacre of 1860 aroused Christian European sympathy and interest, which found expression in the founding of orphanages, dispensaries and boarding schools. Once started, such establishments tend to become permanent features. American educational work culminated in the Syrian Protestant College (1866, now American University of Beirut), considered the most influential institution of its kind abroad. In 1964-1965 the university had enrolled in its college and schools of medicine, nursing, public health, pharmacy, engineering and agriculture 3115 students, male and female, from sixty-five countries. In the same year seven Arab ambassadors to the United Nations happened to be graduates of the institution.

By way of implementing its educational program the American Mission established in Beirut (1834) an Arabic printing press which was soon matched by the Imprimerie Catholique of the Jesuits. Both establishments are still among the best equipped in the Arab East. While in both cases the motivation was religious, it later expanded to other aspects of knowledge. Both presses made the translation of the Bible into what may be called neo-classical Arabic their first major project, and were eminently successful. While grammatically correct, the Arabic used was not beyond the comprehension of the unschooled. This is the kind of idiom now used in the press and from the platform.

As the wave of new ideas splashed over the eastern Mediterranean, Iraq got only a spray. Its intellectual life remained anchored in Najaf and Karbala, both medieval in their concept and radiating conservatism throughout the Shiite world. A limited number of Iraqi young men did have a glimpse of Western culture throughout the back door of Constantinople, where they had military training. But such training is not normally conducive to the liberation of the individual from the treble shackle of provincialism, prejudice and ignorance. Catholic missionary activity by its nature found more response among the Jacobites and Nestorians of Iraq. Carmelite and Dominican mission schools in Mosul and Baghdad were patronized mostly from these two Christian communities. As early as 1552 a Uniat community, Chaldean, was established with a patriarchate at Mosul. An Arabic printing press was established in Baghdad. The Jesuits entered the field late. In 1932 they founded a college in the capital city and attracted students from all faiths. Southern Iraq benefited from Protestant work in the Persian Gulf area starting in 1889. Later Basra had an American Protestant secondary school.

Until well into the eighteen century the educational system of the entire Arab East may be said to have been still in the traditional, conventional pattern. The society it served was living in the past. Educational support came largely from religious endowments (wakf) and partly from state revenues. Literary productions displayed the characteristic features of a decadent intellectuality. They concentrated on theology, scholasticism and linguistics. Originality was lacking. Scientific productions, in the real sense of the term, were non-existent. Myth, magic, astrology and other pseudosciences were in occupation of the field. The practice of medicine was generally hereditary, passed by word of mouth from father to son and by the written word going back to ibn-Sina and al-Razi.

As the eighteenth passed into the nineteenth century, internal change was already taking place. Native schools following the European models were in evidence. In the absence of adequate Arabic texts, especially in the sciences, translations from French and English were used. One of these languages or both were introduced into the curriculum. Concurrently literary and scientific societies, again inspired by Western patterns, were organized. One such society in Beirut drew members, Christians, Moslems and Druzes, from Damascus and Cairo, and held meetings in which papers were read and published in a monthly bulletin. In a secret meeting of this society (1868) a twenty-year-old Christian Lebanese, Ibrahim al-Yaziji, recited an original poem which was passed from mouth to mouth and sparked the earliest Arab nationalist feeling against Ottoman rule. In due course the spark ignited a flame.

Outstanding among the pioneers in this period of intellectual renaissance was Butrus al-Bustani (1819-1883), co-translator of the Bible, author of textbooks in grammar and mathematics, journalist and editor of the first Arabic encyclopedia. The newspapers and magazines al-Bustani published were among the earliest and most learned in the Arab East. By 1892 Beirut had seen the birth and demise of twenty-eight newspapers and periodicals, some of which had moved to Cairo.

Egypt after the British occupation (1882) offered a more congenial climate for intellectual activity. To it in 1885 moved a magazine, *al-Muqtataf*—founded by two graduates of the American University of Beirut—which in its seventy-six-year career served as an extension school in science and literature wherever Arabic was read. Its two learned editors, Yaqub Sarruf and Faris Nimr, also published a newspaper, *al-Muqattam* (1889-1952), which for years had for rival another Christian Lebanese-founded paper *al-Ahram*. *Al-Ahram* is still considered the most influential paper in the Arabic language. Historical studies received their first extensive critical treatment from the pen of another Beirut-educated emigrant, Jurji Zaydan, founder of *al-Hilal* (1892), still current. Zaydan authored the earliest historical novels. His multi-volume history of Arabic literature was republished recently.

With educational and intellectual reforms went economic and social changes. Economic change normally precedes social change and moves at a more rapid pace. It involves less emotional strain. Usually a person is more ready to give up camel in favor of train or bus than he is to give up his ingrained loyalty to family, tribe or sect.

Down to the eighteenth century Arab industry was generally based on handwork and crude machinery. The typical craftsman produced enough for his village. Agriculture was mainly of the subsistence variety; the farmer produced enough for his family. Urban settlements were few in number and small in size. The onslaught of wholesale technological products, such as textiles from Manchester and machine-made home articles from Paris, wrought havoc in the native economy. As village handicraft dwindled, migration to towns increased, swelling the towns into cities.

A new class was born. Its membership consisted of modernized businessmen, lawyers, physicians, teachers and other professionals. It inched its way into a middle position between the two traditional groups of privileged large landowners and officeholders in government or church and the underprivileged group of manual laborers and soil tillers. As it grew, this middle class gathered into its hands the forces of social as well as economic control. Political control first escaped it.

With the structural change in Arab society went radical change in its unit, the family. Hitherto family organization had remained basically patriarchal and endogamous, just as it was in biblical days. The senior member of the family, usually the grandfather, controlled it. Family property was held by him as a joint possession. Marriages were arranged by him and the immediate parents and were usually limited to cousins. Family loyalty, a dominant force in Arab community life, was hard to crack under the impact of the West. It did not yield until the twentieth century. First in urban settlements, the smaller type of family unit, the biological, began to displace the older expanded type.

Equally if not more dominant in Arab community life was devotion to ancestral religion. Religion was all-pervasive. It explained past events as well as present happenings both human and natural. The interpretation was Providential as against the scientific or secular. As education spread, rational and scientific explanations began to encroach upon what was considered exclusively divine domain. Even today one can hardly go through a four-page Arabic paper without coming across the name of God in connection with such events as births, deaths, weddings, storms and drought—a linguistic fossil of earlier thinking. This change in attitude was far reaching in its affects. It started what could be called the revolution of rising expectations, the expectations of peoples who realized for the first time that those adverse conditions under which they lived were not so much due to a law of nature or an act of God as to their own shortcomings, negligence or inactivity.

Westerners were not the only agents introducing modernizing stimuli to the area. Emigrants played a role. This was especially true of Lebanon, whence the stream of emigration flowed more copiously. Syria came next.

In Lebanon emigration started early and continued to the present. In the United States it was checked by the quota legislation of the early 1920's. The movement served as a safety valve to an overpopulated mountain whose soil was less fertile than its women. Besides, Lebanese had a seafaring tradition, and being Christians could more easily adjust themselves to the Western way of life. Egypt, we noted before, was the earliest goal, but its attraction was almost limited to the Western-style educated. The masses struck farther into the Americas, Australia and West Africa. The flow which began as trickles in the 1870's swelled into a stream in the years before the first World War.

With as light baggage in his head as in his hand, the typical emigrant landed in New York or Rio de Janeiro, began as a peddler, developed into a shopkeeper and ultimately into a national if not international merchant. Lebanese and Syrian Americans, first and second generations, number about a quarter of a million in the United States and slightly more in Brazil. It is estimated that half of the Lebanese live abroad. Lebanon prides itself in its being two: Lebanon the resident and Lebanon the emigrant. Although almost all emigrants adopt American citizenship with its full measure of responsibility and loyalty, they keep for Lebanon a warm spot in their hearts. Remittances to the folks back home and to philanthropic and educational enterprises decrease but do not cease. By their private correspondence, return visits, Arabic newspapers and periodicals—scores of which appear in New York, São Paulo, Rio de Janeiro, Buenos Aires and Mexico City—Lebanese abroad have contributed inmeasurably to the modernization of the homeland. They encouraged opposition to Ottoman rule and enhanced and accelerated the urge for self-rule under democratic processes.

Of all ideas introduced from the West, nationalism and independence stand out among the most dynamic. The two are interrelated. Nationalism is anchored in emotion that may easily flare up into passion. To that extent it partakes of the nature of religion. In another sense it is individual egotism inflated to group dimensions.

Nationalism, as used in this context, implies transcendent loyalty to a politically and territorially defined unit. It is purely secular with predominantly economic values. It is historically a product of the French Revolution of 1789. As such it stands in conflict with Islam, which inculcates loyalty to the Moslem fraternity irrespective of nationality or territory and which emphasizes spiritual values. Negatively, Arab nationalism rose in resistance to Ottoman oppression and to the Young Turks' policy of Turkefication. The mandates added another negative stimulus: opposition to "Western imperialism." On the positive side the newly planted idea was nourished by the growing knowledge of the past glory of the Arab empire and culture and of the vague consciousness of a pseudo-ethnic identity among Arabic-speaking peoples. Its pioneers and advocates were Christian Lebanese and Syrians with Western education. The base therefore was wide, encompassing Pan-Arabism.

With the political division of the Arab East, consequent upon the first World War, Arab nationalism suffered fragmentation. The Egyptians under British occupation faced problems different from those of the Syrians and Lebanese under the French mandate, or the Iraqis and Palestinians under British mandate. Nationalism tended to become provincial in these areas. It was not until the creation of Israel (1948) that the trend toward unity reasserted itself. But then it did not maintain its purity. It became indistinguishably mixed with Islamism, and acquired further coloring by serving as a vehicle for the rising expectations of an awakened people.

The impact of the West, interrupted by the war of 1914 to 1918, was resumed and escalated in the mandatory period. A new dimension, military-political, was added. Of all the dimensions, including the economic, social and cultural, this was the least fortunate, the unhappiest.

The mandate system, created by the League of Nations (1919), was a novel experiment in international affairs. Noble in concept but difficult of execution, it purported to make of the mandatory power a trustee, one primarily interested in and concerned with the future of its charge. This was especially true of the mandate styled class A, imposed on the Arab Crescent. In the words of the covenant of the League this type was given to people who had reached a stage of development where their existence as "independent nations can be provisionally recognized, subject to the rendering of administrative advice and assistance by the mandatory until such time as they are able to stand alone." It all sounded good on paper.

France entrusted its administration of the mandate over Syria-Lebanon to generals whose chief credentials must have been distinction in the war just ended. High commissioners, as they were titled, followed one another in rapid succession. Their aides were recruited mainly from colonial service. Admittedly, even with the best implementation the task was gigantic and the path bristled with thorny difficulties. The mandated territories, whether under the French or British, were just emerging from a calamitous war. They stood at the lowest ebb in their modern history economically and socially. None other than Lebanon had experienced home rule, developed democratic institutions or laid the foundations of modern nationhood. As late as 1933 over forty-one per cent of the Syrian population was still illiterate.

Syrian opposition to the mandate began before the mandate was imposed. In fact, the imposition was against the people's expressed will. Three months after the landing of the first high commissioner, Henri Gouraud, in Beirut (December 1919), a national Syrian congress was held in Damascus and proclaimed Faysal king of an independent greater Syria. Gouraud's troops had no difficulty in entering Damascus and chasing out the newly crowned king, on whom the British the following year placed a new crown, that of Iraq. French-Syrian relations continued to deteriorate. Nationalist leaders and political agitators were imprisoned or banished.

Grievances accumulated. The new republican government set up was but a façade. Censorship and espionage were maintained. One party or sect was pitted against another. French was promoted at the expense of Arabic. On the credit side the mandatory power did set up the machinery of a modernized government, improve communications, widen the areas of cultivation, extend the facilities of sanitation and up-to-date education. From all these benefits, however, Lebanon drew the larger share.

Mandated Lebanon was not as restless as its sister. From the beginning it had no serious objections to the new order. In 1920 General Gouraud in an eloquent proclamation announced the formation of Grand Liban by restoring to it the coastal and inland plains lost in 1861. Long before the mandate, French companies had invested in Lebanese public utilities, railways and banks. New contracts and concessions now went increasingly to French concerns or Lebanese with French connections. On the whole, Lebanese could and did tolerate a heavier dose of French culture, including French language.

Six years after its proclamation, greater Lebanon was made a republic, the first in the Arab world. A representative council drew up a constitution providing for an elective parliament, a president elected by it and a responsible cabinet. Amended several times, this is the constitution still in force. Unlike other constitutions of neighboring states, the Lebanese contains no provision for a state religion. By convention, however, the president has been a Maronite, the prime minister a Sunnite and the speaker of the house a Shiite. Druzes usually hold one or more cabinet posts.

The French-Lebanese honeymoon was not of long duration. As the native government tried to exercise what it considered its legitimate functions, it received increasing resistance on the part of the mandatory power. The second World War interrupted the course of events. On the economic side it was not as disastrous as its predecessor. In fact Lebanon and Syria suffered but little. But on the political side the picture was different. After the collapse of France in 1940 and the rise of the Free French under Charles de Gaulle, his representative proclaimed (1941) the termination of the mandate for Syria and Lebanon and the independence of their peoples. But when Lebanon in 1943 elected Bisharah al-Khuri (Khoury) its president and proceeded to purge its constitution of references to the mandate, the French arrested him and sent him with members of the cabinet to a castle on the frontier. An infuriated public staged strikes, demonstrations and disturbances that did not cease until his return on November 22. This is memorialized as independence day. Syria fixed on November 27, 1941, as its first day of independence, though it was not able to exercise full sovereignty till 1945.

Iraq, though less developed, fared better under the British. One month after the imposition of the mandate a violent insurrection started, spread and was not suppressed till the following year (1921), after a loss of millions of pounds and hundreds of lives. The British learned their lesson early. In March of that year they put the country under civilian administration and chose Faysal of Hejaz as king. The setup was similar to that of Egypt. The king was to be guided by the high commissioner. In spite of difficulties inherent in his anomalous position as king over a mandated state, Faysal in eleven years managed to lead his country through the steps toward full independence and sovereignty. In 1932 Iraq qualified for membership in the League of Nations. Two years earlier a twenty-five-year treaty with Britain was signed, stipulating mutual aid in time of war and giving Britain certain advantages in financial and educational matters.

By this time Iraq was becoming economically independent. For this it had petroleum to thank. Hitherto the principal product of the country had been dates, the Basra variety of which was world famed. Shortly after oil was discovered (1929) by the Iraq Petroleum Company, approximately fifty per cent of the government revenues accrued from royalties. This enabled the country to launch an extensive development program. As it developed into a world oil center, Iraq maintained its leadership in dates, whereas Kuwait and Bahrain lost their pre-oil pearl-fishing industry.

Of the four mandated territories Palestine was the unhappiest. Not only was its mandate, approved by the League of Nations in 1922, unrecognized by the people, but it was stubbornly resisted from beginning to end. Throughout, the Arab struggle continued against the British as mandatory power and against intruding Zionists, whom the mandate was committed to support. At that time the Palestine Arabs outnumbered the Jews by ten to one—700,000 to 70,000. By 1939 the Arab population had increased by natural growth to 1,044,000, but it had reduced its majority to only two to one, thanks to Zionist-instigated, British-facilitated immigration from all lands. In the twenty years ending 1939 Zionist groups had spent some $79,000,000 on land purchase, agriculture and other pursuits in the furtherance of their plan. In their struggle against such odds Palestine Arabs remained disorganized, impoverished, with no substantial aid from outside. Moslems everywhere, to whom Jerusalem was the third holiest city, resented Jewish intrusion, but did nothing about it.

In the second World War the Zionist movement shifted its center from England—to which it had shifted from the continent in the first World War—to the United States. There it gained new strength, financially and numerically. At a New York conference in 1942, its new position was made clear: unlimited immigration, converting Palestine into a Jewish commonwealth and organizing a Jewish army to implement the program. Hitler's persecution of German Jews aroused new and wide sympathies among gentiles and Jews. In New York and Washington, as in London, politicians competed to win what they considered the Jewish vote. Arabs everywhere viewed Zionism as an inimical movement encouraged by the imperialist West to plant in the heart of their land an intrusive alien state. Moslem reaction everywhere was anti-Zionist.

The year 1947 was crucial. A hastily assembled, ill-equipped and inadequately trained "army of liberation" was put in the field by the Arabs. The fight was more on the company and battalion level rather than the brigade or divisional level. As Arabs attacked Jews, Jews attacked Arabs and Britishers. The jinni let loose by the British could no longer be contained. On May 14, 1948, the birth of a new state was announced in Tel Aviv. The United States lost no time in recognizing it. Others followed. The head of the new government was Russian-Polish-born David Ben-Gurion, who, except for a two-year interruption, led his country till 1963. At the time of his retirement the Arab population had been reduced to a minority of about nine per cent (about 240,000). Approximately a million of the original population is still languishing in alien camps, the object of charity.

As Israel was being conceived another state was rising in Palestine, the Hashimite Kingdom of Jordan. This state began (1920) as the amirate of Transjordan, amputated from mandated Palestine by the British and put under Abudllah, son of King Husayn of Hejaz and elder brother of Faysal. The new state was intended as a buffer against Bedouins. Amman was chosen as capital. The amirate evolved in 1946 into a kingdom, and three years later it was expanded west of the Jordan and given its present name. The added territory was acquired during the war of 1947-1948 in which the British-trained Arab legion of King Abdullah fared relatively well. Hemmed in between Israel and the desert, the country is hardly viable. It has to depend on outside support, mainly from Britain and the United States. The throne has been held by Abdullah's progeny.

25

Independence

If the first World War yielded the mandates, the second resulted in independence for the Arab Crescent. In the inter-war period Egypt attained its full independence.

In Egypt the ending of the British protectorate and the instituting of a monarchy in 1922 did not assure complete sovereignty. There were reservations made by the British. A three-corner struggle for power ensued, involving an autocratic king, Fuad (1917-1936), a Wafdist party clamoring for constitutional processes and a great foreign power with vested interest. It was not until 1936, when a new Anglo-Egyptian treaty limited British interest to the Suez Canal, that the country could be considered as fully independent. This last toe hold was not loosened until 1956. In 1937 Egypt abolished the capitulations and in the following year gained admittance to the United Nations. Soon after the outbreak of European hostilities (summer of 1939) Egypt under Fuad's successor Faruq (Farouk) broke off diplomatic relations with Germany and proceeded to implement its treaty obligations with Britain. Both Cairo and Alexandria were subjected to air raids from Italy. By the autumn of 1942 a German corps, especially trained under Erwin Rommel for desert warfare, had swept through Libya, entered Egypt and threatened Alexandria. The fate of the country hung in the balance. Victory was snatched by Allied troops under General Bernard Montgomery. A monument on the battlefield (al-Alamayn) for the 13,000 killed reads: "They preserved for the West the link with the East and turned the tide of war."

War-time Egypt served as a supply center for the entire Near East and as a base of preparation for the Allied campaign against Japan. Consequently it did not suffer economically. In fact it prospered. In the Arab-Zionist war its troops occupied the Gaza strip, which they still hold. Otherwise their performance was discreditable. Charges of nepotism and corruption involving even royal courtiers and relating to the supply of troops with defective weapons gained currency. The scandal prompted the military coup of July 1952, the coup that ended the monarchy, established the present republic and put Colonel Nasser (Jamal Abd-al-Nasir) into power.

The new regime was a revolutionary one in name and in deed. It aimed at a thorough break with the past and a remodeling of the society. One after another of the established institutions tumbled down. The incumbent of a century-and-a-half-old throne was sent out of the country. The constitution was abolished. Political parties were dissolved. Pashas and beys lost their titles; before long they were to lose their extensive landholdings. No such changes had been experienced in a land that had witnessed probably more changes in its five-thousand-year history than any other land.

In June 1956, with only his name on the ballot, Nasser was elected president of the republic for a six-year term. He has since been reelected. In 1958 he succeeded in transferring the Suez Canal base to native authorities. Hailed as a national hero, he was soon to become a Pan-Arab one. Under him, the Egyptians, new converts to Arabism, became its leaders.

Feeling politically secure, the regime turned its attention to economic and social problems. The country's population in 1956 reached 22,000,000 and was increasing at the rate of half a million a year. There was no parallel increase in land or economy. Estates seized from wealthy owners offered no solution. The government's request for financial aid from the United States was brusquely rejected. England also rejected it. With a view to increasing its revenue, the government nationalized the Suez Canal. Vociferous protests and threats were raised from England and France; and when in October 1956 Israel launched an abrupt military campaign through Sinai, these two powers collaborated. Their planes attacked Egyptian objectives and landed troops in Port Said. President Eisenhower took the initiative in condemning the triple assault, and under pressure from the United Nations it was given up.

Egypt now turned for financial support to the Soviet bloc, from which it had been receiving arms to balance the increasing armament of Israel from the West, particularly France. Like other neighboring countries Egypt felt insecure with Israel on its border. Russia obliged by initially advancing 60,000,000 Egyptian pounds for a development program featured by the building of a dam across the Nile at Aswan. The dam was calculated to reclaim a vast territory from the desert and ease the pressure from overpopulation. A new formulation of the regime's policy emerged: the achievement of a "nationalist, democratic, socialist, cooperative society." In this context democracy meant freedom for the national —not the individual—will to act independently; socialism meant employment of the state machinery to achieve public welfare in the varied aspects of economic and social life. By nationalization, industrialization and decree legislation, the regime sought to reform the society. In 1960 the government imposed new restrictions on the Moslem husband and decreed new rights for the wife. Three years earlier it had abrogated the shariah courts, as well as the religious courts of non-Moslem communities. It provided that all litigation be conducted in the ordinary courts but under the relevant personal law.

Egypt under Nasser assumed the leadership of the nationalist Pan-Arab movement. In February 1958 it joined with Syria to form the United Arab Republic. The attempt was hailed as the first step toward the realization of the long-sought-after plan for a union among the eastern Arab states. The union turned out to be premature. Three years later it was dissolved, but Egypt maintained the new name. Its hopes then centered on Iraq, whose new revolutionary regime had destroyed the monarchy, verred to the left and clamored for Arab unity.

Monarchic Iraq had an auspicious beginning under Faysal I (d. 1933) but a tragic ending twenty-five years later under his grandson

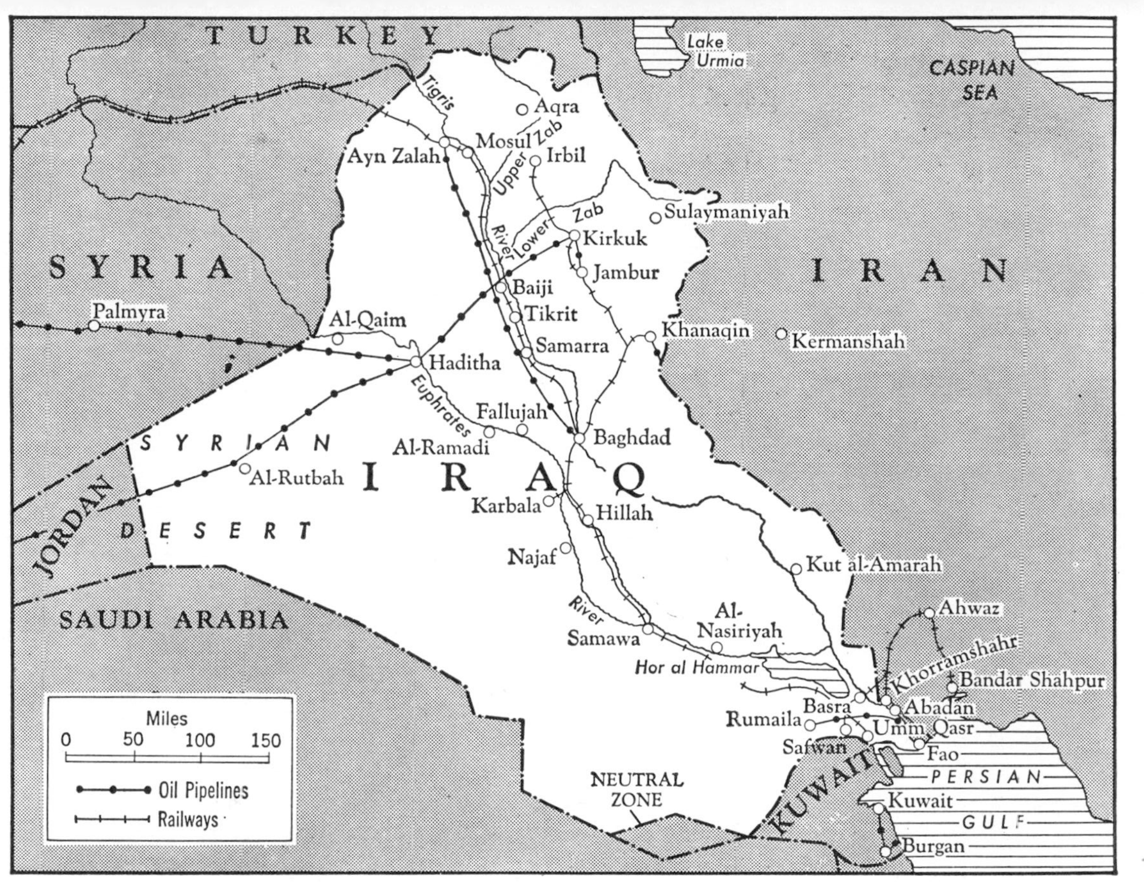

TURKEY
Lake Urmia
CASPIAN SEA
SYRIA
IRAN
IRAQ
SYRIAN DESERT
JORDAN
SAUDI ARABIA
NEUTRAL ZONE
KUWAIT
PERSIAN GULF
Tigris
Euphrates
River
Upper Zab
Lower Zab
Hor al Hammar
Aqra
Mosul
Irbil
Ayn Zalah
Sulaymaniyah
Kirkuk
Jambur
Baiji
Tikrit
Samarra
Palmyra
Al-Qaim
Haditha
Khanaqin
Kermanshah
Fallujah
Al-Ramadi
Baghdad
Al-Rutbah
Karbala
Hillah
Najaf
Kut al-Amarah
Samawa
Al-Nasiriyah
Ahwaz
Khorramshahr
Bandar Shahpur
Basra
Abadan
Rumaila
Umm Qasr
Safwan
Fao
Kuwait
Burgan
Miles
0
50
100
150
Oil Pipelines
Railways

IRAQ

and namesake. Foremost among the problems was the maintenance of the prestige of independence and the dignity of sovereignty while receiving financial and military aid from a foreign power. The problem was complicated by the fact that that power, Britain, was a sponsor of Zionism and Israel, against whom Iraqis were particularly bitter. Two years after the start of the second World War anti-British nationalist feeling rose to such a pitch tha it could establish a temporary pro-German regime at Baghdad. The capital was then reoccupied by British troops, and thereafter the country, considered vital for the Allied cause as a base for the movement of war supplies to Iran and Russia, fulfilled its obligations as an ally.

On the domestic side there were the difficulties of ruling a people one-sixth of whom were nomads and nine-tenths illiterate. Then there was a small minority of Christians and a majority of Moslems, the latter divided into two almost numerically equal camps. Among the Sunnites were the Kurds, restless and eager to join other Kurds in Iran and Turkey to form an independent unit. Among the Christians were the Assyrians (Nestorians) in the Lake Van region whose insurrection in 1933 ended in their virtual destruction as a community. On the economic side Iraq fared better than most of its neighboring states. The rapid development of its oil industry was responsible for that. In the 1930's new concessions in Mosul and Basra were given to companies, and pipelines conveyed the oil to Tripoli and Haifa. In 1950 a development plan was created to use seventy per cent of oil revenue for digging canals and building dams, bridges and highways as well as for educational and military purposes. But the long-range development program did not give the low-income group immediate relief.

In its inter-Arab relations monarchic Baghdad kept especially cordial relations with Amman and Beirut. The thrones of both Iraq and Jordan were held by Hashimites. For a time, beginning in 1949, Iraqi-Syrian relations seemed so close as to encourage a merger of the two countries. But estrangement set in after Iraq's joining (1955) with Turkey and other neighbors in the Baghdad Pact. Syria hwas still embittered by Turkey's acquisition of its

Alexandretta region. When Syria three years later united with Egypt to form the United Arab Republic, Iraq hurriedly consummated the long-discussed federation with Jordan.

But this was a federation of governments rather than of peoples. Under the two successors of Faysal I political intrigues and cliques became rife. Cabinets rose and fell. A new aristocracy of office-holders and tribal shaykhs arose. Faysal II, who attained majority in 1953, lacked the experience and maturity to cope with the deteriorating situation. To the clamor of the economically and socially dissatisfied was added that of the Arab nationalists who resented Iraq's continued pro-British attitude. The explosion found expression in a military coup of July 1958 which brought about the murder of the king, the crown prince, the prime minister and other high officials. The coup abolished the monarchy and elevated Brigadier Kassem (Abd-al-Karim Qasim) to the premiership of a so-called republic. The new regime found itself confronted with problems created by communists, Nasserites, tribesmen and rebellious Kurds beyond its ability to solve. A confidant and deputy premier of Kassem, Colonel Aref (Abd-al-Salam Arif) used the same techniques against Kassem that they both had used against the king. In February 1963 Kassem was suddenly attacked, captured and shot. Aref was declared president of the republic. His regime was as military as its predecessor. Arab nationalist and Baath army officers gained control. The Baath (ba'th, renaissance) was the socialist party with a strong following in Syria, where it was founded in 1941. The new regime entered into negotiations for federation with Egypt, resulting in signing (1964) an agreement establishing a joint residency council for the two countries. The council's purpose was to coordinate policies and intigrate military and economic planning. By following Egypt's path Iraq was alienated from Jordan.

The Hashimite Kingdom of Jordan, we noted earlier, was an outgrowth of an amirate established by the British mandate in Transjordan. Its first amir, Abdullah, became its first king. Son of the sharif who once declared himself king of the Arabs, and

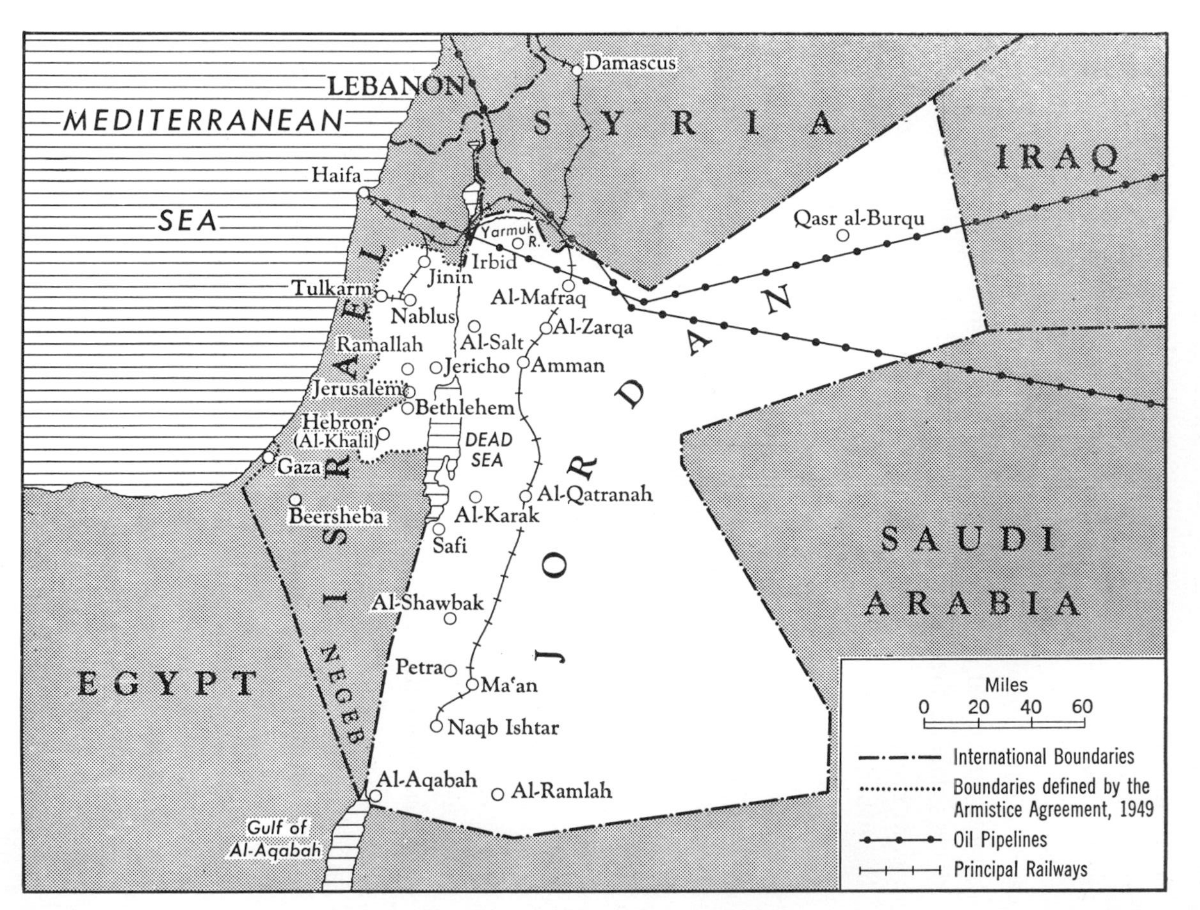

HASHIMITE KINGDOM OF JORDAN

brother of the first king of Iraq, Abdullah exercised influence on Arab affairs out of proportion to the size and importance of his realm. His pet scheme was a "greater Syria"—under him, of course. But his being a British collaborator discredited him in Arab nationalist eyes. Besides, he was considered soft on Zionism, archenemy of Arabism. An assassin's bullet cut short the monarch's life as he was entering the Aqsa Mosque (Jerusalem) in July 1951.

Two years later his grandson Husayn (Hussein), having come of age (18), gave up his military studies in England and ascended the throne. The realm of the young king, who had to become a man before he stopped being a boy, consisted of an eastern part of 400,000 mostly semi-nomads, and a western part of 1,000,000, half of whom were Palestinian refugees from what became Israel. Unsettled conditions discouraged pilgrimage and tourism, a main source of national income. Whatever minerals the Dead Sea put in Jordan could not be exploited for lack of capital and technological knowledge.

Economically anemic, socially unhomogenized and politically unsettled, Jordan invited aggression not only from its enemy but from friendly neighbors. It had the pluck and courage of its youthful king and the unswerving loyalty of its British-trained legion to depend upon. They both served it well in the first crisis, that of 1957, generated by pro-Nasser Arab nationalists, anti-monarchists, leftists and other malcontents. The United States' declaration of interest in the preservation of the independence and integrity of the shaky kingdom helped to steady it. Even more perilous was the crisis of July 1958 precipitated by the Iraq coup and the disturbances in Lebanon. Earlier that year Jordan, it will be remembered, had joined Iraq in a short-lived federation to counterbalance Syria's merger with Egypt. In response to the king's appeal British troops were flown from Cyprus to Amman. British and American arms and money continued to flow into the country.

More coup-prone or crisis-prone than Iraq or Jordan was Syria. Between 1949 and 1955 it saw the rise and fall of four regimes. Religiously the country was more splintered than any other state,

Lebanon excepted. Christians constituted about an eighth of the population, Nusayris a tenth and Druzes had Hawran as their stronghold. More political groupings flourished than in any of its neighboring states, but they lacked a special pole of attraction. Arab nationalism could be considered such a pole, but it had varying schools of thought and developed no stalwart leaders. Some wanted to merge with Jordan, others with Iraq, still others with Egypt. Especially proud as heirs of a most glorious period in Arab history, the Umayyad, Syrian Moslems aimed high at Arab leadership but fell short. They developed xenophobia toward the West and more pronounced animosity toward Israel. Though rich in land and water resources, the country remained poor. The economic policy it followed after its mandate separation from Lebanon, we noted above, led to the opposite results from the policy pursued by Lebanon.

The series of presidents of the republic was inaugurated by Shukri al-Quwatli, elected by the chamber of deputies in 1943, when the Free French declared Syria independent. The nominal independence did not become real till 1945. The infant republic faced problems with all its neighbors—Turkey, Lebanon, Iraq and Jordan—but above all with Zionist Israel. As under the mandate the people's preoccupation was political and military, rather than economic and social. As prices soared, sales dipped. In 1949 the first military coup was staged. Others followed in a row. In the government budget the national defense item escalated year after year. Education, sanitation and communication hardly received their due. Social legislation lagged behind. Resort was made to nationalization. By decree some 4,000,000 square acres of state-owned lands were distributed. Water, electricity and communication companies were put under government control. But relief was not in sight. Business strikes, student demonstrations, political disturbances gained momentum in 1953 and passed into 1954. A Druze uprising sparked a general one against military dictatorship and brought back to power (1955) al-Quwatli, who had fled for refuge in Egypt. Military dictatorship was tried and found wanting—at least for the time being.

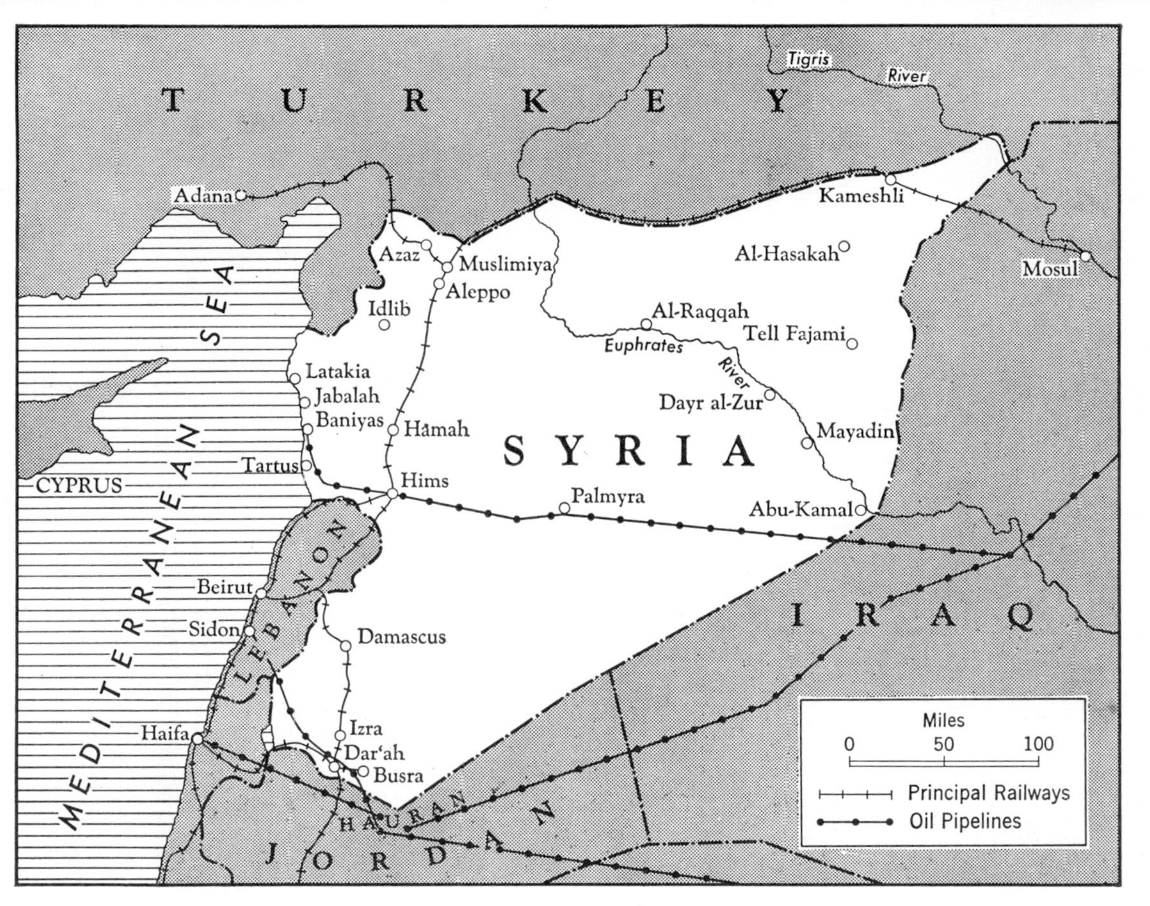
TURKEY
SYRIA
IRAQ
JORDAN
LEBANON
HAURAN
MEDITERRANEAN SEA
CYPRUS
Tigris River
Euphrates River
Adana
Azaz
Muslimiya
Aleppo
Idlib
Latakia
Jabalah
Baniyas
Hamah
Tartus
Hims
Palmyra
Kameshli
Al-Hasakah
Mosul
Al-Raqqah
Tell Fajami
Dayr al-Zur
Mayadin
Abu-Kamal
Beirut
Sidon
Damascus
Haifa
Izra
Dar'ah
Busra
Miles
0 50 100
Principal Railways
Oil Pipelines

SYRIA

Al-Quwatli's second regime pursued the ideal of Arab unity beginning with Egypt. Hostile to Israel, cherishing a grudge towjrd Turkey, alienated from Lebanon and more recently from Iraq, Syria felt isolated and vulnerable. Geographically and traditionally Iraq would have been a natural ally. But Iraq at that time leaned to the West. On the East-or-West issue it was Egypt that saw eye to eye with Syria. The avowed policy of al-Quwatli on this issue was "neutrality": rejection of foreign pacts and readiness to receive arms "with no strings attached." The Soviet bloc was willing to accommodate. Trade agreements were made with Russia, Rumania, Bulgaria, Hungary and Czechoslovakia. Cultural agreements with Russia involved specialists in arts, sciences, education and scholarships. In 1956 arms were received from Russia.

All hope of reconciliation with the West was shattered when in October 1956 Israel attacked Egypt and was seconded by an Anglo-French attack. Syria rushed to the support of its ally. It mobilized its forces and inflicted damage on the oil pipelines from Iraq and Saudi Arabia passing through its territory. Russia offered arms and volunteers to Egypt. Nothing could have more increased communist influence. At last the Soviet Union succeeded in identifying its interests with those of the Arabs on three fronts: opposition to the Western powers, hostility to Israel and the drive for Pan-Arabism.

But reaction soon set in. Though legally banned in Syria, as in other Arab states, the Communist Party now posed a threat to the existing order. On Syria's initiative the long-standing plans for union with Egypt were hurriedly consummated. After February 1958 the Republic of Syria became the northern region of the United Arab Republic. Three years later it seceded from the union to become the Syrian Arab Republic. The military coup by which its secession was effected initiated a new series of coups. Such political spasms may be viewed as growing pains on the part of a people seeking a higher and fuller life.

If Syria holds first prize in military coups, Lebanon holds the booby prize. True, Lebanon did experience a couple of crises, but

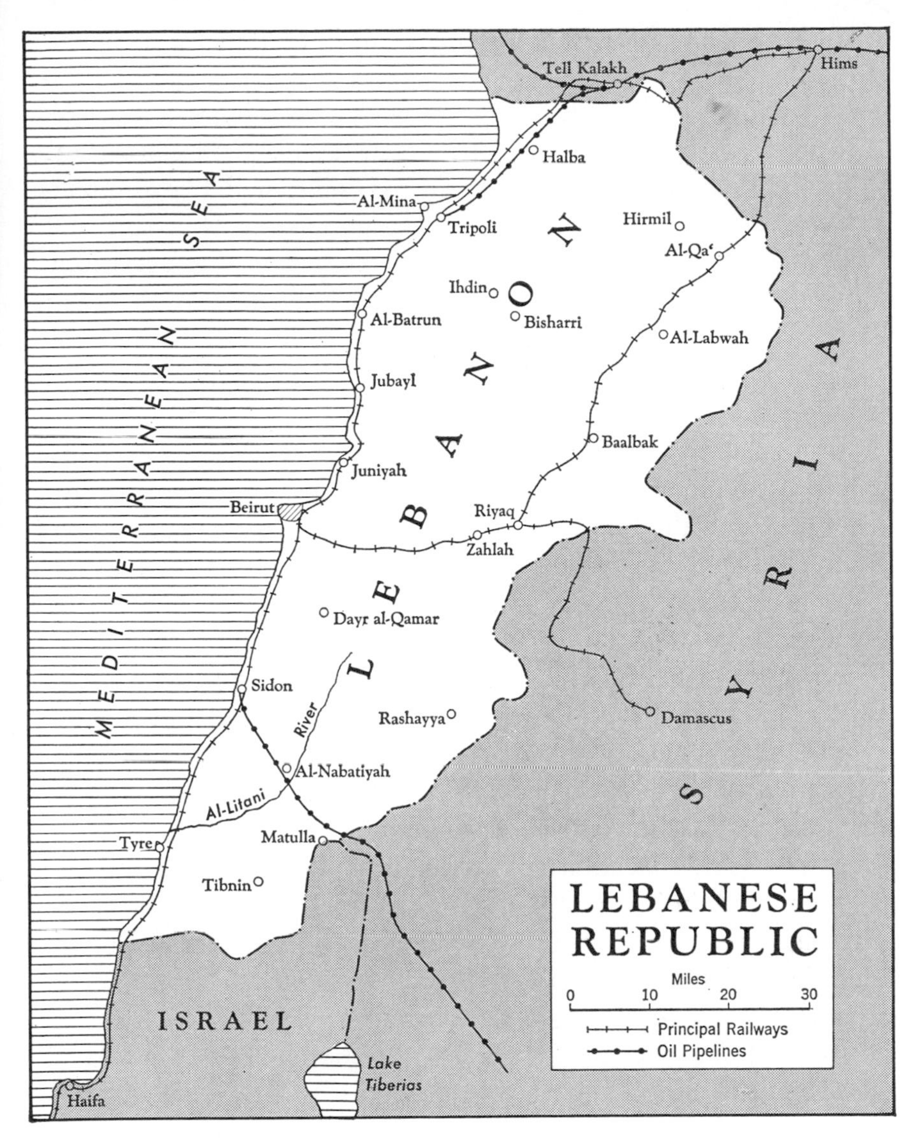

LEBANESE REPUBLIC

throughout, transition in government was in accordance with constitutional procedures.

The reasons are not far to seek. Though a fledgling as a republic, Lebanon had had some experience in self-government since 1861. The backbone of its population was Maronite and Durze mountaineers, imbued with individualism and love of freedom and hardened by climate. The percentage of literacy has been relatively high, thanks to foreign agencies and native individual—rather than state—effort. Also high has been the standard of living, despite the paucity of natural resources. Like their Phoenician predecessors modern Lebanese are commercially, not militarily, minded. Amidst a world of trade restrictions, state economic planning and currency control, the merchant republic has adhered to the principle of free enterprise and the traditional law of supply and demand. Economically and culturally it has remained more attuned to Western influences than its neighbors. Its capital city developed into a window through which the hinterland could look westward, and a gateway through which East and West could exchange commodities and ideas. Lebanese emigrants served as liaison officers.

The fabulous oil boom in Saudi Arabia, Iraq, Kuwait and the Persian Gulf shaykhdoms after the 1930's was a boon to Lebanon. It added to the number of individuals seeking Beirut for pleasure, entertainment, education or investment, and of families resorting to the mountain in summer. In the mid-1960's the city housed four universities and published thirty dailies in Arabic, French, English and Armenian as well as twenty weeklies and ten monthlies in Arabic, French and English. Transit trade, free in Lebanon, added to the national income. In pipelines from Iraq and Saudi Arabi flowed oil to Tripoli and Sidon. Contrary to the prevailing economic pattern in the area, Lebanese made their living not so much from industry or agriculture as from services renedered mainly to non-Lebanese. This dependence on services, naturally, made the country more vulnerable to economic and political crises.

On the political side the republic adhered to democratic processes. It viewed with alarm the emerging military governments around it and with disfavor the Greater Syria project of King Abdullah as well as that of the Fertile Crescent by Iraqi politicians. It feared loss of identity. While in an Arab-Moslem world, it did not feel fully identified with it. It consistently pursued the policy of wholehearted cooperation short of assimilation. It participated in the Arab-Zionist struggle of 1947-1948 and, in common with its allies, maintained a state of war with Israel. It became a charter member of the League of Arab States, founded in 1945, fulfilled its obligations and at times mediated problems among its members. But its over-all attitude remained a source of perennial conflict.

In the East-West tug of war the Lebanese government leaned in a direction that further alienated it from Syria and Egypt. In the Suez episode (1956) it took a firm stand with Egypt but failed to break diplomatic relations with Britain and France. The following year when the Eisenhower doctrine of financial and military aid to Near Eastern states against communist aggression was announced, Lebanon was the only one to accept it.

By then subversive seeds from outside began to find fertile soil inside. The pronouncedly pro-Western regime of Kamil Shamun (Chamoun), who had succeeded Bisharah al-Khuri in 1952, was subjected to sharp attacks from within and without. The regime had made a number of political enemies, including Moslem and Druze ex-ministers who blamed their loss of seats in the chamber of deputies on its interference in elections. Cabinet members were normally recruited from the chamber. The republic's problem became that of retaining its sovereignty while walking a tightrope between the "neutrality" of its Arab friends and its community of interest with the West. In the summer of 1958, when Pan-Arab nationalism had reached a new high pitch, following the Syria-Egypt merger, Shamun's government found itself confronted with strikes, demonstrations and terrorism leading to bloody conflicts and a quasi-chaotic state. The July explosion in Iraq added fuel to the conflagration. In his despair Shamun appealed to the United States to help preserve his country's independence in face of foreigh interference. Ten thousand marines were landed on the beach near Beirut. On the last day of July General of the Army Fuad

Shihab (Chehab) was elected to succeed Shamun at the expiration of Shamun's second term in office. All United States troops were then (October) withdrawn. A new corner was turned.

A military man and scion of an aristocratic family that had lorded it over Lebanon for a century and a half, President Shihab restored the Christian-Moslem equilibrium on which the stability of the country rested. He utilized certain leaders of the opposition in high government places and deviated enough from his predecessor's Western alignment to satisfy all concerned. His adherence to the democratic cause was even more marked than that of the two presidents he succeeded. Especially evident in Shihab's regime was social legislation. Until then four per cent of the population received thirty per cent of the national income, creating a serious inequality in wealth distribution. New laws instituting social security and other benefits for the wage earner were passed. Considerable sums were devoted to providing non-urban communities with electricity, drinking facilities, better sanitation and improved means of transportation. In the fall of 1964 Shihab's term of office expired. He refused to endorse a constitutional amendment allowing his reelection and was succeeded by Charles Hulu (Helou), former minister and ambassador and professionally a lawyer. Hulu pledged himself to follow the Shihabi policies.

Readings

HISTORICAL SETTING (pages 1-5)

Childe, V. Gordon, *New Light on the Most Ancient East*, 4th ed. (London, 1952).

Coon, Carleton S., *The Story of the Middle East*, rev. ed. (New York, 1958).

THE SETTING OF THE STAGE (pages 6-11)

Fisher, W. D., *The Middle East*, 3rd ed. (London, 1956).

Hogarth, D. G., *The Nearer East* (London, 1902).

Semple, Ellen C., *The Geography of the Mediterranean Region* (London, 1932).

Smith, George A., *The Historical Geography of the Holy Land*, 11th ed. (New York, 1934).

EARLY STAGES OF CULTURAL EVOLUTION (pages 12-18)

Childe, V. Gordon, *The Dawn of European Civilization*, 5th ed. (London, 1950).

Frankfort, Henri, *The Birth of Civilization in the Near East* (London, 1951).

Turner, Ralph, *The Great Cultural Traditions*, vol. I, *The Ancient Cities* (New York, 1941).

THE IMPERIAL AGE (pages 19-32)

Hall, H. R., *Ancient History of the Near East*, 8th ed., rev. (New York, 1952).

Moscati, Sabatino, *Ancient Semitic Civilizations* (London, 1957).

Steindorff, George and Seele, Keith C., *When Egypt Ruled the East*, 2nd ed. Chicago, 1957).

Wilson, John A., *The Burden of Egypt* (Chicago, 1951).

RELIGION, SCIENCE AND LITERATURE (pages 33-46)

Finegan, Jack, *Light from the Ancient Near East* (Princeton, 1946).

Kramer, Samuel N., *From the Tablets of Sumer* (Indian Hills, Col., 1956).

Peet, T. Eric, *A Comparative Study of the Literatures of Egypt, Palestine and Mesopotomia* (London, 1931).

PHOENICIA AND PALESTINE: THEIR CONTRIBUTIONS (pages 47-57)

Bevan, Edwyn R. and Singer, Charles, eds., *The Legacy of Isreal* (Oxford, 1928).

Bright, John, *A History of Isreal* (Philadelphia, 1959).

Philip K. Hitti, *A Short History of Lebanon* (New York, 1965).

Scott, Robert B. Y., *The Relevance of the Prophets* (New York, 1944).

Wright, George E., and Filson, Floyd V., *The Westminister Historical Atlas of the Bible*, 2nd ed. (Philadelphia, 1956).

UNDER ALEXANDER AND HIS SUCCESSORS (pages 58-66)

Hitti, Philip K., *History of Syria including Lebanon and Palestine* (New York, 1951).

Robinson, Charles A., *The History of Alexander the Grea*t (Providence, 1953).

Tarn, W. W., *Hellenistic Civilization*, 3rd ed., rev. (London, 1952).

Hitti, Philip K., *Lebanon in History*, 2nd ed. (New York, 1962).

UNDER THE ROMAN CAESARS (pages 67-75)

Bailey, Cyril, *The Legacy of Rome* (Oxford, 1928).

Bell, Harold I., *Egypt from Alexander the Great to the Arab Conquest* (Oxford, 1948).

Bouchier, E. S., *Syria as a Roman Province* (Oxford, 1916).

Chapot, Victor, *The Roman World* (New York, 1928).

CHRISTIANITY ON THE MARCH (pages 76-80)

Cumont, Franz, *The Oriental Religions in Roman Paganism* (New York, reprint 1956).

Hatch, Edwin, *The Influence of Greek Ideas on Christianity* (New York, 1957).

Pfeiffer, Robert H., *History of New Testament Times* (New York, 1949).

IN BYZANTINE DAYS (pages 81-89)

Byron, Robert, *The Byzantine Achievement* (New York, 1929).

Hussey, Joan M., *The Byzantine World* (London, 1957).

Wilber, Donald N., *Iran: Past and Present*, 4th ed. (Princeton, 1958).

THE ARABIAN PROPHET (pages 90-95)

Andrae, Tor, *Mohammed: The Man and His Faith*, tr. Theophil Menzel (New York, 1936).
Bell, Richard, *The Origin of Islam in Its Christian Environment* (London, 1926).
Jeffery, Arthur, *The Koran as Scripture* (New York, 1952).
Katsh, Abraham A., *Judaism in Islam* (New York, 1954).
Pickthall, Marmaduke, *The Meaning of the Glorious Koran* (New York 1953).
Roberts, Robert, *The Social Laws of the Qurān* (London, 1929).
Robson, James, *Christ in Islam* (London, 1929).
Torrey, Charles C., *The Jewish Foundation of Islam* (New York, 1933).

ISLAM ON THE MARCH (pages 96-101)

Gibb, H. A. R., *Mohammedanism* (London, 1949).
Guillaume, Alfred, *Islam* (Harmondsworth, 1954).
Levy, Reuben, *The Social Structure of Islam* (Cambridge, 1957).

THE CALIPHAL EMPIRE (pages 102-118)

Arnold, Thomas W., *The Caliphate* (Oxford, 1924).
Hitti, Philip K., *History of the Arabs*, 8th ed. (New York, 1964).
Lewis, Bernard, *The Arabs in History*, 3rd ed. (London, 1956).
Tritton, A. S., *The Caliphs and Their Non-Muslim Subjects* (London, 1930).

BAGHDAD: POLITICAL AND INTELLECTUAL WORLD CENTER (pages 119-137)

Arberry, Arthur J., *Sufism: An Account of the Mystics in Islam* (London, 1950).
Arnold, Thomas, and Guillaume, Alfred, *The Legacy of Islam* (Oxford, 1947).
Hitti, Philip K., *Islam and the West* (Princeton, 1962).
Le Strange, Guy, *Baghdad During the Abbasid Caliphate* (London, 1924).
Nicholson, Reynold A., *The Mystics of Islam* (London, 1914).
O'Leary, De Lacy E., *Arabic Thought and Its Place in History*, rev. ed. (London, 1954); *How Greek Science Passed to the Arabs* (London, 1949).

DISMEMBERMENT AND SUCCESSION (pages 138-151)

Arberry, A. J., ed., *The Legacy of Persia* (Cambridge, 1953).
Atiya, Aziz S., *Crusades: Commerce and Culture* (Bloomington, 1962).

Hitti, Philip K., tr., *An Arab-Syrian Gentleman and Warrior in the Period of the Crusades* (Beirut, reprint 1964).
Lane-Poole, Stanley, *Saladin and the Fall of the Kingdom of Jerusalem* (New York, 1898).
Monro, Dana L., *The Kingdom of the Crusades* (New York, 1935).

UNDER THE OTTOMAN CRESCENT (pages 152-163)

Alderson, A. D., *The Structure of the Ottoman Dynasty* (Oxford, 1956).
Jackh, Ernest, ed., *Background of the Middle East* (Ithaca, 1952).
Merriman, Roger H., *Suleiman the Magnificent* (Cambridge, Mass., 1944).
Wittek, Paul, *The Rise of the Ottoman Empire* (London, 1938).

CULTURAL INSTITUTIONS (pages 164-169)

Brown, John P., *The Derwishes*, ed. Horace A. Rose (London, 1927).
Hasluck, F. W., *Christianity and Islam under the Sultans*, ed. Margaret Hasluck, Vol. I (Oxford, 1929).
Miller, Barnette, *The Palace School of Muhammad the Conqueror* (Cambridge, Mass., 1941).
Patmore, Derek, *The Star and the Cresent: An Anthology of Modern Turkish Poetry* (London, 1946).

FROM ABSOLUTISM TO REPUBLICANISM (pages 170-179)

Hoskins, Halford L., *The Middle East*, 2nd ed. (New York, 1959).
Lewis, Bernard, *Turkey Today* (London, 1940).
Thomas, Lewis J., and Frye, Richard N., *The United States and Turkey and Iran* (Cambridge, Mass., 1951).
Webster, Donald S., *The Turkey of Atatürk* (Philadelphia, 1939).

IMPERIAL PERSIA (pages 180-186)

Arberry, A. J., ed., *The Legacy of Persia* (Oxford, 1953).
Lockhart, Lawrence, *Nadir Shah* (London, 1938); *Famous Cities of Iran* (Brentford, 1939).
Pope, Arthur U., *An Introduction to Persian Art* (New York, 1931).

QAJAR PERSIA AND EUROPEAN INVOLVEMENT (pages 187-198)

Elwell-Sutton, L. P., *Modern Iran* (London, 1941).
Frye, Richard N., ed., *Iran* (New York, 1953).
Haas, William S., *Iran* (New York, 1946).
Lambton, Ann K., *Landlord and Peasant in Persia* (London, 1953).

OTTOMAN BACKGROUND OF ARAB STATES: EGYPT (pages 199-210)

Hazard, Harry W., *Atlas of Islamic History*, 3rd ed. (Princeton, 1954).
Longrigg, Stephen H., *Four Centuries of Modern Iraq* (Oxford, 1925).
Miller, William, *The Ottoman Empire and Its Successors* (Cambridge, 1936).
Ziadeh, Nicola A., *Syria and Lebanon* (London, 1956).

THE ARABIAN PENINSULA (pages 211-218)

Armstrong, H. C., *Lord of Arabia* (London, 1938).
Hazard, Harry W., ed., *Eastern Arabia* (New Haven, 1956).
Lawrence, T. E., *Revolt in the Desert* (New York, 1927).
Longrigg, Stephen H., *Oil in the Middle East* (London and New York, 1954).
Philby, H. St. John B., *Arabia of the Wahhabis* (London, 1928).
Winder, R. Bayly, *Saudi Arabia in the Nineteenth Century* (New York, 1965).

THE ARAB CRESCENT (pages 219-225)

Hourani, A. H., *Syria and Lebanon* (London, 1946).
Kohn, Hans, *Nationalism and Imperialism in the Hither East* (London, 1932).

MODERNIZATION AND MANDATES (pages 226-237)

Haddad, George, *Fifty Years of Modern Syria and Lebanon* (Beirut, 1950).
Hanna, Paul L., *British Policy in Palestine* (Washington, 1942).
Hurewitz, J. C., *The Struggle for Palestine* (New York, 1950).

INDEPENDENCE (pages 238-252)

Badeau, John S., *The Emergence of Modern Egypt* (New York, 1953).
Hitti, Philip K., *Lebanon: A Short History* (New York, 1965); *Syria: A Short History* (New York, 1959).
Khadduri, Majid, *Independent Iraq, 1932-1958*, 2nd ed. (London, 1960).
Qubain, Fahim I., *The Reconstruction of Iraq, 1950-1957* (New York, 1958).

Chronology

	B.C.
Charcoal in a Carmel cave	*ca.* 150,000
Earliest pottery, Tell al-Halaf	*ca.* 5000
Potters' wheel in use	*ca.* 4000
Use of metal spread	*ca.* 3000
Near East copper reaches Europe	*ca.* 2000
Iron tools in Hittiteland	*ca.* 1350
Bronze age ended	*ca.* 1200
Earliest written document, Mesopotamia	*ca.* 3000
Lower and Upper Egypt united by Menes	*ca.* 2900
Mesopotamia united under king of Uruk	*ca.* 2255
Sargon of Akkad	fl. *ca.* 2350
Zoser builds first pyramid, Egypt	*ca.* 2650
Cheops, founder of Fourth Dynasty	fl. *ca.* 2550
Twelfth Dynasty inaugurated	*ca.* 2200
Sesotris III connects Nile with Red Sea	d. 1840
Ahmose chases Hyksos out, ushers in imperial age	r. 1570-1545
Thutmose III reaches Euphrates	r. *ca.* 1502-1448
Ikhnaton removes capital from Thebes to Akhetaton	r. *ca.* 1377-1361
Tutankhamon returns to Thebes	r. *ca.* 1361-1352
Ramses II wars against Hittites	r. *ca.* 1301-1234
Hebrew exodus under Merneptah	r. *ca.* 1234-1215
Hammurabi, Babylonian lawgiver	fl. *ca.* 1686
Babylon falls under Hittite attack	*ca.* 1530
Hittites occupy north Syria	*ca.* 1350
Egypto-Hittite treaty	1280
Rise of Nineveh	*ca.* 1100
Tiglath-pileser I makes first essay at empire building	r. 1116-1093
Shalmaneser III wins indecisive victory in north Syria	r. 859-824

	B.C.
Damascus captured	732
Samaria submits	722
Sennacherib occupies Egyptian Delta	671
Nineveh destroyed	612
Nebuchadnezzar, Neo-Babylonian, destroys Jerusalem	586
Babylon destroyed by Cyrus of Persia	539
Cambyses adds Egypt to Persian Empire	525
Darius the Great reaches the Indus	r. 521-586
Battle of Marathon	490
Battle of Thermopylae	480
Zoroaster, founder of Persian religion	fl. *ca.* 600
Ptahhotep, early Egyptian sage	fl. *ca.* 2375
The story of Sinuhe	*ca.* 1960
Canaanites enter Syria	*ca.* 2900
Phoenician trade flourishes	*ca.* 1000-700
Gades, colony in Spain, founded	*ca.* 1000
Carthage founded	814
Hannibal flees to Tyre	196
Hebrews in Palestine	*ca.* 1225
King David	r. *ca.* 1004-963
Solomon	r. *ca.* 963-923
Sargon II destroys Kingdom of Israel	722
Amos, earliest monotheist	fl. *ca.* 750
Alexander the Great victor at Issus	333
He gives Persian capital Persepolis to the flames	331
Seleucus I, Alexander's successor in Syria	r. 312-280
Antiochus the Great defeated at Magnesia	190
Maccabean rebels capture Jerusalem	164
Pompey administers death blow to Syrian Kingdom	64
Cleopatra, last Ptolemy	d. 30
Euclid of Alexandria, geometrician	fl. *ca.* 300
Zeno, founder of Stoicism	d. 261

	A.D.
Near East under Augustus Caesar	d. 14
Caracalla, a Syrian Roman emperor	r. 211-217
Alexander Severus born in Lebanon	r. 223-235
Petra destroyed by Trajan	106
Zenobia of Palmyra taken captive by Aurelian	274
Apostle Paul dies in Rome	67
Church Fathers in Alexandria	*ca.* 190-300
Constantine favors Christianity	r. 306-337
Council of Nicaea	325
Council of Chalcedon	451
Persian Shapur I reaches Cappadocia	r. 240-272
Khosrau I reaches the Black Sea	r. 531-579
Heraclius rolls back Persians	r. 610-641
Muhammad born in Mecca	570
Umar ibn-al-Khattab, caliph	634-644
Decisive battle of the Yarmuk	636
Egypt reached	640
Yazdagird, last Persian emperor	d. 651
Uthman ibn-Affan, caliph	644-656
Caliph Ali ibn-abi-Talib	d. 661
Mu'awiyah, caliph in Damascus	661-680
Qayrawan (Kairwan) founded	670
War against Byzantines	674-680
Abd-al-Malik, caliph	685-705
Constantinople under siege	716-717
Moslem army enters Spain	711
Pyrenees crossed	718
Battle between Tours and Poitiers	732
Abu-al-Abbas, founder of Abbasid caliphate	r. 750-754
Caliph al-Mansur, builder of Baghdad	r. 754-775
Translations from Greek under al-Mamun	r. 813-833
Al-Khwarizmi, algebraist	d. 850
Humayn ibn-Ishaq, dean of translators	d. 873
Al-Razi, physician	d. 925
Ibn-Sina (Avicenna), physician and philosopher	d. 1037
Ibn-Rushd (Averroës), Aristotelian commentator	d. 1198

	A.D.
Ismail, seventh Shiite imam	d. 760
Al-Ghazzali, restorer of orthodoxy	d. 1111
Hasan al-Sabbah, founder of Assassin order	d. 1124
Abd-al-Qadir, founder of first Sufi order	d. 1166
Mawlawi order founded	1173
Arab army enters Sicily	909
Fatimid caliphate established	909
Caliphate at its height under al-Aziz	r. 975-996
Caliphate destroyed by Salah-al-Din (Saladin)	1171
Samanid regime ended	999
Firdawsi, epic poet of Persia	d. 1020
Saljuqs in Baghdad	1055
Decisive battle of Manzikart	1071
Umar al-Khayyam, poet of wine	d. 1123
Crusaders capture Edessa and Antioch	1098
Jerusalem stormed	1099
Raymond captures Tripoli	1109
Decisive battle of Hittin	1187
Salah-al-Din dies	1193
Mamluks in Egypt and Syria	1250-1517
Baybars captures Antioch	1268
Raymond Lull initiates missionary work	d. 1315
Vasco da Gama rounds southern tip of Africa	1498
Salim I destroys Mamluk kingdom	1516-1517
Uthman, father of Ottoman Turks	d. 1326
Constantinople captured	1453
Empire at its height under Sulayman the Magnificent	r. 1520-1568
Algeria added	1518
Vienna besieged	1529, 1683
Printing press introduced	1728
Reforms of Mahmud II	r. 1808-1839
First government newspaper	1860
Abd-al-Hamid, reactionary sultan-caliph	r. 1876-1909
Constitution promulgated	1908

	A.D.
Young Turks seize power	1909
Balkan wars	1912-1913
Turkey sides with Central Powers	1914
Sharif Husayn of Hejaz revolts	1916
Peace treaty of Sèvres	1920
Mustafa Kemal heads provisional government	1920
Ismet Inönü, second president of the Republic	1938
Military coup	1960
Safawid dynasty	1501-1736
Abbas the Great	r. 1587-1629
Afsharid dynasty	1736-1796
Sadi, classical Persian poet	d. 1292
Bihzad, master miniature artist	d. 1537
Qajar dynasty	1779-1925
Anglo-Persian treaty	1814
Russo-Persian treaty	1828
Foreign control of Persian economy under Nasr-al-Din	d. 1896
Revolution spread under Muzaffar-al-Din	d. 1907
Convocation of general assembly	1906
Oil found in commercial quantities	1909
United States sends economic adviser	1911
Independent Persia admitted to the League of Nations	1920
A theologian proclaims himself the Bab	1844
Baha-Allah, founder of Bahaism	d. 1892
Jamal-al-Din al-Afghani, Pan-Islamist reformer	d. 1896
Carmelite mission in Persia	1604
Protestant mission	1811
Presbyterians found College of Tehran	1925
Reza Khan Pahlawi seizes power	1925
University of Tehran organized	1935
Russian troops occupy northern Persia	1941
Muhammad Reza installed Shah	1941
Allied summit conference, Tehran	1943
Oil industry nationalized	1951
Ali Bey of Egypt semi-independent	1769
Napoleon Bonaparte attacks Egypt	1798

	A.D.
Muhammad Ali, viceroy	d. 1849
Egyptian expedition against Syria by Ibrahim Pasha	1831
Suez Canal opened	1869
Rifaat al-Tahtawi, early scholar in Europe	1873
The British occupy Egypt	1882
The Mahdi controls Sudan	1881
Sudan declared independent	1956
Egypt pronounced a protectorate	1914
Fuad assumes title of king	1922
Muhammad Abduh, modernist reformer	fl. 1890
Yemen independent of Turkey	1918
Imam Yahya, first ruler	d. 1948
Ahmad, conservative imam-king	d. 1962
Civil war begins	1962
Ibn-Abd-al-Wahhab, Arabian reformer	d. 1793
Riyad seized by Wahhabis	1773
Damascus attacked	1808
Abd-al-Aziz ibn-Saud, creator of Saudi Arabia	d. 1953
Oil concession to an American company	1933
Faysal displaces his brother Saud	1964
Oil in Bahrain	1932
Kuwait declared independent	1961
Ahmad al-Jazzar of Acre	d. 1804
Midhat Pasha, liberal wali of Iraq	d. 1883
Fakhr-al-Din II, fuedal lord of Lebanon	r. 1590-1635
Bashir II, feudal lord of Lebanon	r. 1788-1840
Civil disturbances ending in massacre	1860
Lebanon under mutasarrifs	1861-1915
American University of Beirut founded	1866
French mandate over Syria and Lebanon	1919-1943
Faysal of Hejaz, King of Iraq under British mandate	1921
Oil discovered in Iraq	1929
Shukri al-Quwatli, president of the Syrian Republic	1943
Bisharah al-Khuri, president of Lebanon	1943-1952
Military coup establishes a republic in Iraq	1958

	A.D.
British mandate over Palestine approved by League of Nations	1922
Transjordan made amirate	1920
Transjordan declared kingdom	1946
Israel born	1948
Abdullah establishes Hashimite Kingdom of Jordan	1949
Egypt fully independent	1936
King Faruq	r. 1936-1952
Military coup establishes a republic	1952
Nasser elected president	1956
Egypt and Syria join in United Arab Republic	1958-1961

Index